GAZETTEER
OF THE
COAL MINES
OF
SOUTH WALES
& MONMOUTHSHIRE
FROM 1854

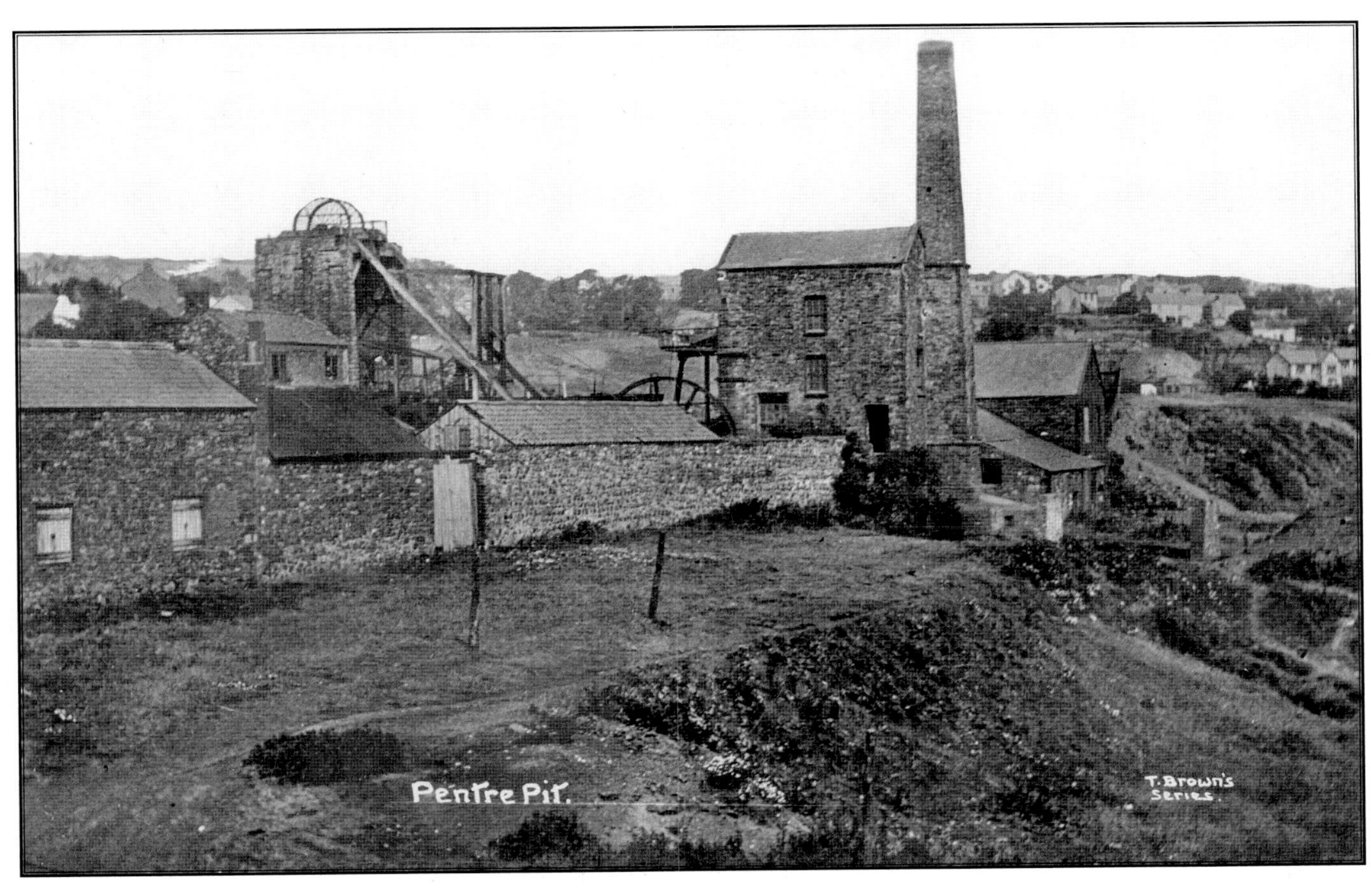

Designed by Ian Pope

British Library Cataloguing-in-Publication Data. A catalogue record for this book is available from the British Library:

ISBN 9781911038 37 5

Published by Lightmoor Press
Unit 144B Harbour Road Industrial Estate, Lydney, Gloucestershire GL15 4EJ

Printed in Poland www.lfbookservices.co.uk

GAZETTEER
OF THE
COAL MINES
OF
SOUTH WALES
& MONMOUTHSHIRE
FROM 1854

R. A. Cooke

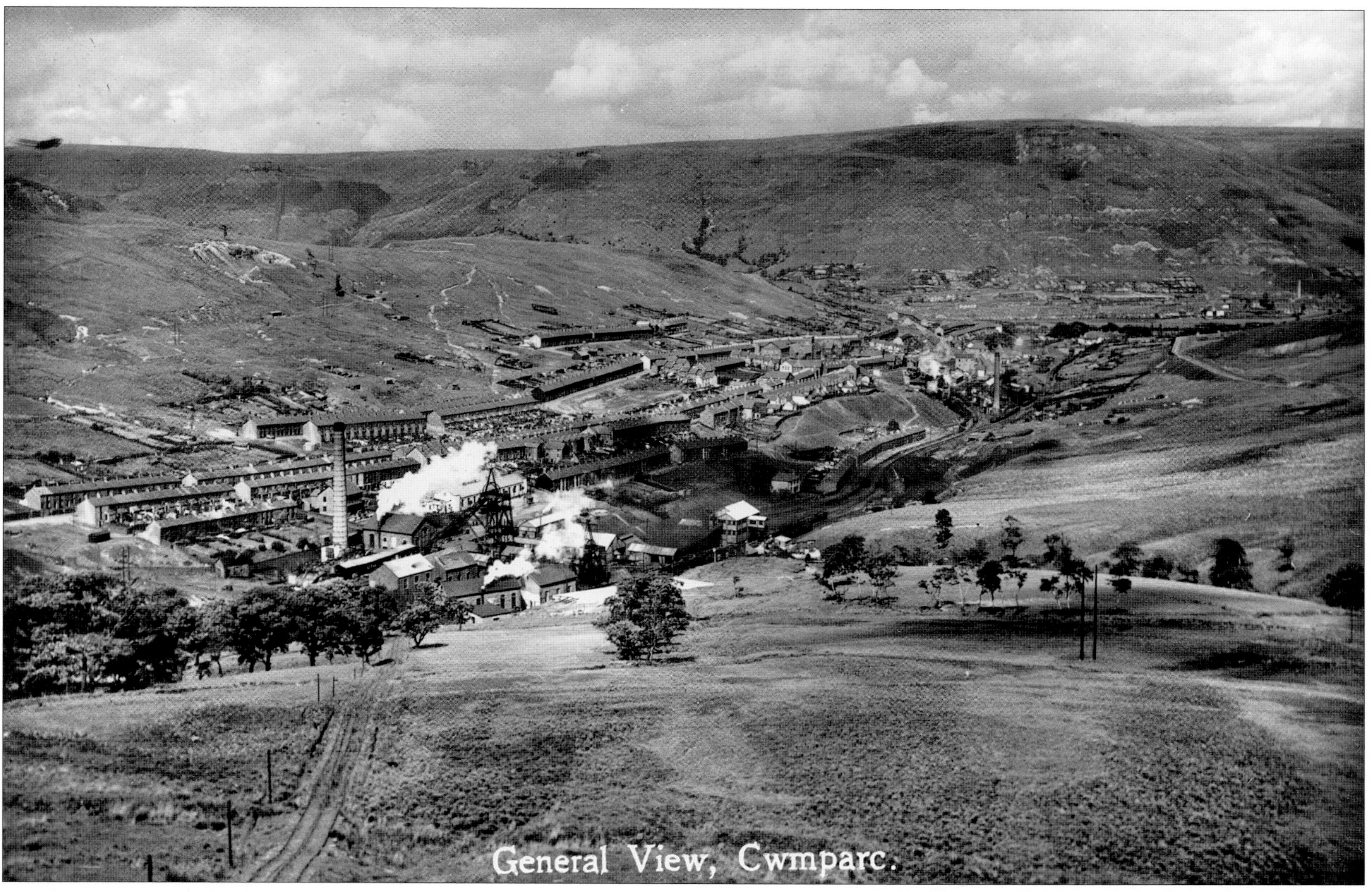
General View, Cwmparc.

CONTENTS

PREFACE

There is a well known and often quoted remark of Dr Johnson, which it seems appropriate to repeat here.

"In all places where there are objects worthy of detail or observation, there should be a short printed Directory for the use of strangers."

Well, his objective still seems to me to be very worthy, but my attempts to produce a Directory of the coal mines of South Wales has failed to produce something which is short, and time has produced changes that we are all familiar with today. So, instead of a printed Directory, which now totals some 1,500 pages, it has been placed on that modern-day convenience, a compact disc.

Why a Gazetteer of South Wales coalmines? During nearly forty years researching the Great Western Railway, I became increasingly sceptical of the accuracy of some railway and Railway Clearing House details appertaining to coal mines (See Appendix F). When the opportunity arose in September 1998, to check out some specific instances, these suspicions were largely confirmed and I realised that some of the data that I had previously collated was less than useful. When an attempt was made to consult published works, I was surprised at the paucity of information and, with a few exceptions, at the poor quality of the information that was available.

Thus, was born this attempt to put some meat on the bare bones of what was once the most important industry of South Wales. The task was daunting, more especially as I had no experience in coal mining and even elementary aspects have had to be patiently explained to me. I am especially grateful to all the people who have contributed and who attempted to keep me on the straight and narrow. Certainly, without their help and support this work would have been far poorer.

It is not a complete history of each mine, rather a compendium of available data, warts and all. The project has turned out to be far larger than I had originally envisaged and over time has grown and grown. It is inevitable that errors of transcription or interpretation will be discovered and despite all the willing help that I have received, such errors remain mine alone. There is still a vast amount of material awaiting researchers, so this volume is not the complete story. Perhaps though, others will be able to build on these foundations.

ACKNOWLEDGEMENTS

To the staff of all the following institutions I owe a very great debt and in particular to Dave Clarke and Brian Thornton and their staff at the Coal Authority, whose tireless efforts to keep me continually supplied with material must at times have sorely tested them. Also to John Holden, at the time, Chief Executive of Companies House, for privileged access to their records.

Aberdare Library
Birmingham Library
Bodleian Library, Oxford
British Geological Survey
British Library (at St. Pancras and Colindale)
Brunel University, Uxbridge (Special Collections Dept)
Cardiff Library (Reference & Local History Depts)
Coal Authority, Mansfield (formerly at Bretby)
Companies House, Customer Services Section, Cardiff
Geological Museum, Earth Sciences Library, London
Glamorgan Archives, Cardiff
Guildhall Library, London
Imperial College Library, London
Llanelly Library
National Archives, formerly Public Records Office, Kew
National Library of Wales
National Museum of Wales (Department of Industry)
Neath Library
Newport Library
Ordnance Survey
Port Talbot Library
Railtrack Mining Engineer, Derby
Railtrack Records Centre, Swindon
Salvation Army (Correspondence over Blackmill Level)
Science Museum Library, London
Swansea Library (Reference & Local History Depts.)
Treorchy Library
West Glamorgan Archives, Swansea
Wiltshire & Swindon Archives, Chippenham

to John Williams, Phil Cullen, Steve Dumpleton and many, many other members of the Welsh Coal Mines Forum for their unstinting help on a myriad of questions,

to John Mann for his prodigious efforts to supply vast amounts of railway siding related material,

to Ian Pope and Keith Turton for generous access to their extensive work on railway wagons,

to Robert Protheroe Jones for very extensive guidance and access to his researches over a long period of time, both generally and on the mines of Carmarthenshire,

to Ifor Coggan for access to his comprehensive records on the Fochriw area,

to the Rev. Dr. M. R. Connop Price for help on the mines of Pembrokeshire,

to Ian Pope for the production of all of the maps.

INTRODUCTION

CONTENT

There are approximately 3,300 entries included in this work, which probably represent over 4,000 sites. In addition, there are over 1,600 cross referencing entries. Regrettably it has not been possible to give cross references for every alternative or erroneous form of spelling, so vast is the sheer number involved. For instance, Danyderi appears in various lists and reports as Dan Deri, Danderir, Danderry, Dandery, Dandiri, Dangderre, Danyderre and Dan-y-derri.

The extraction and collation of information from so many sources has inevitably produced conflicts, not just in ownership (see Section 9 of the guidance notes), but on the dates of events. Where no positive evidence has been found to support one date or company, rather than another, then the information is reproduced without comment

The layout is less than ideal, as compression of the mass of information available was paramount in order to keep the size of an ever growing volume to a minimum and yet include sources for every item of information. The widespread use of abbreviations (see Appendix 'A') has therefore been necessary to conserve space.

USE OF THIS GAZETTEER

As the gazetteer is in strict alphabetical order for the whole of South Wales, if the name of the colliery is known, then clearly you go direct to that entry. If the mine name is unknown, but the name of the owner is available, then the Index of Owners should help locate the mine name. Should only the approximate geographical area be known then try consulting the maps.

Note that opencast sites are not included within this gazetteer and that no research has been directed towards them. However, any information uncovered in respect of them was not discarded and has been placed in the incomplete Appendix 'H'.

SOURCE DATA

This gazetteer is based upon the Lists of Mines starting in 1854. Any material relating to the period before this date, which was encountered during the research, was noted and in the main included.

1854-1872	Annual lists in *Hunt's Mineral Statistics* (HMS)	
1873-1883	Lists in Annual Reports of H.M. Inspectors of Mines, with any variations against HMS annotated alongside	
1884-1887	Lists in the annual volumes of Mining & Mineral Statistics	
1888-1919	Annual lists prepared by Mineral Statistics Branch, Home Office	
1920 -1938	Annual lists prepared by Mines Department, Board of Trade	The period 1938 to 10.1947 also covered by unpublished monthly update lists (at the National Archives) * 1940-44 not published
1939	List in *Colliery Yearbook & Coal Trades Directory*	
1940-1941	Annual lists prepared by Mines Department, Board of Trade*	
1942-1945	List issued by the Ministry of Fuel & Power *	
1946	List in *Colliery Yearbook & Coal Trades Directory*	
1947	List issued by the Ministry of Fuel & Power and Coal Authority Licence records.	
1948-1949	*Guide to the Coalfields* (1949 & 1950 editions) and Coal Authority Licence records.	
1950	List issued by the Ministry of Fuel & Power and Coal Authority Licence records.	
1951-1996	*Guide to the Coalfields* (1952-97 editions) and Coal Authority Licence records	
1997-2010	Coal Authority records	

The *Hunt's Mineral Statistics* (HMS), covering the early period, are an invaluable source, but as they were voluntary they are certainly not comprehensive (e.g. Ferndale was not listed for 1866-68, yet it was a large established colliery where an explosion killed 178 in 1867) and even when the information is included, it can be prone to error especially of updating (e.g. Tylacoch shown for 1856-67 as Carr & Co. and 1868-69 as Thomas Jones. However, the pit was reported in the *Cambrian* of 8.12.1865, as being sold to Thomas Jones, thus 1866 & 67 are incorrect).

Despite the submission of information to the Mines Inspectors being mandatory, the early 'Lists' also leave much to be desired and clearly some owners failed to submit the necessary information. The lists themselves vary in format, and boundary changes occurred to the Inspectors' districts. Some were in alphabetical order of mine name and others by the name of the owner. In some lists the order was totally random and sometimes mines were grouped out of order (See Appendix 'C' for details). Over time, the information about each mine, recorded in the lists, changed and throughout errors occur (especially of spelling).

Although HMS was the basis used up to 1872, where an entry is shown as 'HMS', it relates to the period of overlap from 1873 to 1881 and is included because the entry is at variance with the Inspector's list.

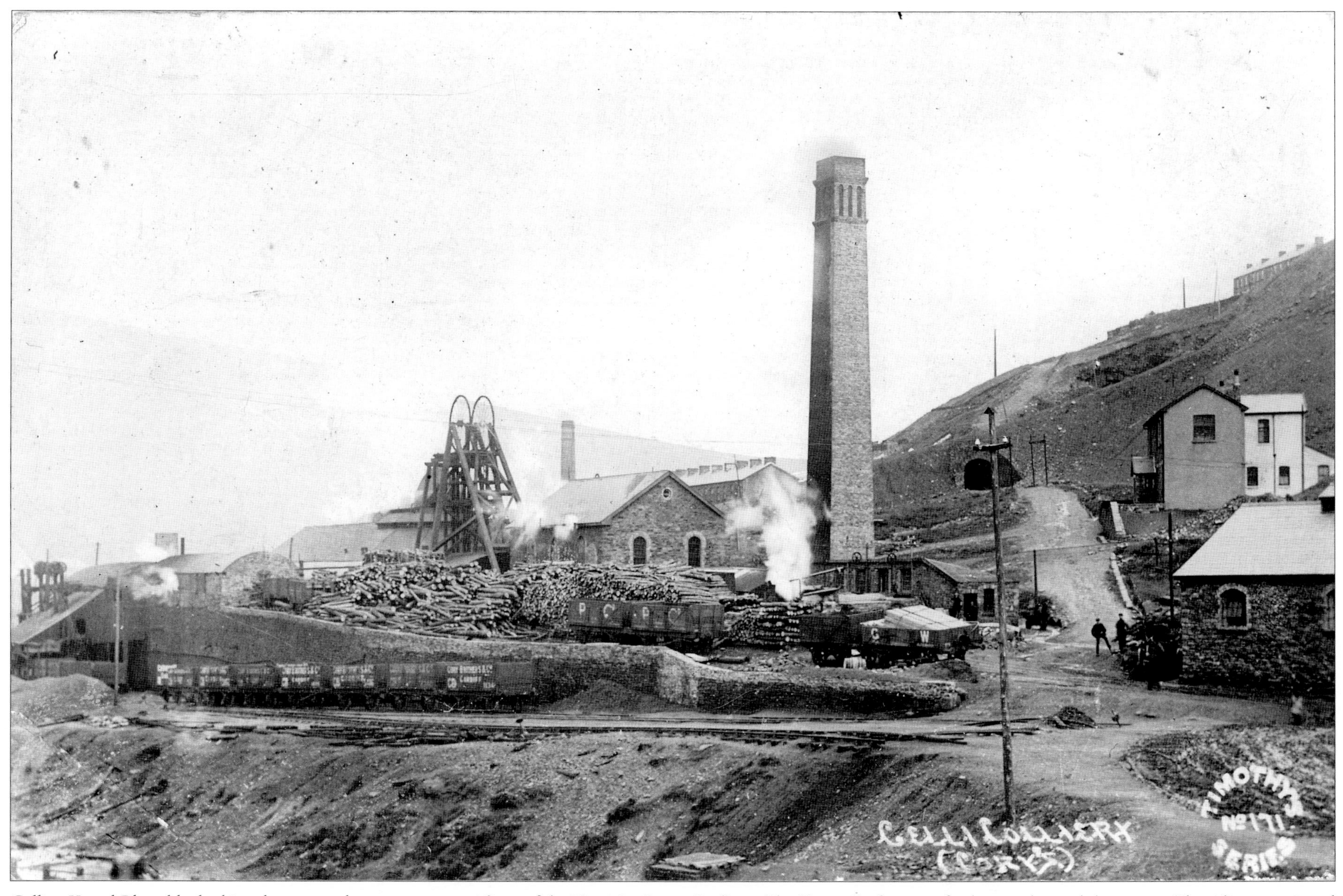

Gelli at Ystrad Rhondda, looking due east at the empty wagon sidings of the No. 1 (or Steam Coal) pit. The House Coal pit was further east beyond the screens. The sidings continued to join the Taff Vale Rly between Ystrad Rhondda and Llwynypia. Started in 1877 (previously worked by levels) it lasted until 1962. [Map 3 G4]

GUIDANCE AND EXPLANATORY NOTES

In order to aid the interpretation of this gazetteer the following fictitious example explains where to find the appropriate guidance notes. Numbers (1) refer to the sections which follow. However, there are a few points outside the content of these notes that also warrant explanation.

Each element of general historical data is in italics and has been enclosed in single apostrophes merely to clearly segregate it from following entries. Any which are verbatim quotes, and there are not many, are enclosed in double apostrophes.

Any company or personal names mentioned in the historical data and shown in non-italics, indicates the first appearance of that name.

Where manpower is shown in tabular form at the end of an entry, a vertical line merely indicates that the years are non consecutive.

BLACK HOLE (1) **WORKS,** (2) **Nelson** (3)

Glam. 20SW, ST 137957, Map 27 B6 (4)

DA – CG 12.5.1894 (5)

Minerals worked: (6) Steam Coal

Seams worked: (7) 1894-95 No. 1 Vein

1878	*Not listed* (*HMS gives* J. Bloggs)
1879 (8)	J. Bloggs (9) (*HMS gives J. Bloggs & Co.*)
1880-85	J. Bloggs & Co. Ltd. (10) (Reg. 1.3.1880, Capital £10,000, Dirs. Joe Bloggs, Fred Bloggs & A. N. Other, RN J. & W. Bloggs & Co. Ltd. 15.10.1882, VL 25.5.1885, COWU 12.12.1885, COD 1.9.1886, WU 7.12.1886, BT31 L.d. 9.7.1889 "Firm sold property in 1887.")
1886	*Not listed. ('It is expected that Black Hole mine will be reopened on* (11) *[23.12.1886]* (12) *.'- SWDN 17.12.1886)*
1887-90	J. Bloggs (*'Opened 1.1887.'* (13) , *'James Bloggs.'- PSA 1.2.1888* (14) , *'J. Bloggs & Son.'- FAL 6.6.1889,* (15) *'Explosion 22.1.1890, 11 killed.'*)
1891-95	J. Bloggs & Co. (*'Nine Foot seam struck [6.4.1891].'- SWDN 12.4.1891,* (16) *'Not listed 1891.'- Gelligaer PPL,* (17) *1892 22 employed, 1894 22/5,* (18) *1895 2/1*)
1896	***Abandoned*** (*'Upcast 8ft x12ft 260 yards and Downcast 10ft x 12ft.* (19) *Abandoned* (20) *6.2.1896.'- CA Ref SW896*) (21)
1932-39	Smith & Co. (*'Application for classification of coals* (22) *for Smith & Co., Black Hole Colliery.'- Min. 9.6.1933 NA Coal 4/30, 'Application of Smith & Co. for Standard Tonnages* (22) *for Black Hole Colliery.'- Min 16.10.1933 NA Coal 4/4*)
1951-59	Coal Mining Ltd. (*"Licence* (23) *granted 1.4.1951, expired 1959."- CA records*)

1951	1952	1953	1954	1955	1956	1957	1958	1959	
4/1	4/1	3/2	3/1	5/2	5/2	5/1	4/1	-/-	(18)

---

1. COLLIERY NAME

Order The locations are listed in alphabetical order. Where the terms 'Drift', 'Level', 'Slope', 'Slant' or 'Pit' (See Appendix 'B' for definitions) formed part of the colliery name in the source lists, then they have been included in the title, but the alphabetical listing ignores the suffix. Thus Garn Level comes before Garnbicca.

Where there was a combination of these terms used, then the term 'colliery' has been adopted. The many entries without any distinction are just listed by name. Even when specified, this can sometimes be misleading, as some had new pits, slants, etc; added to the existing facilities. Very often a single named site contained multiple pits/levels, etc; without specifying so. A further complication is the generalised use of 'level' when it might actually be more correctly identified as a 'slant' or 'drift'.

Incorrect spelling Incorrect spelling of colliery names (and of locations and owners) is common throughout the early lists and in the press, (e.g. Sonda for Tondu, Llanmibrwg for Glanmwrwg, Tydd Lewd for Tyllwyd, Detty Siencyn for Lletty Shenkin, etc;). Many can be deduced, but would you arrive at Fforchaman, for a reference to Foxchange? What is to be made of entries for Cefnfaithryn, Cefnaithryn, Cefn Eithram, Cefn Eithrim, Eithran, Eithrim, Ithram and Ithrun, nine apparent variations on what may have been one, or more, associated sites. No doubt many of these arise from interpretation of unclear handwriting or poor typesetting. Extreme errors are easily spotted, but many subtler errors are not so easily detected.

The South Wales Daily Post of 13.12.1899 says it all when it reported "A Welsh name worried our contemporaries. It was Glanmwrwg Colliery. For instance, the *Daily Chronicle* calls the pit **Glanmerrwg**, the *Daily Telegraph* has **Glanmerriog**, the *Morning Herald* and *Daily Telegraph* agree on **Glanmwrrwy**, the

Bristol Mercury says **Glanmurrwy**, the *Bristol Press* gives **Glanmyrrwy**, the Yorkshire Post gives **Glannwrwg**, whilst the **Glanmurray** of the *Liverpool Post* has quite a Scottish flavour."

Even supposedly authoritative maps can contain errors. The Cambrian dated 5.4.1907 reported "All Welsh maps are not printed in Wales. One of Port Talbot Docks and the South Wales coalfield contains these horrible examples; - Ynysybwll, Pidwallt, Yochriw and Yiniswen."

Alternative spelling The major problem of English versus Welsh forms occurs throughout. In particular the use of 'i' or 'y' (as in Tir/Tyr, Gelli/Gelly) and of 'f' or 'v' (as in Felindre/Velindre) will cause difficulties. Should a location not be found under one form of spelling then it may be necessary to look under the alternative.

Hyphenated names Yet another problem is the use, misuse and lack of hyphens in a location name. Again, there is no easy answer and perseverance in trying alternatives is often the only solution.

Implications Increasingly, old newspapers are being made available on-line and are fully searchable. Clearly, poor originals, dirty, creased and sometimes torn pages and varying type-faces can result in missed search results. Even if the word is perfectly clear, but spelt incorrectly, then it will not show up in a specific search. The extent of errors in typesetting or misreading is surprisingly large and currently (June 2017) the NLW newspaper website returns 2,633 instances of 'coliiery', 728 of 'collery', 678 of 'coliery' and 197 of 'colliry'.

2. 'WORKS'

Definition The Inspector's report for the South-Western District for 1873 concluded that "previous lists appear to have treated the great iron works of Monmouthshire as if each was but one mine." For instance, he states "Blaenavon appears as but one, whereas those vast works are made up of seventeen different, distinct and distant mines". Although no comments were made in the South Wales District report, the same rule appears to have been applied to the other counties. 'Works' is therefore a generic term applying to many mines located within the control of one works. The expression continued to be used in Hunt's Mineral Statistics in respect of Monmouthshire, as late as 1880.

Locations The locations where the term 'Works' was used is given below. Where figures follow the works' name, then the first figure is the number of mines previously appearing in the listings and the second is the actual number of mines involved.

Abercarn, Abersychan 1/4, Beaufort/Nantyglo 2/14, Blaenavon 1/17, Blaina 1/7, Brynamman, Bryndu, Cefn Cwsc, Clydach, Coalbrook Vale, Cwmaman, Cwmavon, Cwmcelyn & Blaina, Cyfarthfa, Ebbw Vale 1/13, Gadlys, Golynos, Hirwain, Llantwit, Llynvi, Maesteg, Pentyrch, Penydarran, Plymouth, Pontypool, Rhymney/Bute 4/17, Risca, Sirhowy 1/8, Tondu, Tredegar 3/20, Varteg, Victoria 1/5, Yniscedwyn, Ynysgeinon and Ystalyfera.

3. LOCATION

General In the early lists, the location was given simply as the nearest postal town or export port, which is not particularly helpful (e.g. Cardiff). In some years, only the county or parish was given and in a few instances even this can be wrong (e.g. Hafod Ellwood Colliery was listed under Monmouthshire until 1919 when it was moved to the Brecknockshire listing). Examples of the entirely wrong location being given are rife in Hunt's Mineral Statistics. For example, Sisters Pit at Llansamlet was stated for 1870-72 as being in the Rhondda and Tyr Glandwr at Landore for 1877-81, was shown as being at Caerphilly.

Irrespective of what was stated in the lists, an attempt has been made to give a more accurate indication of the actual location.

Alternative Locations However, there are some instances where it is not easy to be certain about a mine's location. There are plenty of examples of two mines with the same name, but some distance apart, for example Cefn Mawr at Clyne and Cefn Mawr at Resolven. There are also mines where a shaft would be closed and a new shaft bearing the same name opened in a different position, sometimes significantly further away. For example, at Mynydd Newydd "The Swansea Five Feet has been struck at Mynydd Newydd Colliery. As it had proved uneconomic to work from the old shaft, *over a mile away*, it was decided to drive a slant."

Working from two sides of a mountain There are also examples of mines being worked from both sides of a mountain, giving two geographically separate sites a substantial distance apart. (e.g. Wenallt Merthyr).

Multiple owners using one site See Appendix 'D' for examples of several owners working coal from one entrance.

Incorrect County There are a few mines where even the County was incorrectly recorded. This occurred even as late as the 1920s. Correspondence (C.A.Ref. 11568) concerning Nantgwyn, near Cwmllynfell, records that "In the List of Mines as under Glamorgan, but it is in Carmarthen."

4. MAP REFERENCES

Interpretation The Location References given against each entry e.g. (Glam. 12SW, SN 607104, Map 12 G7) means:

- Glam. Pre-1974 County
- 12SW Sheet Number for Ordnance Survey County Series Six Inch map.
- SN 607104 National Grid Reference (NGR) taken from the above map. In those instances, where the NGR is given as four characters as in:
  60x10x then the location is believed to lie with that square.
  In those cases, where four characters are shown contained in square brackets as in [60x10x] then the location is believed to lie within that square or the surrounding squares.

In this example, on the appropriate sheet, find '60' along the top or bottom edge and read off to the right for 7/10ths (Eastings). Then along the left or right edge, locate 10 and move 4/10ths up the sheet (Northings). Where these two readings intersect would be 607104, where the mine was located.

- Map 12 G7 The number of the map in this volume showing the location of this site. G7 refers to the appropriate grid square within that map. (If this is shown as **, then the precise location has not been established and the mine is not shown on the map, but listed separately.

The NGR has been calculated for as many sites as possible, although inevitably, the precise location of many mines has not been pin-pointed. Abandonment plans were not submitted for a surprisingly large number of sites, especially in the early years. Even where abandonment plans have been consulted, some, even as late as the 1920's do not show any surface features or even give which direction is North, thus frustrating attempts to pinpoint the exact position. As the base information has been culled from a variety of sources, most which date from well before the introduction of the National Grid system, the NGR quoted should, especially for the earlier sites, be treated with caution, but hopefully will be sufficient to enable the approximate position to be located.

The maps in this volume No attempt has been made to portray contours. The colouring is merely an attempt to give a generalised indication of higher ground. The majority of rivers and brooks have been included, to assist with the positional relationships and to give a further 'feel' to the lie of the land.

The boundary of the coalfield has been included on the appropriate maps and has been reproduced from the work of Robert Protheroe Jones, to whom I am very grateful.

Hundreds of sites are shown on original maps without names, especially levels. Some would have been trial sites, some older and therefore outside the scope of this publication, some new workings to replace ones closed down and others, multiple levels, operated under a single name. Each entry, therefore, may be a composite covering several individual locations.

Erroneous rounding For a few NGRs it may well be that the source data quoted a six figure reference which had been derived from the incorrect rounding up of 'Eastings' and Northings' from an eight-digit number, thus potentially shifting the true location of the site. Again, any documented information which would help refine this information would be appreciated.

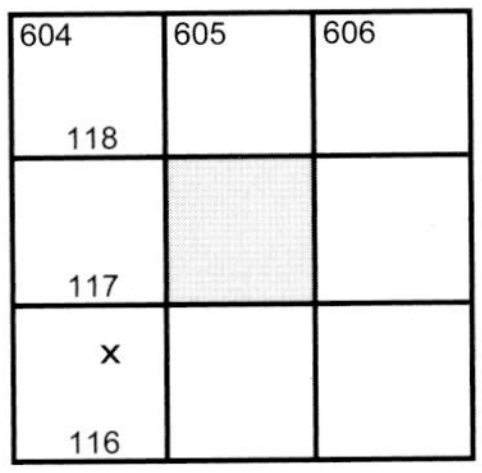

604	605	606
118		
117	(shaded)	
x 116		

Location 'X' at 60471168 if incorrectly rounded up produces 605117 thus shifting the position of location 'X' to the shaded square.
Correct shortening of the eight figure reference would be 604116.

Pre 1854 sites For some mines with multiple site references, it may well be that one or more of the site references may represent sites which were abandoned before 1854 and therefore pre-date the period covered by this volume. Unfortunately, there is no easy way to identify these. Likewise, it may not have been possible to identify the appropriate NGR, when two or more are known, for sites which have multiple entries in this volume.

5. DESCRIPTIVE ARTICLE

General Over the years, many very detailed articles appeared in newspapers and journals and many of these were accompanied by photographs, diagrams and/or plans. For instance, between 5.7.1895 and 29.4.1898 the *Colliery Guardian* published a series of forty-one articles on individual mines (or groups of mines). These extensive articles covered most aspects of the mines concerned. Unfortunately, the idea of providing references in this volume only crystallised late on in the research, so not all were noted. Where they were, references to them have been annotated in the listings as DA = Descriptive article. In addition, articles, with varying degrees of detail, are also referenced which appeared in the *South Wales Coal Annual* (SWCA), *South Wales Coal Field* (SWCF), *Welsh Coal Fields* (WCF), *Syren & Shipping* (S&S) and the *Proceedings of the South Wales Institute of Engineers* (SWIE). In total over 260 entries in this gazetteer are provided with such references.

Photographs Some two hundred photographs of mines have been included in the main volume. Thus, the term 'See volume for photograph' is self-explanatory. See also the notes at the introduction to the 'A Glimpse of the Coalfield' section.

6. MINERALS WORKED

Type of coal For each site, where it was stated in the List of Mines, the type of coal or mineral worked has been specified. For coal, the types are Anthracite, Coking, Gas, Household, Industrial, Manufacturing and Steam, although Annealing has sometimes also been used.

Other minerals Where another mineral was worked, this too has been listed (i.e. Fireclay, Ganister, Iron Pyrites, Ironstone, Ochre, Sandstone and Stone). A few sites were included in the 'Lists' that did not work any coal, but any site included in the source listings, appears in this publication.

7. SEAMS WORKED

Basis The base data for "seams worked" was not included in HMS and is thus not available pre 1874 and is then highly variable. It was not provided for all years and varied between the different inspectors' areas. For some early years, whilst 'Type of coal' was given, information on seams was excluded.

The seams listed were supposed to be the seams that were being worked. Many mines also had other seams that were either not being currently worked or had been abandoned at the time (details of pre 1850 abandonments are not included in this gazetteer). In later years, information was not updated on an annual basis, the previous year's data being carried forward. So far as this publication is concerned the seams listed are given in random order, not in any portrayal of depth. This sequence has been used to simplify comparison year on year.

Where "*Known to have worked .... seams.*" is shown, it refers to entries in the Catalogue of Plans which do not have any abandonment date appended to them.

Seam names Seam names are very confusing. Many had local names, some with alternatives. From the mid 1950's the N.C.B. introduced a set of standard names. Some sites refer to old names whilst others refer to the new classification.

Abandonment Where possible the abandonment dates of seams have been included. These are not comprehensive as many seams were abandoned without a date being recorded and indeed, many mine abandonments went totally unrecorded altogether.

A seam may well have been abandoned and then reopened, perhaps several times. Note however that the reappearance of a seam in the lists does not necessarily imply a working of the seam from the same opening, as it could well have involved an entrance at a new location.

8. FIRST DATE

The first date shown against an entry does not necessarily mean that the mine was not in existence before that date. This is especially true of the earlier years when the records were notoriously inaccurate. Not being listed in HMS or the Lists, could be merely errors or indicate that the mine was in development or was not working. Pre 1880, a mine may not have been listed because it was simply included under a 'Works' entry (See under para. 2). Even in later years, a mine may not have been included in the lists despite it being under development.

9. OWNER

Source The owner is given as shown in the primary source records as detailed above, with any conflicts being detailed. This is supplemented mainly by details from (1) Company Registration Records, but also from (2) Trade Directories, (3) Fatal Accident Listings, (4) Parish Production Lists, (5) Press reports or

advertisements and (6) other sources such as railway private siding records, railway minute books, wagon orders, and of course from Coal Authority Licensing records. Discrepancies have not been corrected, even when clearly incorrect. The two exceptions to this are in respect of:
(a) Sims, Willyams, Nevill, Druce & Co. who traded from 1837 to 1873, after which it was Nevill, Druce & Co. These, the correct forms, have been used throughout and are confirmed by the Nevill papers at the National Library of Wales (These two undertakings were also known as the Llanelly Copper Co.)

(b) the various renderings of the Ebbw Vale Co., Ebbw Vale Co. Ltd. (from 1864) and Ebbw Vale Steel, Iron & Coal Co. Ltd (from 1868)

In many cases where the source lists give a surname and only an initial, and the Christian name has been ascertained from secondary sources (Trade Directories, etc;) then this has been incorporated in the entry without reference to the source.

Owners' names taken from Trade Directories cannot be taken as indicating that the mine was open and working at that time. Owners were listed in the directories because they owned a mine, even though it may at that time have been currently closed.

Some owner details are shown as 'Wagon order dated xx.xx.xxxx for XYZ Co."- GWO Records' These have been sourced from a vast amount of material relating to the Gloucester and the Western wagon companies, together with a few relating to the Monmouthshire Co., kindly made available by Ian Pope. Again, details are shown when they are at variance with other sources and the expression 'Wagon order' may relate to purchase or hire, repair or maintenance and the dates quoted should be taken as being approximate as they relate to four weekly periods.

Conflicts

Conflicts between sources may result from;

- actual change during the course of the year.
- an impending change with the alteration pre-empted. (e.g. Wyndham, did not change to Cory Bros. until 1.1.1907, but was given as Cory Bros in the 1906 list).
- owner given as 'A' may well be trading under the name 'B'.
- wholly owned subsidiary, when the parent company may be named.
- company taken over, but former name retained.
- only one of two or more partners named.
- sub leases or tenant.
- being worked under contract, with the contractor's name being quoted.
- for a company or individual in bankruptcy, the owner may be given as the Receiver. (see below)
- Shortening of a long company name, when reporting an event, to a shorter version.
- plain errors.

Transfer of ownership

Change of ownership could take place at any time, not necessarily on the 31st December, so there will always be an element of overlap and effectively two owners during the course of a year during which the change took place. In some cases, a mine may have changed hands two or three times in the course of a year, with three or more owners therefore being involved. It is exceedingly rare for any of the intermediate owners to appear in the official listings.

Frequent changes

Given that there are many well documented modern examples of a mine changing hands almost yearly, then it is more than likely that the same thing happened in the early days, more especially to those small workings employing few men. Few of these may have been documented and the full details may never come to light.

To illustrate a modern example, Mount Pleasant level near Bedwellty had seven sets of owners, and thus seven licences, in less than the nine years between 1957 and 1966.

Auctions

Advertisements for the sale of a mine by an auction on a given date, do not necessarily mean that it was sold on that date. Provision was usually made in such advertisements for "*unless previously sold privately*", or it may have failed to sell at auction. Even if 'sold', it may have been subject to finalising arrangements, which may have fallen through. The dates of over 800 auctions are included.

A very rich source on auctions is the series of sales ledger books of Stephenson & Alexander auction sales covering 1878-1982. These can be found at Glamorgan Record Office under Ref D/D SA8/.

On liquidation

With companies either forced or going voluntarily into liquidation, the liquidator would effectively become the owner. Under Section 122 of the Coal Mines Act, "*Owner includes Receiver in the case of a mine where the business is carried on by the Receiver.*"

Death In the case of the death of the owner, the executors would become the temporary owners.

On closure Ownership did not cease with closure or abandonment. If, as was often the case, there was an intention to reopen the site, entries would be made in succeeding years in the following format: 'temporarily closed 1894', 'idle 1895', 'idle 1896', 'idle 1897' and then no listing for 1898. If the site was subsequently given in the Abandonment Listings as 'Abandoned 1894', then no entries appear in my listing beyond that date.

Limited companies See under Section 10 below.

Same name Quite often, what appears to be one company existing for a long period of time can in fact be a series of companies with the same name. More often than not these would have different directors, capital and constitution. For example, the 'Glyncorrwg Colliery Co. Ltd.' was listed from 1869 to 1930 but during this time three companies were registered successively on 1.11.1869, 13.3.1880 and 9.1.1890.

Apparent errors There are a few examples of company names appearing to be incorrectly spelt, but where examination clearly shows that the spelling was that used at registration. Powell's Lantwit Collieries was Registered on 7.6.1864 with Llantwit containing a single 'l' and the Corwg Merthyr Coal Co. Ltd was Registered on 26.11.1892 with Corrwg containing only a single 'r'.

Similar names There are numerous examples of a mine listed as being owned by a string of companies with very similar names. The difficulty is in knowing where errors had been made or whether the ownership did in fact change through a series of legitimate companies. The Merthyr Aberdare Steam Coal Colliery Co., the Aberdare Merthyr Steam Coal Colliery Co. or was it the Aberdare Merthyr Colliery Co. or even the Aberdare Merthyr Collieries Co.? In fact, only the first appears to be an error, the other three being registered on 7.1.1873, 16.8.1886 and 1.7.1891.

However, of the Forest Iron & Steel Co. (1873), the Forest Steel & Iron Co. (1874), the Treforest Steel Co. (1875) and the Forrest Steel & Iron Co. (1876), only the first is correct. All the others were errors in the listings, as were the use of Forest Iron & Steel Works Co. Ltd in *Worrall's* 1875 directory and Treforest Steel & Iron Co. in *Fatal Accident Listing* for 30.7.1875 and Forest Steel Co. in 22.8.1878.

Index The Index to Owners should help to track down specific individuals or companies and hopefully should include all names appearing in the main gazetteer. Should any omissions or errors be found, I would be very grateful to receive details.

10. LIMITED COMPANIES

Sources Theoretically at least, two sets of papers should exist. Those of the limited company itself and the file for that company at the registration authority (Board of Trade or later Companies House). Unfortunately, it seems to have been the norm that when a company was Wound Up, the liquidator was instructed, at the Winding Up Meeting, that all papers should be destroyed. Thus the registration file is all that might be available.

Scale of the task The sheer number of companies involved in working coal is overwhelming. Just for 'Limited Companies' over 1,500 firms had been involved. Unfortunately, the availability of information is variable and records, where they exist, are split between Companies House at Cardiff and the National Archives at Kew. Regrettably before the files were moved to Kew many were destroyed as the PRO/NA only accepted files on a sample or representative basis. Of those that survived, considerable 'thinning' took place, although it must be said that within a file, most of the important documents survive. Thus, it is a matter of luck as to whether the records of a particular company still exist. Having said that, over 800 Company Registration Files were examined together with 300 summary records and over 200 'still live' records checked and I need to record my very special thanks to both organisations.

Apart these two main sources, some information has also been obtained from the Stock Exchange Register of Defunct & Other Companies and the Stock Exchange Annual Year Book.

Portrayal of company history The details of the company's history are shown in summary form against its first appearance within an entry and are repeated whenever that company's name appears in another entry. This duplication is provided to overcome the need to search for the details elsewhere on the disc. There are one or two exceptions to this and in such cases a cross reference is provided.

The downside of providing the full history against each entry is that some of that history will not be relevant to those sites which operated for only a short period of the company's existence.

Registered The date 'Registered' is the same as the date the company was incorporated.

Capital The Capital shown was that contained in the Incorporation Documents (Memorandum and Articles of Association). This may well have changed over the period of the company's life, either by increase or by reduction. No details of such subsequent changes have been recorded in this volume.

Directors The Directors listed are, in the main, those that were appointed at the time of Incorporation. These served for a fixed term and were either re-elected or replaced by new directors at frequent intervals. Of course, some directors resigned or died before their term had expired and had to be replaced. Again subsequent changes have not been recorded.

Renaming Changing a company's name usually involved three steps. Firstly, the proposal was put to a special meeting of shareholders and the motion passed. This was then usually confirmed at a second meeting of shareholders. Finally, the proposed name had to be registered with the Board of Trade and the date given in this volume is that date. Note also that in the case of a proposed name closely resembling that of an existing name, formal written permission had to be sought from the existing company for the use of the new name. This was usually just a formality.

Liquidation There are three types of winding-up (1) Compulsory – by order of the Court, (2) Voluntary, which may be initiated either by the members or by creditors, and (3) subject to the supervision of the Court, which can be applied in either types of Voluntary winding up.

Dissolution A company can be dissolved either by the formal winding-up of the firm, by an order of the Court or by the Registrar striking the name from the Register if he believes the company to be defunct. So a 'Dissolved date' is very often just the formal removal of the company name from the Register, many years after it ceased trading. Many companies quietly faded away with no formal liquidation or winding up at all.

BT31 The index of owners provides a tool for anyone wishing to carry out further research on specific limited companies, as the company number and National Archives (PRO) reference is given where appropriate and where it was found.

The N.A. description of BT31 is '*Files of dissolved companies registered with the Board of Trade from 1856 onwards. The files cover those dissolved companies of all kinds incorporated between 1856 and 1931 and dissolved before 1932. Some files of companies incorporated between 1856 and 1900 and dissolved between 1933 and 1948. Files of public and private non-exempt companies incorporated up to 1970 and dissolved between 1948 and 1971 with a one per cent sample of files of exempt private companies.*'

BT41 A few companies' records were filed under reference BT41. The N.A. description is '*This series contains the files of all Joint Stock Companies which were registered under the Act of 1844 and dissolved before 1856, and of those re-registered under the 1856 Act.*'

Qualifications

- Some entries are shown in the source lists as not being 'Ltd.' when clearly they were. Likewise, the reverse can be true.
- Where a company name is followed by '(Error?)', then a Limited Company of the same name as that given was registered on the date shown, although it can not be definitely be taken that the Limited Company took over immediately, or in some cases, even took over at all.
- Some companies which were not 'Limited' were Registered and some companies which were 'Limited Companies' had dispensation under the Act to omit the 'Ltd.' from the company name. Clearly it was impossible to check every one.
- Before a new company was registered, invariably the mine (or proposed mine) was in the name of the individual/s involved in launching the company (the subscribers).
- Date of registration of a 'Limited Company' was inevitably not the date of change of ownership. Very often the requisite capital was not raised or agreements with the newly registered company had to be completed (and were very often not). Once a colliery was sold, the new owners may not have taken possession until a later date. Equally, an agreement may have contained a provision for ownership to be deemed to be backdated to an earlier date.

Short life companies Some companies were registered, went to share allocation, but then failed after a very short time. e.g. Ystalyfera Tin-Plate Co. Ltd. Reg. 8.2.1907, VL 2.5.1907, less than three months after incorporation, to be replaced by Ystalyfera Tinplate Co. Ltd. Reg. 3.5.1907: and Cilfynydd Colliery Co. Ltd. Reg. 17.2.1914, VL 28.12.1914 (ten months).

Failed Companies Many companies, whilst being Registered, apparently failed in that they never achieved an existence by the allocation of shares, or because they were unable to achieve their objectives in the acquisition of the desired property. A list of such firms (some 170) is given in Appendix 'G'

11. GENERAL HISTORY

General Apart from the base sources already mentioned, together with newspapers and journals and records of Companies House and the Coal Authority, information has been gleaned from a very wide range of sources. So vast is the material available that it is not practical to list and discuss each individual item here. Suffice to say that the National Archives at Kew, the Welsh Archives at Aberystwyth and the County Archives at Cardiff, Swansea, Llanelli, Carmarthen and Ebbw Vale each contain papers, reports and plans on an immense scale and other locations contain large collections on specific matters. Attention is drawn below to a selective few very important sources not mentioned elsewhere.

Important Sources The National Coal Board papers (and those of the Coal Commission) are held at in the National Archives at Kew in prodigious numbers. One example, Position of Small Mines at Primary Vesting Date. (Coal 29/5) a summary detailing each small mine.

Glamorgan Records Office (Cardiff) holds some eighty bound volumes of the *Annual Report of the Mineral Agent to Lord Windsor* covering 1863 to 1940. After 1906 they are titled 'Earl of Plymouth' rather than 'Lord Windsor'. Note that although dated for a year end (e.g. 30.6.1905) some of them were clearly written a considerable time later and sometimes they reflect events which occurred after that date. Also, reference to a certain activity, relates to how it affected the colliery take within the land owned by his lordship and not necessarily to the whole seam or colliery.

At the Guildhall Library in London are held the *Annual Reports of Limited Companies* from 1873 to 1911. Many, but nothing like all, of the South Wales Limited Companies are included in these archives.

A major failing in this research has been the lack of time (compounded by the distance, and cost) to visit the very extensive records of the National Library of Wales at Aberystwyth. This is very much to be regretted, as examination of their catalogue reveals a great deal that is clearly of significant interest.

12. INTERPRETED DATES

The problem The majority of quoted dates from newspapers and journals, apart from those for auctions, have been interpreted from the day of week quoted in the report. There is therefore a possibility of the actual date being one or two weeks earlier, if there was a delay in printing the report. Such interpreted dates are shown in square brackets thus [ ]. In the event, many hundreds of dates would have been inferred incorrectly, if it were not for the fact that the event appeared in another report some weeks earlier. Even given a string of reports, in many cases no certainty can be put on the inferred date.

Undoubtedly there will be instances where only a single report has been found and without alternative reports to confirm or refute this, the validity of the inferred date must be treated with some caution.

An example To illustrate the pitfalls, a report appeared in the *Colliery Guardian* of 1st September 1866 that "Last week, the first cargo of coal from Aber Coal Co.'s Colliery." i.e. in late August. However, both the *Cambrian* of 3rd August and the *Mining Journal* of 4th August said that the shipment took place on 18th ultimo, i.e. in July).

13. OPENED

Definition A reference to a mine being 'Opened' can mean anything, from sinking, working coal, coal first raised or coal first forwarded. The term has been used indiscriminately in records and reports and if possible such references need to be read in the context of other reports.

Sinking does not necessarily mean a new pit or shaft. It can refer to deepening an existing shaft deeper. In particular, note that reference to 'sinking a staple shaft' always refers to the sinking of a shaft within an established mine (see Appendix 'B' for definition).

Two sinking dates For some mines two 'start of sinking' dates may be given. Usually the first is when the owner commenced sinking and the second is when the contractor took over to complete the undertaking. For example, "*Sinking operations for Britannia Pit, Pengam commenced on 19.9.1910.*" from the ICTR 30.9.1910, but sinking had actually started three months earlier, "*Preparations for sinking were commenced in June 1910 and the shafts sunk to 185 feet with a crane, when sinking was stopped until the winding machinery was ready. The sinking with the winding engine has recently been commenced.*" from CG 22.9.1910.

Reopened date Note that reopened on a given date does not necessarily mean that production re-commenced from that date. Very often it is the date that repairers commenced work.

14. RAILWAY RECORDS

General

There is much useful information to be found regarding commercial, operating and legal matters relating to collieries and colliery companies in the minute books of the various railway companies. Where such records have been consulted, information has been included selectively, if relevant and helpful in building a fuller picture. In some cases, the content of the minute is immaterial; it is included because of the party named. Minute books consulted cover the following companies:

Aberdare Valley; Barry; Brecon & Merthyr; BP&GV; Great Western; GWR&PT; GWR&R&SB; Llynvi & Ogmore; Llynvi & Ogmore & GWR Jt.; Llantrissant & Taff Vale Junction; Llanelly Railway & Dock Co.; LM&SR; London & North Western; Midland; Monmouthshire Railway & Canal Co.; Neath & Brecon; Port Talbot Railway & Dock Co.; Rhondda & Swansea Bay; Rhymney, Sirhowy; South Wales Mineral; Taff Vale; and the Vale of Neath. (See section B of Sources & Bibliography for details and dates of these Minute Books.)

Private Siding Agreements

A great number of collieries had railway facilities, even many small ones and most of these were covered by a Private Siding Agreement (PSA). The usual problem associated with using these is in knowing whether the agreement was implemented in the form set out in the document. However, in the context of this volume this is immaterial, as details quoted from agreements relate only to the parties named at a given date, indicating that they were active at the time the agreement was signed. Information from PSAs has therefore only been used when the party is at variance (or is more complete, e.g. full Christian names instead of just initials) with the data obtained from the prime sources; or if the date of the agreement (a) predates the source material, (b) is useful in defining when a site changed hands or (c) postdates the source material. Only occasionally are other references included, which are felt to be pertinent to the activity of the firm or the colliery. Much of the detail shown as 'PSA papers' comes from John Mann's extensive records or from material and records in my own collection.

Transfer of ownership

Siding agreements covering the transfer of ownership can be very misleading, in that quite often the railway company was 'catching up' with a previously unrecorded change of ownership. There are also numerous examples where such changes went totally unrecorded.

Authority for facilities

The provision of siding facilities invariably involved the appropriate railway body in approving the terms and conditions associated with an agreement and also in authorising the necessary expenditure (in most cases recouped from the prospective siding user). As with PSAs above, many such authorities reveal useful information regarding the individual or company involved.

Railway Lists of collieries

Seven "Lists of Collieries" published by railway companies have been consulted (A(N&SW)D& Rly 1902, GWR of 1907/1924/1932, LM&SR 1924 and 1937 and BR 1954) and, where information conflicted with the base source material, appropriate notes have been included. There are several instances of colliery names appearing only in these lists. 'Gloda' for example, is listed as an alternative name for 'Glyncorrwg'. Many instances occur of collieries being included in these lists after they have been closed or abandoned. There are various possible explanations for this:

- railway facilities were retained for clearance of stock coal or more likely for the disposal of scrap following demolition.
- the company was still in existence and finalisation of commercial matters (e.g. outstanding debts) had not been completed.
- railway facilities retained pending possible sale and transfer to a purchaser.
- and of course just plain errors.

15. FATAL ACCIDENT LISTS

Disasters

Brief details are included of incidents which involved five or more deaths. This is an arbitrary cut-off, as regrettably deaths were a common occurrence and to have reproduced details of all of them would have swamped many entries. Most of these resulted from explosions, but some were occasioned by shaft accidents and others by inundation of water. On this basis, from 1851 to 1971 123 disasters occurred, taking 3,883 lives. (See Appendix 'E')

Fatal Accident Listings

In terms of all fatal accidents, brief details are only included where (1) there is a variant in the mine owner's name, (2) the owner's name is the same, but the date assists in indicating when a change between owners took place or (3) when no entry has otherwise appeared in the listings for the year concerned. (Two dates separated by a comma indicate two accidents, whilst those separated by a hyphen indicate several other accidents were reported between the two dates given)

16. PRESS EXTRACTS (Also read '12 Interpreted Dates')

General

Wales was not only rich in coal, but in the range and number of its newspapers. Apart from the *South Wales Daily News*, the *Cambrian* and the *Western Mail*, there were numerous local papers covering the majority of South Wales. Regrettably most of these local papers were not consulted, because of the lack of time. No doubt many of the entries in this gazetteer would have been considerably enhanced had that not been the case. If anyone has researched any of these and can supply additional reports, I would be very pleased to hear from them.

Likewise, there were a number of Welsh language newspapers which no doubt contain much valuable material, but which, with my lack of knowledge of the language, were not consulted. Any material from these sources would be very welcome.

In addition to the newspapers, there were the national specialized journals, the *Colliery Guardian* and the *Mining Journal*, which have contributed so much to this publication.

Later in my researches the NLW newspaper website became available. This has grown considerably as more papers have been digitized. It has proved to be an absolute boon and has been extensively used. It is highly recommended as an invaluable aid to all types of research. (Note comment at end of para 1.)

Extracts have been taken, from amongst others, from the following:

- the one hundred and thirty years of the *Colliery Guardian* from 1861 to 1990 (weekly; monthly from 1968).
- thirty-seven years of the *Mining Journal* (weekly) from 1853 to 1889 when it became primarily concerned with Metallic mining.
- thirty-five years of the *South Wales Daily News* (Daily)
- twenty years of the *Cambrian* (weekly, taken from the excellent computerised index at Swansea Library).
- eleven years of the *Cardiff Times* (weekly)

A full list of all the newspapers and journals consulted will be found under 'Sources & Bibliography'

With the sheer size of the task, it would be impossible to say that nothing had been missed in the volumes consulted, especially those that were on micro-film. Also, some volumes were incomplete or others had odd pages or issues missing.

The only reason that further years or papers were not covered was time. Nonetheless, over nineteen and a half thousand extracts have been taken (not all of which have needed to, or could, be used). Those covering the earlier years are especially useful, helping to amplify the sometimes sparse data in the listings. Additionally, there were plenty of reports that could not be identified to a specific site.

What was reported, especially in the early days, is just a matter of luck. Some mines were covered profusely (e.g. between 1868 and 1873 Gnoll Colliery gets mentioned on at least 16 occasions); on other mines, not a word. Pressure of space in some editions no doubt resulted in reports being 'squeezed out'. Major news items and especially general elections took over many pages, often for over a week, to the detriment of the reporting of local happenings.

Some of the quoted reports are included, not for the matter being reported, but to indicate that the colliery was active or inactive at that time, or to confirm, or otherwise, the owner.

In the interests of space saving, all extracted reports have been paraphrased or abbreviated

London Gazette

The one publication that has not so far not been mentioned is the *London Gazette*, which is without doubt one of the most important sources. Amongst other things, this publication details bankruptcies and the Winding Up of companies, but perhaps the most valuable contribution it makes is in the recording the dissolution of partnerships, wherein are listed the full names of all the members. Over 300 such entries were extracted.

It should be especially noted that the recording of names in the *Gazette* is the most accurate and reliable source and should take preference over most other sources.

In total over 2,700 extracts were taken from the *Gazette* covering the period from 1840 to 2007.

Uncertainty over correct site

Whilst every effort has been made to ensure that ambiguous or vague press reports have been allocated to the appropriate entry, some have been endorsed 'Query this site'. It is inevitable that some reports, entered in good faith to one site, will turn out to have been incorrectly allocated.

Infuriatingly, many advertisements made no mention of the mine name, the owner or even the location. They just refer to 'A splendid anthracite colliery in Glamorgan' or 'A fine bituminous pit in South Wales.' All these had to be ignored.

Duplicate reports

When an event was reported in two or more papers (of those examined), all references are given, as very often the content of these reports varied and the detail shown in this volume will be a composite of these differing reports. Even when different papers/journals gave the same information, all sources are given, as readers wishing to consult a source may have easier access to one rather than another.

Erroneous reports Examples of errors are rife. The Mining Journal reported on 8.2.1868 'The whole of the collieries of the Dynevor Coal Co. have been purchased by Messrs Evan & Bevan'. The *Colliery Guardian* reported the same, one week later on 15th. However, on the 15th the Mining Journal issued a correction 'The report of the 8th re Dynevor Coal Co. is incorrect. The property remains in possession of Mr. E. A. Moore'. Such are the traps and it is inevitable that some of the reports included in this work will turn out to be erroneous. By the same token, some reports were clearly based on rumours and a report quoted one week may be denied in the following week's issue.

Interpreted dates References, such as 'happened on Tuesday' can be very misleading and need to be treated with caution. (see 12 above)

Auctions With advertisements for auctions, the date of the paper quoted may not have been the earliest edition in which it appeared. Sometimes these advertisements appeared weeks or even months before the date of the auction, thus providing an earlier indication of the situation at that particular mine. See also under 'auctions' in 9 above.

17. PARISH PRODUCTION LISTS

Returns of coal worked It seems that Parish Overseers produced and published an annual 'Return of coal worked (and or raised)' by each mine within a parish. How extensive these returns were, has not been established and the only ones (which I have termed 'Parish Production Lists' = PPL) for which detailed data has been located are the following:

Aberdare	1861-81, 1902,1905, 1906, 1910 & 1912.
Llanwonno	1866-81.
Ystradyfodwg	1866-81.
Gelligaer	1860-61, 64-65, 67-81 & 83-87, 1908-10, 1917.

together with Merthyr 1866-75, and 1887 data for the above four plus Llantrissant from '*The South Wales Coal Trade*' by Wilkins 1888.

The data for up to 1881 has come from *Hunts Mineral Statistics* and that for other years from reports in various newspapers.
I would be delighted to hear of the location of any further sources.

18. NUMBER EMPLOYED

Figures first provided First provided comprehensively from 1894, although

- for 1888 one of the two South Wales Inspector's Districts gave the total employed at each site,
- for 1891 the South Wales District (but not the South Western) gave the number of men employed (in a separate table),
- for 1893 the South Wales District (but not the South Western) gave the number of men employed underground for some mines.

Delegates meetings Between 1879 and 1881 a number of union meetings of miners' delegates were reported in the SWDN of 12.7.1879, 16.7.1879 and 25.1.1881, where the number of men represented was recorded. These have been reproduced in this volume, although it must be stressed that the number represented may be considerably fewer than the total workforce.

Post 1939 figures Note that from 1939 many companies' figures remained unchanged year after year. Even under the N.C.B., some districts' figures were not updated year on year. The last year of any pretence to provision of accurate manpower figures was 1971. After this time, the 1971 figures are merely carried forward with only occasional changes. A comparison of the reported figures for Licenced mines, compared with the details recorded in the 1960 Licenced Mines Survey, amply illustrates just how misleading these reported figures can be.

Portrayal of the figures The number of men employed is given in the form X/Y where X = the number below ground and Y = those above. Some entries may be shown with only a single (X/Y) and in such cases the manpower relates to the year (or years) in question for that line of entry. Where an entry is shown in the form '1960-70 4/3', the manpower figures 4/3 apply to each year from 1960 to 1970 inclusive. In most cases the figures are given in tabular form for clarity.

Variations exist between different sources, especially post war, and sometimes these can be significant. Which may be correct is impossible to say and indeed both may be correct in that the figures may have been supplied at different times in the course of a year.

Private mines A special point needs to be made with the figures for private mines. Where the owner/owners actually worked the mine, in terms of reporting the 'Number employed,' it is clear that in some (many) cases they excluded themselves from the figures, thus distorting the figures for the number working at that mine. Where examples have been found, details have been highlighted.

None employed Some entries will show the number of men employed as -/- (nil). There are several possible reasons for this:

- The mine may not have been working for various reasons.
- Only the owners worked in the mine, thus nobody was 'employed'.
- Sinking was in progress and if shown as -/-, may be explained by the use of contractors (i.e. no direct employment)
- For the year of abandonment, very often given as -/-, but this can mean that the return was sent in after abandonment and therefore there were none employed at that time. Effectively therefore, in such cases, manpower figures for the year of abandonment are not available. There is no means of knowing whether -/- was correct or not.

Year on year variations There are many examples of a very significant variation between years. An odd year with a lower or 'nil' figure may sometimes be explained by the press extracts (e.g. temporary closure, sinking deeper or dispute, etc;). In other cases, a significant drop in manpower might have resulted from the abandonment of one or more seams which may be explained by details given under 'seams worked'. Some of these, where a date has been ascertained, have been annotated by way of a note. Likewise, a significant increase may be down to the opening of additional seams or faces.

Value of the figures Although the number of men employed is merely a snapshot at the time the return was sent in, their value, at least up to the mid 20th century, is in the following;

- providing an indication of whether a mine was working or not,
- the relative size of the undertaking,
- trends, year on year and
- enabling some crude estimation to be made of production capability.

Caution As with nearly all other data gathered for this publication some caution needs to be exercised. In some cases, manpower figures are given, even though the mine was idle the whole time because of a strike. e.g. Deep Navigation was shown for 1927 as employing 1824/358 and for 1928 as 1852/371. However, the Colliery Guardian of 8.2.1929 stated that "*It has been decided to restart work at Deep Navigation Colliery after a stoppage of two years.*"

19. SHAFT SIZES

In the main, shaft diameters were provided 'in the clear', but there is evidence that some, especially in press reports, quoted a diameter which included the brickwork walling. Some caution needs to be exercised. It should also be noted that shafts could be oval, elliptical, square or oblong, and it is not always clear from the data provided which is involved in a particular report. Any clarification on such instances would be appreciated.

20. ABANDONED

Abandoned Sources do not define 'Closed', 'Abandoned', 'Discontinued', 'Suspended', 'Not working', 'Idle' and 'Standing', each being used interchangeably and indiscriminately. This is probably more so for the term 'Abandoned' where the rules applicable have changed considerably over time.

Note also that when the term 'Not listed' is used, it does not infer that the site was closed for the full year, only that it was not operating (or details had not been sent in) when the returns were made at the end of the year.

Closures There does not seem to have been any standard rule for including a mine in the lists when it was not working. Some were excluded, some included and of these, only some are annotated 'Not working.'

Mines were very often closed for a period of weeks or months, when changing hands to allow the various formalities to be completed.

Note also that when the term 'Not Listed' is used, it does not infer that the site was closed for the full year, only that it was not operating (or details had not been sent in) when the returns were made at the end of the year.

Royalty plans The Catalogue of Plans of Abandoned Coal Mines lists all deposited plans. Whilst the great majority are true abandonment plans, a small proportion are working or royalty plans with termination dates that do not relate to closure of the mines they record. Time constraints did not permit an examination of the many thousands of individual plans to distinguish the few that were not abandonment plans. This will have resulted in a few spurious abandonment dates being given in the entries.

21. COAL AUTHORITY

Many references are given as 'C.A. Ref, xxx' and these refer to the very extensive archives maintained by the Mining Records section of the Coal Authority at Mansfield (formerly located at Bretby, Burton on Trent). In excess of 1,000 abandonment plans and several hundred colliery files have been seen, together with various other miscellaneous records, but it is stressed that this is only a fraction of those held by the Authority.

22. CLASSIFICATION OF COAL & STANDARD TONNAGES

General Under the Coal Mines Act 1930, which came into operation on 28th October 1930, the production, supply and sale of coal were regulated. This was controlled through the South Wales District (Coal Mines) Scheme 1930 which operated an Executive Board and a number of committees. The majority of the records of this organisation survive at the National Archives (under reference Coal 4) and provide a vast amount of information relating to the mines, especially the small ones, operating in the 1930s.

Classification of Coal The Classification of Coal Committee was remitted to determine the various classes to which any coal produced in the district belonged and to allocate the coal produced at each mine into the appropriate classes. In the course of this work the Committee was advised of new openings, changes in ownership and of closures.

Standard Tonnages The Standard Tonnages Committee fixed the standard (output) tonnage on a quarterly basis for each mine.

Whilst this at first glance appears relatively straight forward, the rules were lengthy and complex. Once again the committee was kept advised of changes as above.

23. LICENCE DATA

Background From 1947 all coal mines, other than those shown as the National Coal Board, were licensed by the N.C.B. and the data in respect of them comes from a variety of sources. Apart from 1947 and 1950, for which lists (dated 1948 and 1950) were issued by the Ministry of Fuel & Power, the original base was the Guide to the Coalfields. This guide is useful, but more accurate information is available from the Licence records themselves, where they exist and where an opportunity was available to examine them. In addition, information has also been gleaned from abandonment records, but not comprehensively.

Licenced Mines The information shown for private mines is thus a mixture of the above. Where the details are taken from the Licence records then the 'years' given in Column 1 reflect this and have been used even if other source material gave information to the contrary. Where start and termination dates of the licence were available, then these have been included. Some entries only have details of when the licence started or when it terminated, rather than both.

The expiry date represents the end of the period of permitted operation. It does not mean or imply that work continued right through the permitted period and in fact many mines ceased operation, and were abandoned, long before that date. By the same token the 'end' date does not necessarily mean closure, as very often a new licence would be granted to extend the period of operation.

Examination of these records identified some new mines not previously heard of (or not listed as being in existence at a certain date), some new owners (even for mines previously listed) and some first names for owners where only initials had previously been available.

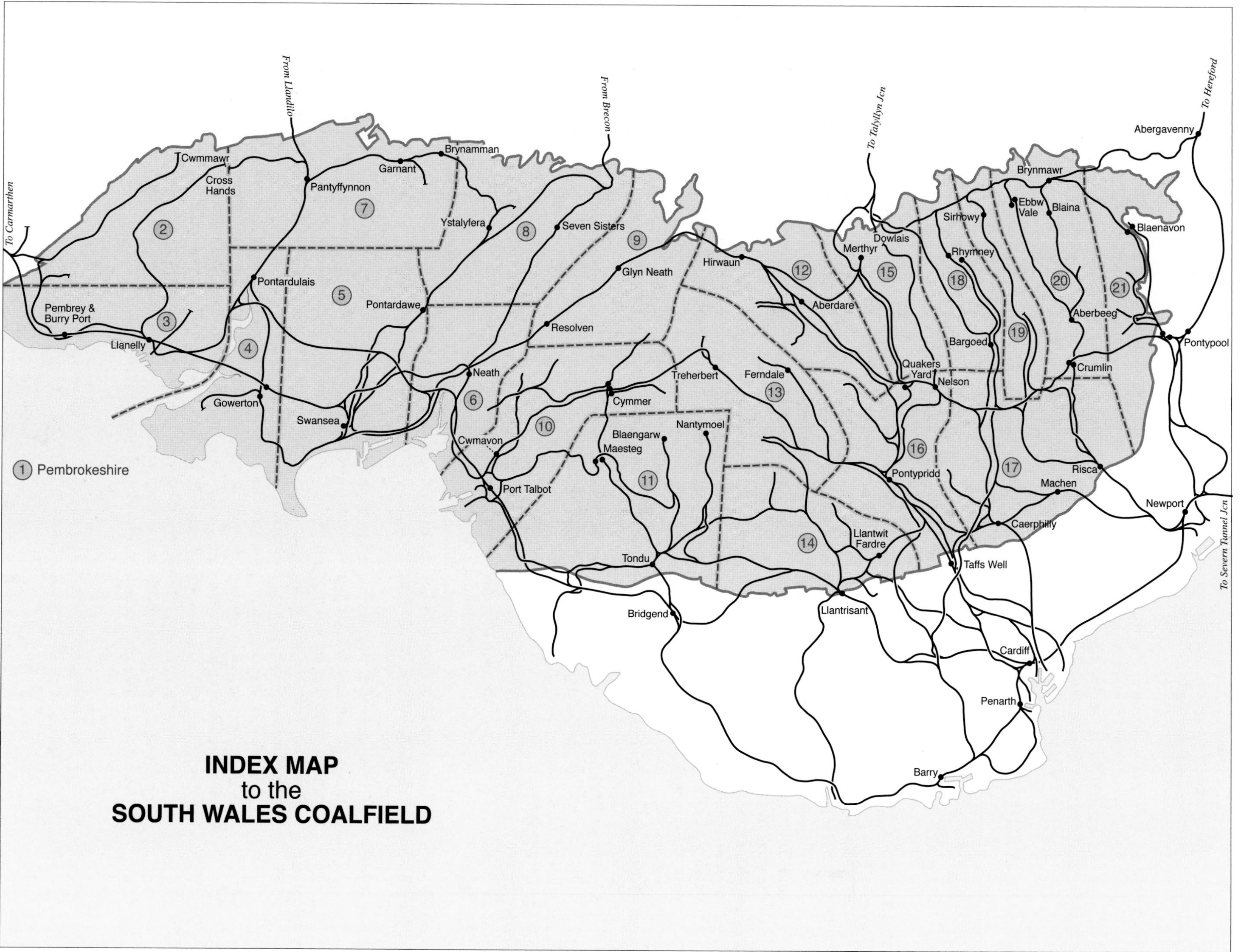

INDEX MAP
to the
SOUTH WALES COALFIELD
1 Pembrokeshire
To Carmarthen
From Llandilo
From Brecon
To Talyllyn Jcn
To Hereford
To Severn Tunnel Jcn
Cwmmawr
Cross Hands
Pantyffynnon
Garnant
Brynamman
Ystalyfera
Seven Sisters
Glyn Neath
Hirwaun
Merthyr
Dowlais
Sirhowy
Rhymney
Ebbw Vale
Brynmawr
Blaina
Blaenavon
Abergavenny
Pontardulais
Pembrey & Burry Port
Llanelly
Gowerton
Swansea
Pontardawe
Resolven
Neath
Cwmavon
Port Talbot
Cymmer
Treherbert
Ferndale
Aberdare
Quakers Yard
Nelson
Bargoed
Aberbeeg
Crumlin
Pontypool
Blaengarw
Maesteg
Nantymoel
Tondu
Bridgend
Llantrisant
Llantwit Fardre
Pontypridd
Taffs Well
Caerphilly
Machen
Risca
Newport
Cardiff
Penarth
Barry
2
3
4
5
6
7
8
9
10
11
12
13
14
15
16
17
18
19
20
21

THE MAPS

To repeat what is stated in the Introduction. No attempt has been made to portray contours. The colouring is merely an attempt to give a generalised indication of higher ground. The majority of rivers and brooks have been included, to assist with the positional relationships and to give a further 'feel' to the lie of the land. The boundary of the coalfield has been included on the appropriate maps and has been reproduced from the work of Robert Protheroe Jones, to whom I am very grateful.

Hundreds of sites are shown on original maps without names, especially levels. Some would have been trial sites, some older and therefore outside the scope of this publication, some new workings to replace ones closed down and others, multiple levels, operated under a single name. Each entry, therefore, may be a composite covering several individual locations.

Railways are shown only in outline and anyone requiring more detail is referred to the *Atlas of the Great Western Railway* 2nd ed. 1997, published by Wild Swan Publications, and for very detailed information, to the series 'Track Layout Diagrams of the GWR and BR WR' originally published by the author and now by Lightmoor Press.

The excellent maps that follow are based on originals by the author but are the skill full work of Ian Pope to whom I am exceeding grateful.

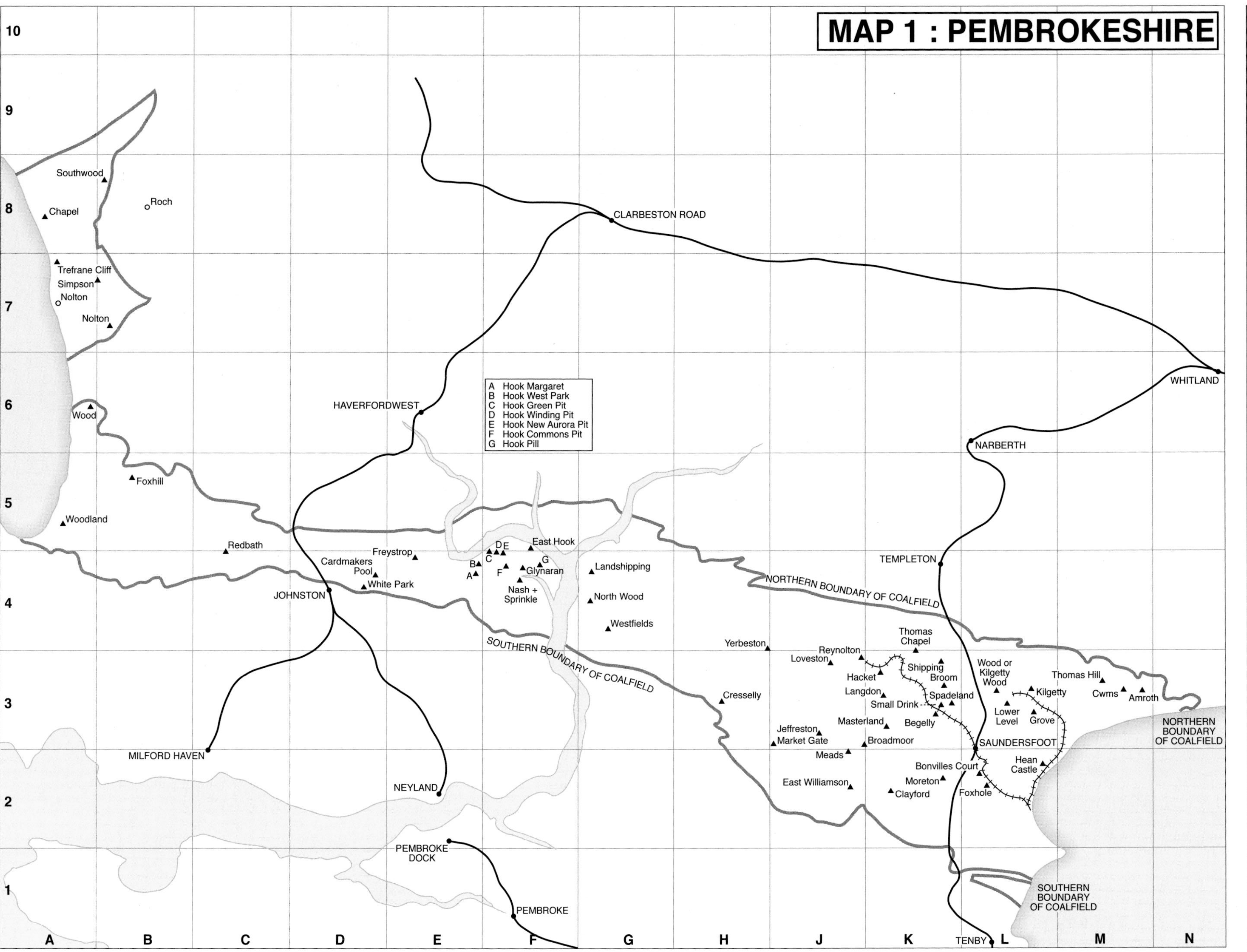

MAP 1 : PEMBROKESHIRE
A Hook Margaret
B Hook West Park
C Hook Green Pit
D Hook Winding Pit
E Hook New Aurora Pit
F Hook Commons Pit
G Hook Pill
Southwood
Chapel
Roch
Trefrane Cliff
Simpson
Nolton
Nolton
Wood
Foxhill
Woodland
Redbath
HAVERFORDWEST
CLARBESTON ROAD
WHITLAND
NARBERTH
TEMPLETON
JOHNSTON
Cardmakers Pool
White Park
Freystrop
East Hook
Glynaran
Nash + Sprinkle
Landshipping
North Wood
Westfields
NORTHERN BOUNDARY OF COALFIELD
SOUTHERN BOUNDARY OF COALFIELD
Yerbeston
Cresselly
Reynolton
Loveston
Hacket
Langdon
Small Drink
Thomas Chapel
Shipping
Broom
Spadeland
Masterland
Begelly
Jeffreston
Market Gate
Broadmoor
Meads
East Williamson
Clayford
Moreton
Bonvilles Court
Foxhole
SAUNDERSFOOT
Wood or Kilgetty Wood
Lower Level
Grove
Kilgetty
Thomas Hill
Cwms
Amroth
Hean Castle
NORTHERN BOUNDARY OF COALFIELD
SOUTHERN BOUNDARY OF COALFIELD
MILFORD HAVEN
NEYLAND
PEMBROKE DOCK
PEMBROKE
TENBY
10
9
8
7
6
5
4
3
2
1
A
B
C
D
E
F
G
H
J
K
L
M
N

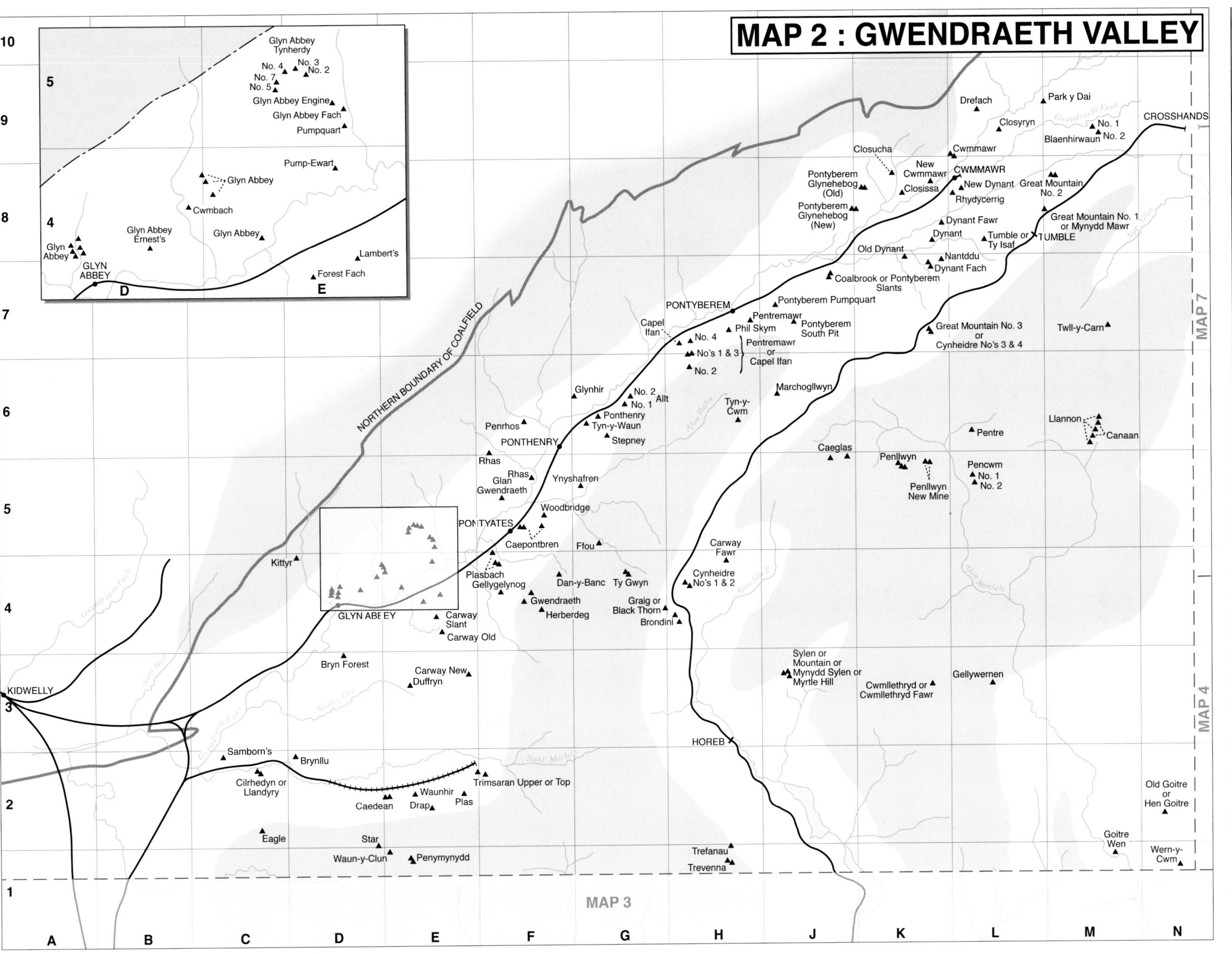

MAP 2 : GWENDRAETH VALLEY
MAP 7
MAP 4
MAP 3
NORTHERN BOUNDARY OF COALFIELD
CROSSHANDS
Park y Dai
No. 1
No. 2
Blaenhirwaun
Closyryn
Drefach
Great Mountain No. 2
Great Mountain No. 1 or Mynydd Mawr
TUMBLE
Tumble or Ty Isaf
Cwmmawr
CWMMAWR
New Dynant
Rhydycerrig
Dynant Fawr
Dynant
Nantddu
Dynant Fach
New Cwmmawr
Closissa
Closucha
Old Dynant
Coalbrook or Pontyberem Slants
Pontyberem Glynehebog (Old)
Pontyberem Glynehebog (New)
Pontyberem Pumpquart
Pontyberem South Pit
Pentremawr
Pentremawr or Capel Ifan
Phil Skym
PONTYBEREM
No. 4
No's 1 & 3
No. 2
Capel Ifan
Twll-y-Carn
Great Mountain No. 3 or Cynheidre No's 3 & 4
Marchogllwyn
Tyn-y-Cwm
Llannon
Canaan
Pentre
Pencwm No. 1 No. 2
Penllwyn
Penllwyn New Mine
Caeglas
Gellywernen
Cwmllethryd or Cwmllethryd Fawr
Sylen or Mountain or Mynydd Sylen or Myrtle Hill
Carway Fawr
Cynheidre No's 1 & 2
HOREB
Graig or Black Thorn
Brondini
Trefanau
Trevenna
Goitre Wen
Old Goitre or Hen Goitre
Wern-y-Cwm
No. 2
No. 1
Allt
Glynhir
Ponthenry
Tyn-y-Waun
Stepney
PONTHENRY
Ynyshafren
Woodbridge
Ffou
Ty Gwyn
Dan-y-Banc
Gwendraeth
Herberdeg
Caepontbren
Penrhos
Rhas
Rhas Glan Gwendraeth
PONTYATES
Plasbach
Gellygelynog
Carway Slant
Carway Old
Carway New
Duffryn
Trimsaran Upper or Top
Plas
Waunhir
Drap
Penymynydd
Caedean
Star
Waun-y-Clun
GLYN ABBEY
Bryn Forest
Kittyr
Brynllu
Samborn's
Cilrhedyn or Llandyry
Eagle
KIDWELLY
Glyn Abbey Tynherdy
No. 4
No. 3
No. 2
No. 7
No. 5
Glyn Abbey Engine
Glyn Abbey Fach
Pumpquart
Pump-Ewart
Glyn Abbey
Cwmbach
Glyn Abbey
Lambert's
Forest Fach
Glyn Abbey Ernest's
Glyn Abbey
GLYN ABBEY
A B C D E F G H J K L M N
1 2 3 4 5 6 7 8 9 10

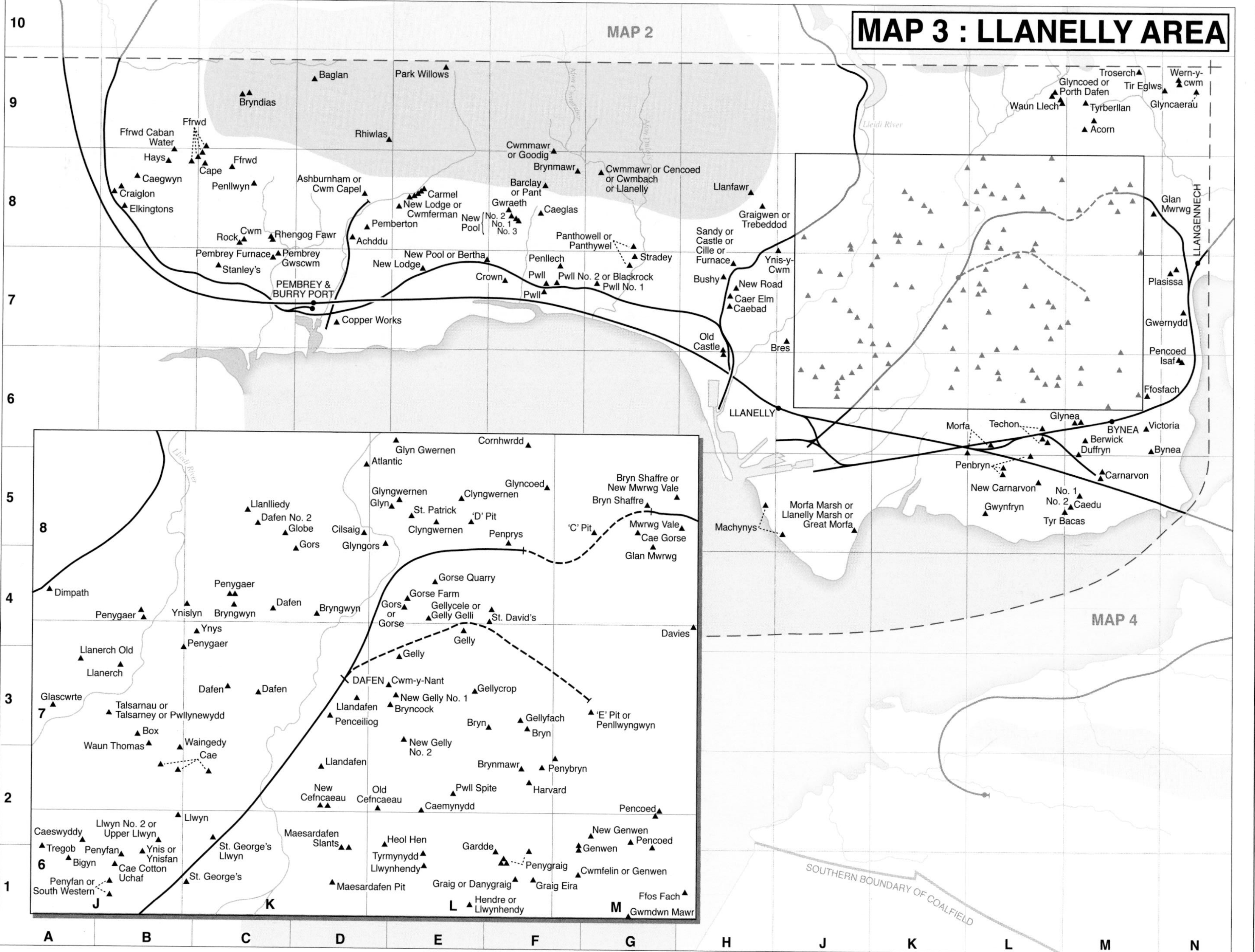

MAP 3 : LLANELLY AREA
MAP 2
MAP 4
SOUTHERN BOUNDARY OF COALFIELD
LLANGENNECH
LLANELLY
BYNEA
DAFEN
PEMBREY & BURRY PORT
Lliedi River
Afon Dulais
Afon Cwmmawr
Wern-y-cwm
Glyncaerau
Troserch
Tir Eglws
Tyrberllan
Acorn
Glyncoed or Porth Dafen
Waun Llech
Glan Mwrwg
Plasissa
Gwernydd
Pencoed Isaf
Ffosfach
Victoria
Bynea
Carnarvon
Berwick
Duffryn
Glynea
Caedu
No. 1
No. 2
Tyr Bacas
Techon
New Carnarvon
Gwynfryn
Penbryn
Morfa
Morfa Marsh or Llanelly Marsh or Great Morfa
Machynys
Graigwen or Trebeddod
Ynis-y-Cwm
New Road
Caer Elm
Caebad
Bres
Llanfawr
Sandy or Castle or Cille or Furnace
Bushy
Old Castle
Cwmmawr or Cencoed or Cwmbach or Llanelly
Stradey
Panthowell or Panthywel
Pwll No. 2 or Blackrock
Pwll No. 1
Brynmawr
Caeglas
Barclay or Pant
Penllech
Pwll
Cwmmawr or Goodig
Gwraeth
No. 2
No. 1
No. 3
New Pool
Crown
New Pool or Bertha
Park Willows
Carmel
New Lodge or Cwmferman
Pemberton
New Lodge
Rhiwlas
Achddu
Copper Works
Ashburnham or Cwm Capel
Baglan
Rhengog Fawr
Pembrey
Gwscwm
Cwm
Rock
Pembrey Furnace
Stanley's
Bryndias
Ffrwd
Cape
Penllwyn
Ffrwd Caban Water
Hays
Caegwyn
Craiglon
Elkingtons
Bryn Shaffre or New Mwrwg Vale
Bryn Shaffre
Mwrwg Vale
Cae Gorse
Glan Mwrwg
Davies
'C' Pit
'E' Pit or Penllwyngwyn
Pencoed
New Genwen
Genwen
Cwmfelin or Genwen
Ffos Fach
Gwmdwn Mawr
Cornhwrdd
Glyncoed
Clyngwernen
'D' Pit
Penprys
St. David's
Gellyfach
Bryn
Penybryn
Harvard
Penygraig
Graig Eira
Glyn Gwernen
St. Patrick
Clyngwernen
Gorse Quarry
Gorse Farm
Gellycele or Gelly Gelli
Gelly
Gellycrop
Brynmawr
Pwll Spite
Caemynydd
Gardde
Graig or Danygraig
Hendre or Llwynhendy
Atlantic
Glyngwernen
Glyn
Gors or Gorse
Cwm-y-Nant
New Gelly No. 1
Bryncock
New Gelly No. 2
Heol Hen
Tyrmynydd
Llwynhendy
Maesardafen Pit
Cilsaig
Glyngors
Bryngwyn
Llandafen
Penceiliog
Old Cefncaeau
Maesardafen Slants
New Cefncaeau
Llanlliedy
Dafen No. 2
Globe
Gors
Dafen
Penygaer
Ynys
Ynislyn
St. George's Llwyn
St. George's
Llwyn
Waingedy
Cae
Box
Talsarnau or Talsarney or Pwllynewydd
Waun Thomas
Llanerch Old
Llanerch
Llwyn No. 2 or Upper Llwyn
Ynis or Ynisfan
Cae Cotton Uchaf
Penyfan
Bigyn
Tregob
Caeswyddy
Penyfan or South Western
Glascwrte
Dimpath
A B C D E F G H J K L M N
1 2 3 4 5 6 7 8 9 10

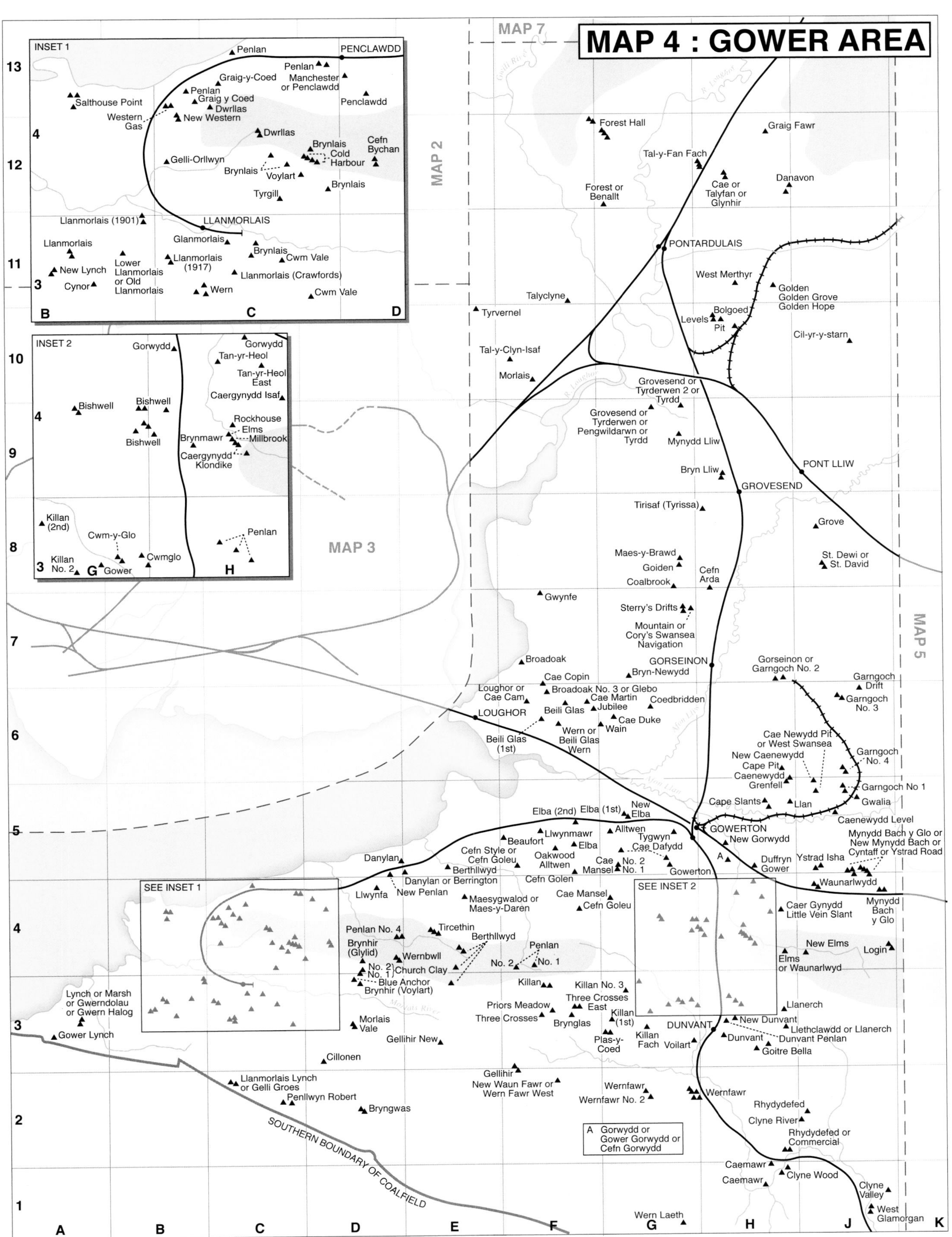

MAP 4 : GOWER AREA
MAP 7
MAP 2
MAP 3
MAP 5
INSET 1
Penlan
PENCLAWDD
Penlan
Manchester or Penclawdd
Graig-y-Coed
Penlan
Graig y Coed
Dwrllas
Penclawdd
Salthouse Point
Western Gas
New Western
Dwrllas
Cefn Bychan
Brynlais
Cold Harbour
Gelli-Orllwyn
Brynlais
Voylart
Brynlais
Tyrgill
Llanmorlais (1901)
LLANMORLAIS
Glanmorlais
Llanmorlais
Brynlais
Cwm Vale
New Lynch
Lower Llanmorlais or Old Llanmorlais
Llanmorlais (1917)
Llanmorlais (Crawfords)
Cynor
Wern
Cwm Vale
INSET 2
Gorwydd
Gorwydd
Tan-yr-Heol
Tan-yr-Heol East
Caergynydd Isaf
Bishwell
Bishwell
Bishwell
Rockhouse
Elms
Brynmawr
Millbrook
Caergynydd Klondike
Killan (2nd)
Cwm-y-Glo
Penlan
Killan No. 2
Gower
Cwmglo
Forest Hall
Graig Fawr
Tal-y-Fan Fach
Cae or Talyfan or Glynhir
Danavon
Forest or Benallt
PONTARDULAIS
West Merthyr
Golden Golden Grove Golden Hope
Talyclyne
Tyrvernel
Bolgoed
Levels
Pit
Cil-yr-y-starn
Tal-y-Clyn-Isaf
Morlais
Grovesend or Tyrderwen 2 or Tyrdd
Grovesend or Tyrderwen or Pengwildarwn or Tyrdd
Mynydd Lliw
PONT LLIW
Bryn Lliw
GROVESEND
Tirisaf (Tyrissa)
Grove
Maes-y-Brawd
Goiden
Cefn Arda
St. Dewi or St. David
Coalbrook
Gwynfe
Sterry's Drifts
Mountain or Cory's Swansea Navigation
Broadoak
GORSEINON
Gorseinon or Garngoch No. 2
Bryn-Newydd
Cae Copin
Garngoch Drift
Loughor or Cae Cam
Broadoak No. 3 or Glebo
Cae Martin
Jubilee
Coedbridden
Garngoch No. 3
LOUGHOR
Beili Glas
Cae Duke
Wern or Beili Glas Wern
Wain
Beili Glas (1st)
Cae Newydd Pit or West Swansea
New Caenewydd
Garngoch No. 4
Cape Pit
Caenewydd
Grenfell
Garngoch No 1
Cape Slants
Llan
Gwalia
Elba (2nd)
Elba (1st)
New Elba
Caenewydd Level
Alltwen
GOWERTON
Llwynmawr
Tygwyn
Mynydd Bach y Glo or New Mynydd Bach or Cyntaff or Ystrad Road
Beaufort
Elba
Cae Dafydd
New Gorwydd
Cefn Style or Cefn Goleu
Oakwood
Alltwen
Cae
Mansel
No. 2
No. 1
A
Duffryn Gower
Ystrad Isha
Danylan
Berthllwyd
Gowerton
Danylan or Berrington
Cefn Golen
Waunarlwydd
SEE INSET 1
Llwynfa
New Penlan
Cae Mansel
SEE INSET 2
Caer Gynydd Little Vein Slant
Mynydd Bach y Glo
Maesygwalod or Maes-y-Daren
Cefn Goleu
Penlan No. 4
Tircethin
Berthllwyd
New Elms
Login
Brynhir (Glylid)
Penlan
Elms or Waunarlwyd
Wernbwll
No. 2
No. 1
No. 2
No. 1
Church Clay
Blue Anchor
Brynhir (Voylart)
Killan
Killan No. 3
Three Crosses
East
Lynch or Marsh or Gwerndolau or Gwern Halog
Priors Meadow
Three Crosses
Llanerch
Killan (1st)
New Dunvant
Bryngals
Morlais Vale
DUNVANT
Llethclawdd or Llanerch
Gower Lynch
Killan Fach
Voilart
Dunvant
Dunvant Penlan
Gellihir New
Plas-y-Coed
Goitre Bella
Cillonen
Gellihir
Llanmorlais Lynch or Gelli Groes
New Waun Fawr or Wern Fawr West
Wernfawr
Wernfawr
Wernfawr No. 2
Penllwyn Robert
Rhydydefed
Bryngwas
Clyne River
SOUTHERN BOUNDARY OF COALFIELD
A Gorwydd or Gower Gorwydd or Cefn Gorwydd
Rhydydefed or Commercial
Caemawr
Caemawr
Clyne Wood
Clyne Valley
Wern Laeth
West Glamorgan
R. Loughor
Afon Llan
Morlais River
A B C D E F G H J K
1 2 3 4 5 6 7 8 9 10 11 12 13

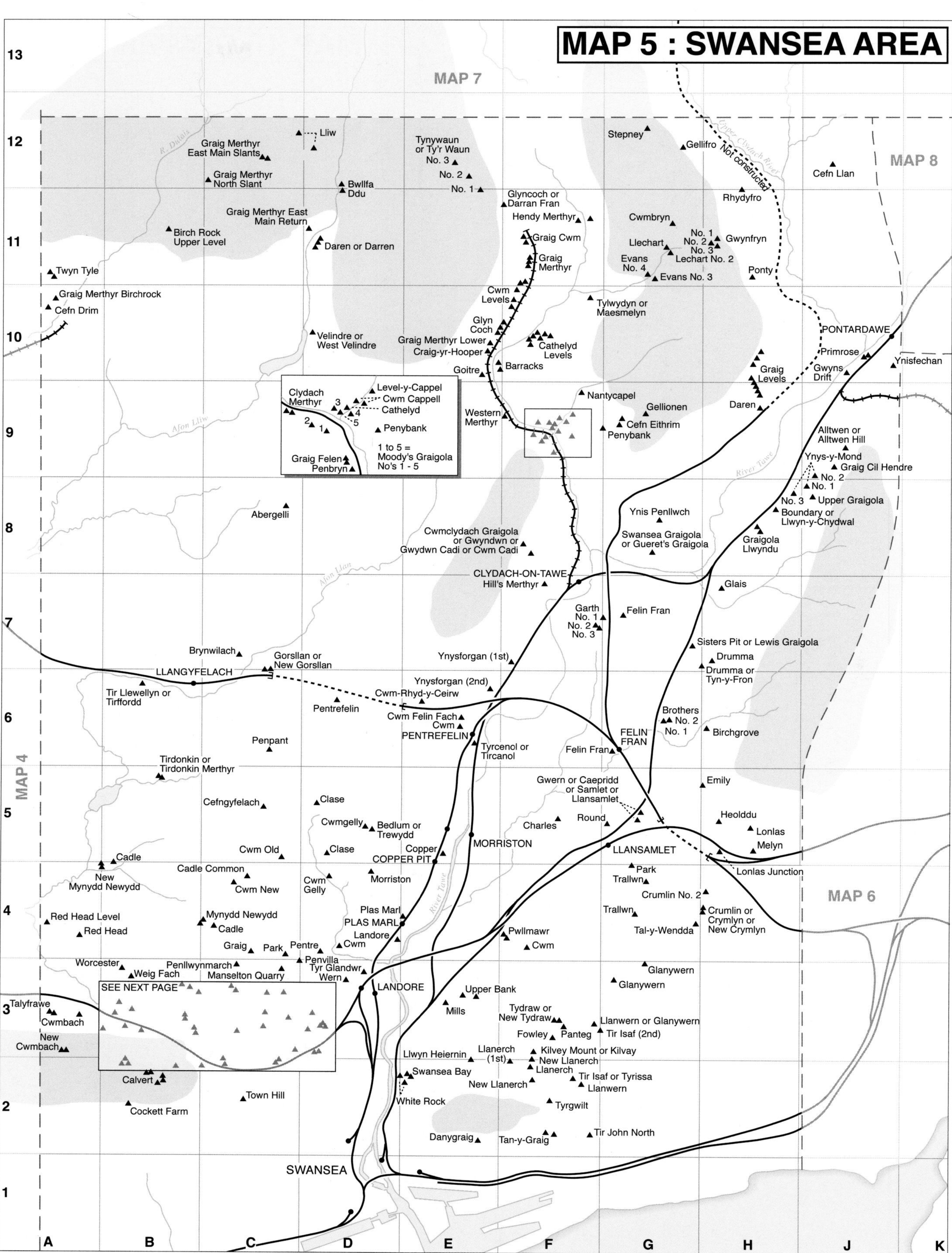

MAP 5 : SWANSEA AREA
MAP 7
MAP 8
MAP 4
MAP 6
Lliw
Graig Merthyr East Main Slants
Graig Merthyr North Slant
Bwllfa Ddu
Tynywaun or Ty'r Waun No. 3
No. 2
No. 1
Stepney
Gellifro
Not constructed
Upper Clydach River
Cefn Llan
Rhydyfro
Glyncoch or Darran Fran
Graig Merthyr East Main Return
Birch Rock Upper Level
Daren or Darren
Hendy Merthyr
Graig Cwm
Graig Merthyr
Cwmbryn
Llechart
No. 1
No. 2
No. 3
Gwynfryn
Lechart No. 2
Evans No. 4
Evans No. 3
Ponty
Twyn Tyle
Graig Merthyr Birchrock
Cefn Drim
Cwm Levels
Tylwydyn or Maesmelyn
Glyn Coch
Velindre or West Velindre
Graig Merthyr Lower
Craig-yr-Hooper
Cathelyd Levels
PONTARDAWE
Primrose
Gwyns Drift
Ynisfechan
Goitre
Barracks
Graig Levels
Clydach Merthyr
Level-y-Cappel
Cwm Cappell
Cathelyd
Penybank
1 to 5 = Moody's Graigola No's 1 - 5
Graig Felen
Penbryn
Nantycapel
Gellionen
Daren
Western Merthyr
Cefn Eithrim
Penybank
Afon Lliw
R. Dulais
Alltwen or Alltwen Hill
Ynys-y-Mond
Graig Cil Hendre
No. 2
No. 1
No. 3
Upper Graigola
Boundary or Llwyn-y-Chydwal
River Tawe
Abergelli
Ynis Penllwch
Cwmclydach Graigola or Gwyndwn or Gwydwn Cadi or Cwm Cadi
Swansea Graigola or Gueret's Graigola
Graigola Llwyndu
Afon Llan
CLYDACH-ON-TAWE
Hill's Merthyr
Glais
Garth No. 1
No. 2
No. 3
Felin Fran
Brynwilach
Gorsllan or New Gorsllan
LLANGYFELACH
Ynysforgan (1st)
Sisters Pit or Lewis Graigola
Drumma
Drumma or Tyn-y-Fron
Tir Llewellyn or Tirffordd
Ynysforgan (2nd)
Cwm-Rhyd-y-Ceirw
Pentrefelin
Cwm Felin Fach
Cwm
PENTREFELIN
Brothers
No. 2
No. 1
Birchgrove
FELIN FRAN
Felin Fran
Penpant
Tyrcenol or Tircanol
Tirdonkin or Tirdonkin Merthyr
Emily
Gwern or Caepridd or Samlet or Llansamlet
Cefngyfelach
Clase
Round
Charles
Heolddu
Cwmgelly
Bedlum or Trewydd
Lonlas
MORRISTON
LLANSAMLET
Melyn
Cadle
Cwm Old
Clase
Copper
COPPER PIT
Lonlas Junction
New Mynydd Newydd
Cadle Common
Cwm New
Cwm Gelly
Morriston
Park
Trallwn
Crumlin No. 2
Red Head Level
Red Head
Mynydd Newydd
Cadle
Plas Marl
PLAS MARL
Trallwn
Crumlin or Crymlyn or New Crymlyn
Tal-y-Wendda
Landore
Cwm
Graig
Park
Pentre
Pwllmawr
Cwm
Worcester
Penllwynmarch
Weig Fach
Manselton Quarry
Penvilla
Tyr Glandwr
Wern
Glanywern
Glanywern
SEE NEXT PAGE
LANDORE
Upper Bank
Talyfrawe
Cwmbach
New Cwmbach
Mills
Tydraw or New Tydraw
Llanwern or Glanywern
Fowley
Panteg
Tir Isaf (2nd)
Llwyn Heiernin
Llanerch (1st)
Kilvey Mount or Kilvay
New Llanerch
Llanerch
Swansea Bay
Tir Isaf or Tyrissa
Llanwern
New Llanerch
Calvert
Town Hill
White Rock
Tyrgwilt
Cockett Farm
Danygraig
Tan-y-Graig
Tir John North
SWANSEA
1
2
3
4
5
6
7
8
9
10
11
12
13
A
B
C
D
E
F
G
H
J
K

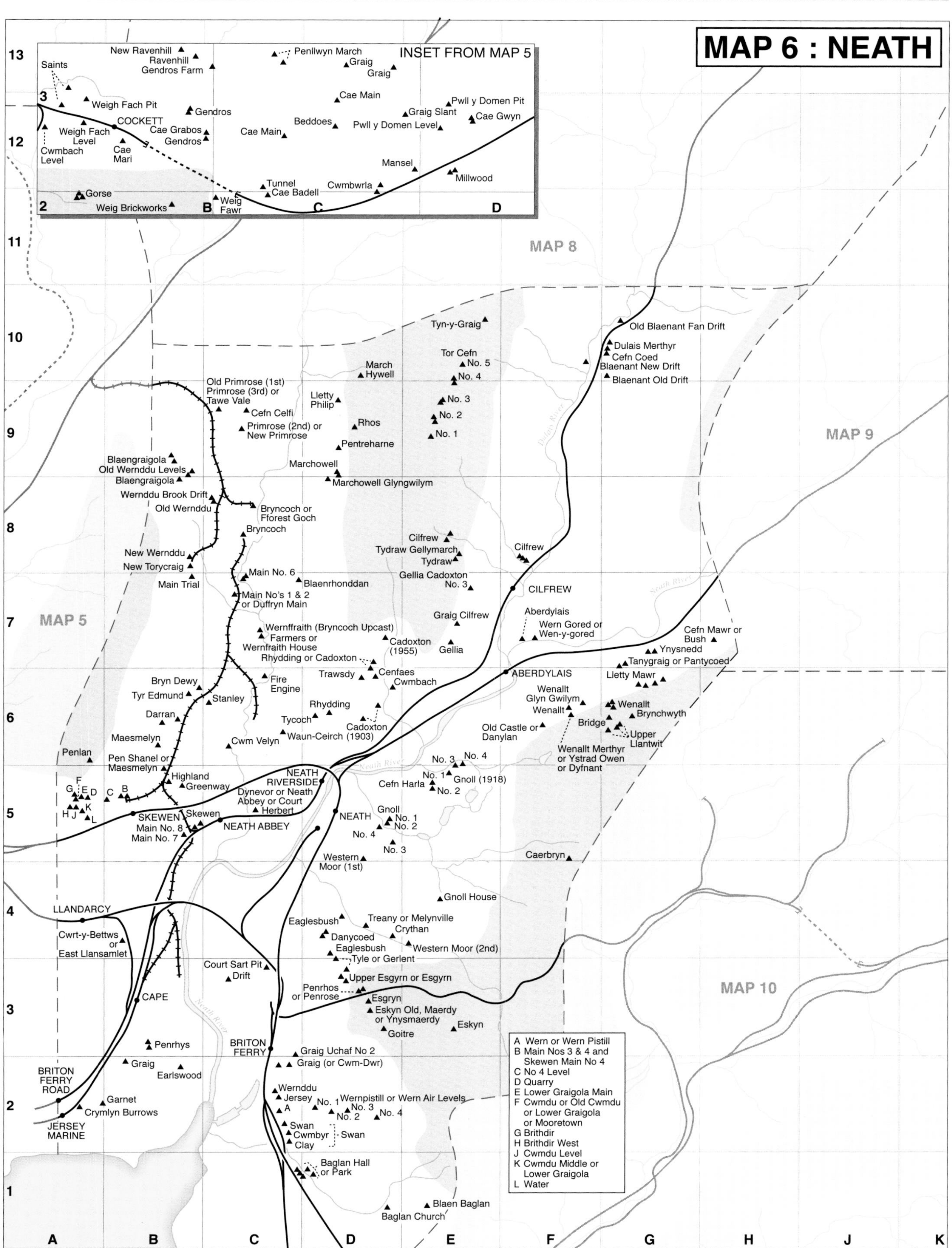
MAP 6 : NEATH
INSET FROM MAP 5
New Ravenhill
Ravenhill
Gendros Farm
Saints
Penllwyn March
Graig
Graig
Weigh Fach Pit
Cae Main
Pwll y Domen Pit
Gendros
Graig Slant
Cae Gwyn
COCKETT
Beddoes
Weigh Fach Level
Cae Grabos
Cae Main
Pwll y Domen Level
Gendros
Cwmbach Level
Cae Mari
Mansel
Millwood
Tunnel
Cwmbwrla
Gorse
Cae Badell
Weig Brickworks
Weig Fawr
MAP 8
Tyn-y-Graig
Old Blaenant Fan Drift
Dulais Merthyr
Cefn Coed
Tor Cefn
No. 5
Blaenant New Drift
March Hywell
No. 4
Blaenant Old Drift
Old Primrose (1st)
Primrose (3rd) or
Tawe Vale
Lletty Philip
No. 3
Cefn Celfi
No. 2
Dulais River
MAP 9
Primrose (2nd) or
New Primrose
Rhos
No. 1
Pentreharne
Blaengraigola
Marchowell
Old Wernddu Levels
Blaengraigola
Marchowell Glyngwilym
Wernddu Brook Drift
Old Wernddu
Bryncoch or
Fforest Goch
Bryncoch
Cilfrew
Tydraw Gellymarch
Cilfrew
New Wernddu
Tydraw
New Torycraig
Main No. 6
Gellia Cadoxton
No. 3
Blaenrhonddan
Main Trial
CILFREW
Neath River
Main No's 1 & 2
or Duffryn Main
Aberdylais
MAP 5
Graig Cilfrew
Wern Gored or
Wen-y-gored
Wernffraith (Bryncoch Upcast)
Cefn Mawr or
Bush
Farmers or
Wernfraith House
Cadoxton
(1955)
Gellia
Ynysnedd
Rhydding or Cadoxton
Tanygraig or Pantycoed
Trawsdy
Cenfaes
ABERDYLAIS
Bryn Dewy
Fire Engine
Cwmbach
Lletty Mawr
Wenallt
Tyr Edmund
Stanley
Glyn Gwilym
Rhydding
Wenallt
Wenallt
Brynchwyth
Darran
Tycoch
Bridge
Cadoxton
Old Castle or
Danylan
Upper
Llantwit
Maesmelyn
Waun-Ceirch (1903)
Cwm Velyn
Wenallt Merthyr
or Ystrad Owen
or Dyfnant
Penlan
No. 3
No. 4
Pen Shanel or
Maesmelyn
NEATH
RIVERSIDE
Neath River
No. 1
Gnoll (1918)
Highland
F
Greenway
Dynevor or Neath
Abbey or Court
Cefn Harla
G
E
D
C
B
No. 2
K
Herbert
H
J
L
SKEWEN
Skewen
Gnoll
NEATH
No. 1
Main No. 8
NEATH ABBEY
No. 2
Main No. 7
No. 4
No. 3
Caerbryn
Western Moor (1st)
Gnoll House
LLANDARCY
Treany or Melynville
Eaglesbush
Crythan
Cwrt-y-Bettws
or
East Llansamlet
Danycoed
Eaglesbush
Western Moor (2nd)
Tyle or Gerlent
Court Sart Pit
Drift
Upper Esgyrn or Esgyrn
MAP 10
Penrhos
or Penrose
CAPE
Esgryn
Eskyn Old, Maerdy
or Ynysmaerdy
Neath River
Eskyn
Goitre
Penrhys
BRITON
FERRY
Graig Uchaf No 2
Graig
Graig (or Cwm-Dwr)
Earlswood
BRITON
FERRY
ROAD
Wernddu
Jersey
No. 1
Wernpistill or Wern Air Levels
Garnet
No. 3
A
No. 2
No. 4
Crymlyn Burrows
JERSEY
MARINE
Swan
Cwmbyr
Swan
Clay
Baglan Hall
or Park
Blaen Baglan
Baglan Church
A Wern or Wern Pistill
B Main Nos 3 & 4 and
Skewen Main No 4
C No 4 Level
D Quarry
E Lower Graigola Main
F Cwmdu or Old Cwmdu
or Lower Graigola
or Mooretown
G Brithdir
H Brithdir West
J Cwmdu Level
K Cwmdu Middle or
Lower Graigola
L Water
13
12
11
10
9
8
7
6
5
4
3
2
1
A
B
C
D
E
F
G
H
J
K

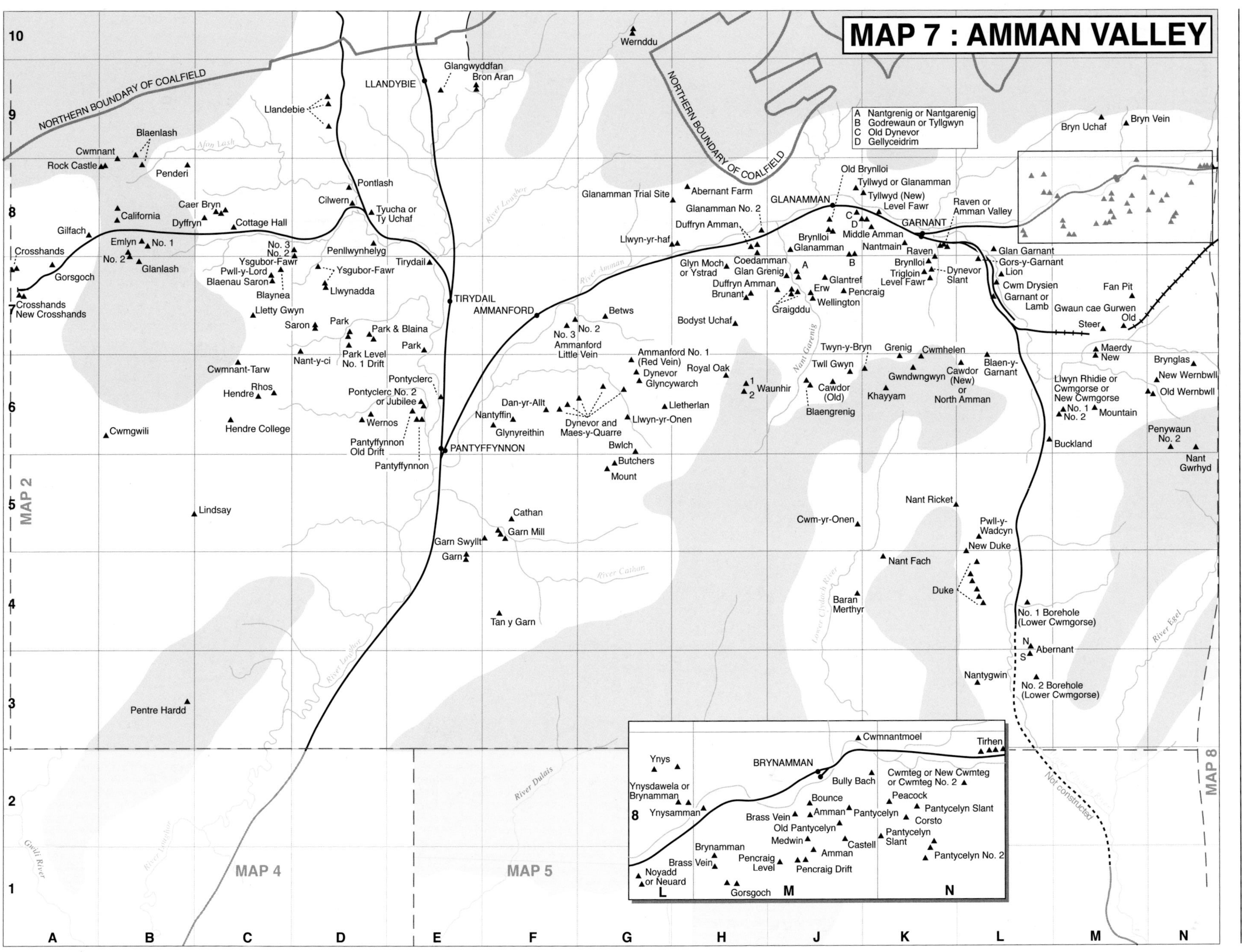

MAP 7 : AMMAN VALLEY
A Nantgrenig or Nantgarenig
B Godrewaun or Tyllgwyn
C Old Dynevor
D Gellyceidrim
NORTHERN BOUNDARY OF COALFIELD
NORTHERN BOUNDARY OF COALFIELD
Wernddu
Glangwyddfan
Bron Aran
LLANDYBIE
Llandebie
Blaenlash
Cwmnant
Rock Castle
Penderi
Caer Bryn
California
Dyffryn
Cottage Hall
Gilfach
Emlyn
No. 1
No. 2
Glanlash
Crosshands
Gorsgoch
Crosshands
New Crosshands
Pontlash
Cilwern
Tyucha or Ty Uchaf
Penllwynhelyg
No. 3
No. 2
Ysgubor-Fawr
Pwll-y-Lord
Blaenau Saron
Blaynea
Ysgubor-Fawr
Llwynadda
Tirydail
Lletty Gwyn
Saron
Park
Park & Blaina
Park
Nant-y-ci
Park Level
No. 1 Drift
Cwmnant-Tarw
Rhos
Hendre
Pontyclerc
Pontyclerc No. 2
or Jubilee
Wernos
Hendre College
Cwmgwili
Pantyffynnon
Old Drift
Pantyffynnon
TIRYDAIL
AMMANFORD
PANTYFFYNNON
Lindsay
Garn Swyllt
Garn
Cathan
Garn Mill
Tan y Garn
Pentre Hardd
Betws
No. 3
No. 2
Ammanford
Little Vein
Ammanford No. 1
(Red Vein)
Dynevor
Glyncywarch
Royal Oak
Dan-yr-Allt
Nantyffin
Glynyreithin
Dynevor and
Maes-y-Quarre
Lletherlan
Llwyn-yr-Onen
Bwlch
Butchers
Mount
Glanamman Trial Site
Abernant Farm
Glanamman No. 2
Duffryn Amman
Llwyn-yr-haf
Glyn Moch
or Ystrad
Coedamman
Glan Grenig
Duffryn Amman
Brunant
Bodyst Uchaf
Waunhir
GLANAMMAN
Old Brynlloi
Tyllwyd or Glanamman
Tyllwyd (New)
Level Fawr
Brynlloi
Glanamman
Middle Amman
Nantmain
Raven
Brynlloi
Triglo
Level Fawr
Dynevor
Slant
GARNANT
Raven or
Amman Valley
Erw
Glantref
Pencraig
Wellington
Graigddu
Twyn-y-Bryn
Twll Gwyn
Cawdor
(Old)
Blaengrenig
Grenig
Cwmhelen
Gwndwngwyn
Khayyam
Cawdor
(New)
or
North Amman
Blaen-y-
Garnant
Glan Garnant
Gors-y-Garnant
Lion
Cwm Drysien
Garnant or
Lamb
Gwaun cae Gurwen
Old
Fan Pit
Steer
Bryn Uchaf
Bryn Vein
Maerdy
New
Brynglas
New Wernbwll
Old Wernbwll
Llwyn Rhidie or
Cwmgorse or
New Cwmgorse
No. 1
No. 2
Mountain
Buckland
Penywaun
No. 2
Nant
Gwrhyd
Nant Ricket
Cwm-yr-Onen
Pwll-y-
Wadcyn
New Duke
Nant Fach
Duke
Baran
Merthyr
No. 1 Borehole
(Lower Cwmgorse)
N
S
Abernant
Nantygwin
No. 2 Borehole
(Lower Cwmgorse)
Not constructed
Ynys
Ynysdawela or
Brynamman
Ynysamman
BRYNAMMAN
Cwmnantmoel
Tirhen
Bully Bach
Cwmteg or New Cwmteg
or Cwmteg No. 2
Peacock
Bounce
Amman
Pantycelyn
Pantycelyn Slant
Corsto
Brass Vein
Old Pantycelyn
Medwin
Castell
Pantycelyn
Slant
Brynamman
Brass Vein
Pencraig
Level
Amman
Pencraig Drift
Pantycelyn No. 2
Noyadd
or Neuard
Gorsgoch
L M N
Afon Lash
River Loughor
River Amman
Nant Garenig
Lower Clydach River
River Cathan
River Dulais
River Egel
Gwili River
MAP 2
MAP 4
MAP 5
MAP 8
A B C D E F G H J K L M N
1 2 3 4 5 6 7 8 9 10

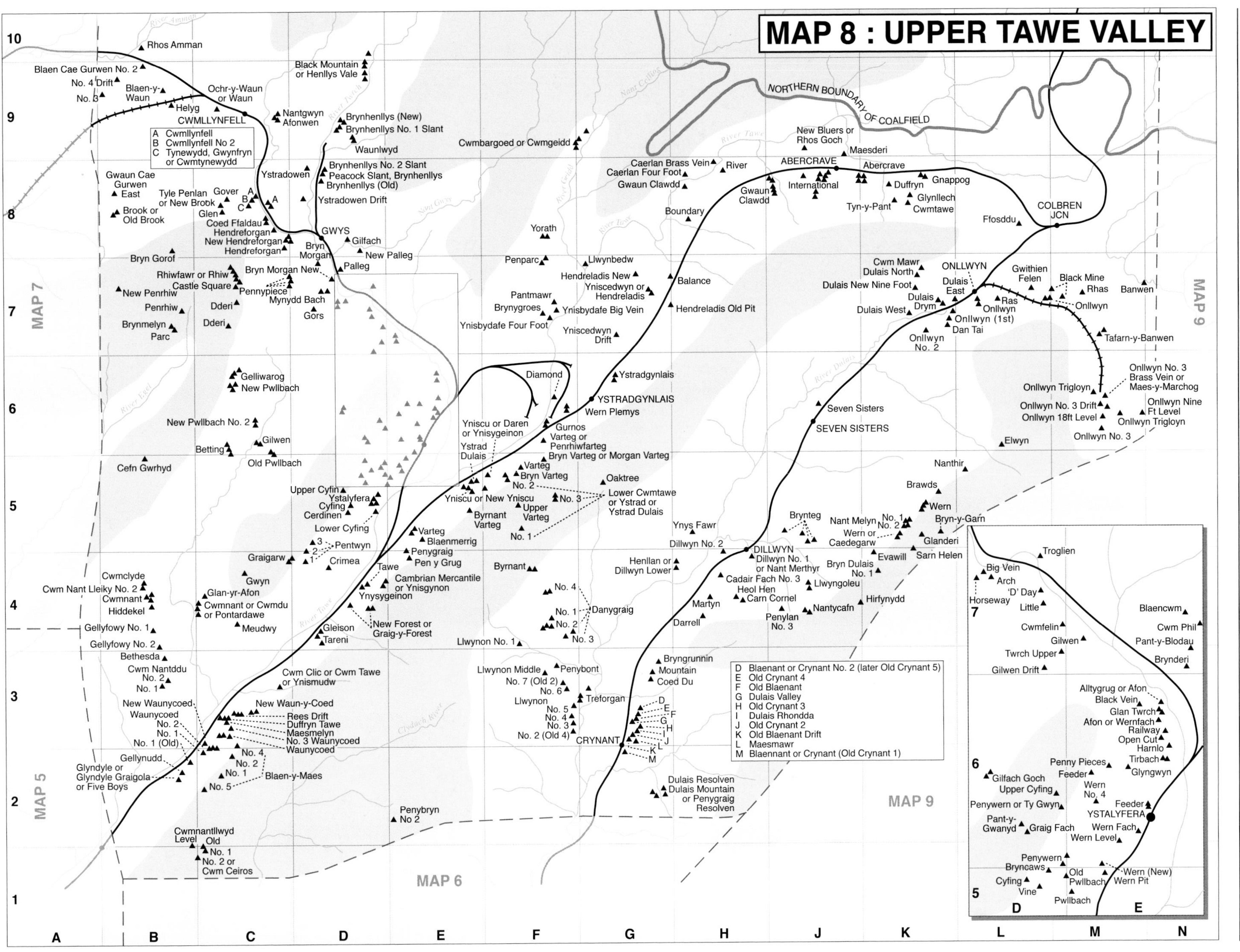
MAP 8 : UPPER TAWE VALLEY
MAP 9
MAP 7
MAP 6
MAP 5
NORTHERN BOUNDARY OF COALFIELD
A Cwmllynfell
B Cwmllynfell No 2
C Tynewydd, Gwynfryn or Cwmtynewydd
D Blaenant or Crynant No. 2 (later Old Crynant 5)
E Old Crynant 4
F Old Blaenant
G Dulais Valley
H Old Crynant 3
I Dulais Rhondda
J Old Crynant 2
K Old Blaenant Drift
L Maesmawr
M Blaennant or Crynant (Old Crynant 1)
COLBREN JCN
ONLLWYN
ABERCRAVE
SEVEN SISTERS
DILLWYN
YSTRADGYNLAIS
CRYNANT
GWYS
CWMLLYNFELL
YSTALYFERA
Rhos Amman
Blaen Cae Gurwen No. 2
No. 4 Drift
No. 3
Blaen-y-Waun
Ochr-y-Waun or Waun
Helyg
Black Mountain or Henllys Vale
Nantgwyn
Afonwen
Brynhenllys (New)
Brynhenllys No. 1 Slant
Waunlwyd
Brynhenllys No. 2 Slant
Peacock Slant, Brynhenllys
Brynhenllys (Old)
Ystradowen
Ystradowen Drift
Gwaun Cae Gurwen East
Tyle Penlan or New Brook
Gover
Brook or Old Brook
Glen
Coed Ffaldau
Hendreforgan
New Hendreforgan
Hendreforgan
Gilfach
New Palleg
Bryn Morgan
Palleg
Bryn Gorof
Rhiwfawr or Rhiw
Castle Square
Bryn Morgan New
Pennypiece
Mynydd Bach
Gors
New Penrhiw
Penrhiw
Dderi
Dderi
Brynmelyn
Parc
Gelliwarog
New Pwllbach
New Pwllbach No. 2
Gilwen
Betting
Old Pwllbach
Cefn Gwrhyd
Cwmbargoed or Cwmgeidd
Yorath
Penparc
Pantmawr
Brynygroes
Ynisbydafe Big Vein
Ynisbydafe Four Foot
Yniscedwyn Drift
Llwynbedw
Hendreladis New
Yniscedwyn or Hendreladis
Balance
Hendreladis Old Pit
Boundary
Caerlan Brass Vein
Caerlan Four Foot
Gwaun Clawdd
River
Gwaun Clawdd
New Bluers or Rhos Goch
Maesderi
International
Abercrave
Duffryn
Gnappog
Tyn-y-Pant
Glynllech
Cwmtawe
Ffosddu
Cwm Mawr
Dulais North
Dulais New Nine Foot
Dulais West
Dulais East
Dulais Drym
Gwithien Felen
Black Mine
Rhas
Banwen
Ras
Onllwyn
Onllwyn
Onllwyn (1st)
Dan Tai
Onllwyn No. 2
Tafarn-y-Banwen
Onllwyn Trigloyn
Onllwyn No. 3 Brass Vein or Maes-y-Marchog
Onllwyn No. 3 Drift
Onllwyn 18ft Level
Onllwyn Nine Ft Level
Onllwyn Trigloyn
Onllwyn No. 3
Elwyn
Diamond
Ystradgynlais
Wern Plemys
Seven Sisters
Yniscu or Daren or Ynisygeinon
Ystrad Dulais
Gurnos
Varteg or Penrhiwfarteg
Bryn Varteg or Morgan Varteg
Varteg
Bryn Varteg
No. 2
Oaktree
Yniscu or New Yniscu
No. 3
Lower Cwmtawe or Ystrad or Ystrad Dulais
Bymant Varteg
Upper Varteg
No. 1
Upper Cyfin
Ystalyfera
Cyfing
Cerdinen
Lower Cyfing
Pentwyn
Crimea
Graigarw
Varteg
Blaenmerrig
Penygraig
Pen y Grug
Tawe
Cambrian Mercantile or Ynisgynon
Ynysygeinon
New Forest or Graig-y-Forest
Gleison
Tareni
Bymant
No. 4
Danygraig
No. 1
No. 2
No. 3
Llwynon No. 1
Cwmclyde
Cwm Nant Lleiky No. 2
Cwmnant
Hiddekel
Glan-yr-Afon
Cwmnant or Cwmdu or Pontardawe
Meudwy
Gwyn
Gellyfowy No. 1
Gellyfowy No. 2
Bethesda
Cwm Nantddu
No. 2
No. 1
Cwm Clic or Cwm Tawe or Ynismudw
New Waunycoed
Waunycoed
New Waun-y-Coed
Rees Drift
Duffryn Tawe
Maesmelyn
No. 3 Waunycoed
Waunycoed
No. 1 (Old)
Gellynudd
Glyndyle or Glyndyle Graigola or Five Boys
No. 4
No. 2
No. 1
No. 5
Blaen-y-Maes
Cwmnantllwyd Level
Old
No. 1
No. 2 or Cwm Ceiros
Penybryn No 2
Llwynon Middle
Penybont
No. 7 (Old 2)
No. 6
Llwynon
Treforgan
No. 5
No. 4
No. 3
No. 2 (Old 4)
Bryngrunnin Mountain
Coed Du
Dulais Resolven
Dulais Mountain or Penygraig Resolven
Ynys Fawr
Dillwyn No. 2
Henllan or Dillwyn Lower
Dillwyn No. 1 or Nant Merthyr
Cadair Fach No. 3
Heol Hen
Carn Cornel
Martyn
Darrell
Penylan No. 3
Nantycafn
Llwyngoleu
Brynteg
Nant Melyn No. 1
No. 2
Wern or Caedegarw
Bryn Dulais No. 1
Evawill
Hirfynydd
Nanthir
Brawds
Wern
Bryn-y-Garn
Glanderi
Sarn Helen
Troglien
Big Vein
Arch
Horseway
'D' Day
Little
Cwmfelin
Gilwen
Twrch Upper
Gilwen Drift
Blaencwm
Cwm Phil
Pant-y-Blodau
Brynderi
Alltygrug or Afon
Black Vein
Glan Twrch
Afon or Wernfach
Railway
Open Cut
Harnlo
Tirbach
Glyngwyn
Penny Pieces
Feeder
Gilfach Goch
Upper Cyfing
Wern No. 4
Penywern or Ty Gwyn
Feeder
Pant-y-Gwanyd
Graig Fach
Wern Fach
Wern Level
Penywern
Bryncaws
Old Pwllbach
Wern (New)
Wern Pit
Cyfing
Vine
Pwllbach
River Amman
River Twrch
Nant Ceillog
River Tawe
River Giedd
Nant Gwys
River Egel
River Dulais
Clydach River
A
B
C
D
E
F
G
H
J
K
L
M
N
1
2
3
4
5
6
7
8
9
10

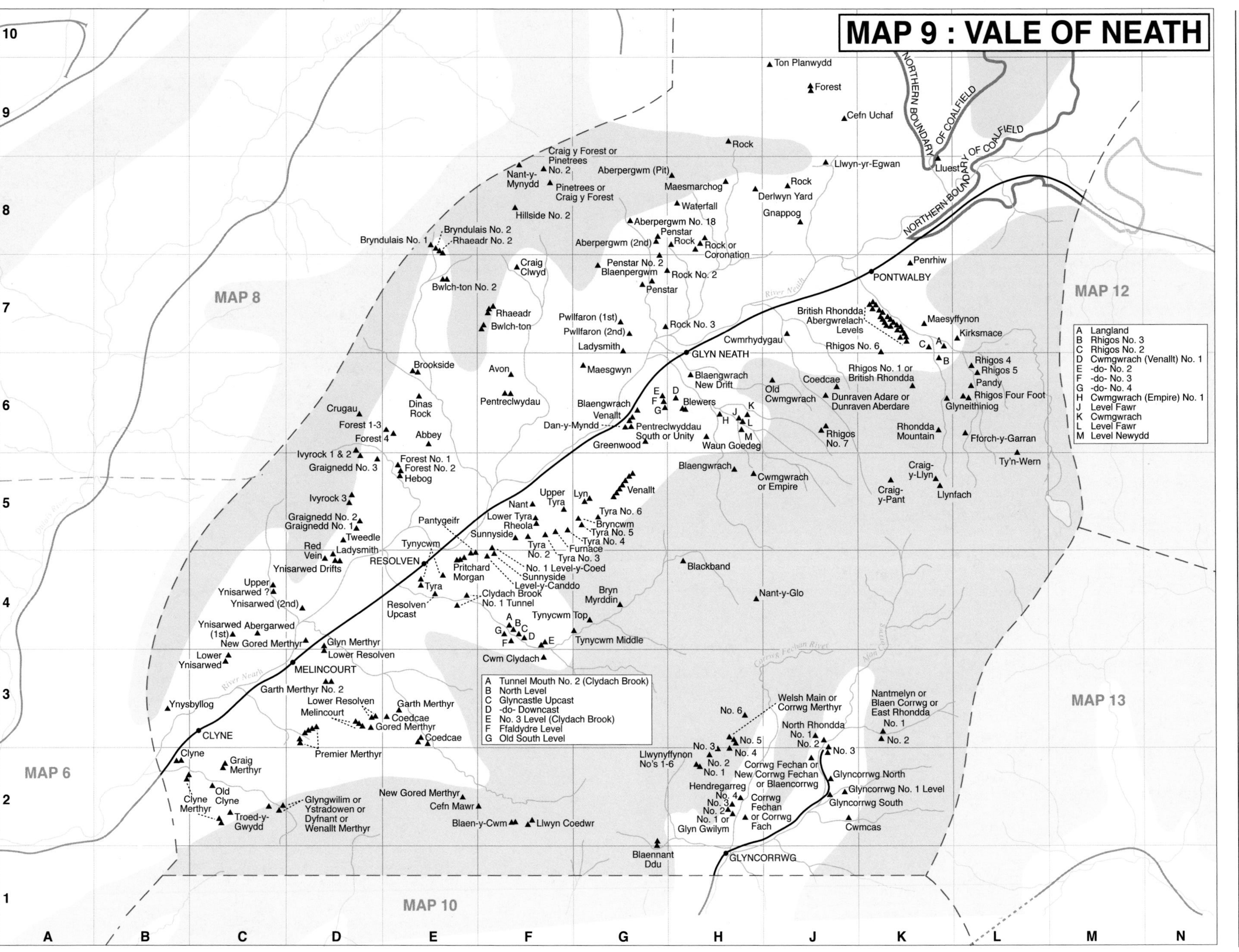

MAP 9 : VALE OF NEATH
NORTHERN BOUNDARY OF COALFIELD
Ton Planwydd
Forest
Cefn Uchaf
Rock
Llwyn-yr-Egwan
Lluest
Craig y Forest or Pinetrees No. 2
Nant-y-Mynydd
Pinetrees or Craig y Forest
Aberpergwm (Pit)
Maesmarchog
Rock
Derlwyn Yard
Waterfall
Gnappog
Hillside No. 2
Aberpergwm No. 18
Bryndulais No. 1
Bryndulais No. 2
Rhaeadr No. 2
Aberpergwm (2nd)
Penstar
Rock
Rock or Coronation
Craig Clwyd
Penstar No. 2
Blaenpergwm
Rock No. 2
Penhriw
PONTWALBY
Bwlch-ton No. 2
Penstar
MAP 8
MAP 12
Rhaeadr
Bwlch-ton
Pwllfaron (1st)
Pwllfaron (2nd)
Rock No. 3
British Rhondda; Abergwrelach Levels
Maesyffynon
Kirksmace
Ladysmith
Cwmrhydygau
Rhigos No. 6
GLYN NEATH
A Langland
B Rhigos No. 3
C Rhigos No. 2
D Cwmgwrach (Venallt) No. 1
E -do- No. 2
F -do- No. 3
G -do- No. 4
H Cwmgwrach (Empire) No. 1
J Level Fawr
K Cwmgwrach
L Level Fawr
M Level Newydd
Brookside
Avon
Maesgwyn
Blaengwrach New Drift
Coedcae
Rhigos No. 1 or British Rhondda
Rhigos 4
Rhigos 5
Pandy
Old Cwmgwrach
Dunraven Adare or Dunraven Aberdare
Rhigos Four Foot
Glyneithiniog
Crugau
Dinas Rock
Pentreclwydau
Blaengwrach Venallt
Blewers
Forest 1-3
Forest 4
Abbey
Dan-y-Myndd
Pentreclwyddau South or Unity
Waun Goedeg
Rhigos No. 7
Rhondda Mountain
Fforch-y-Garran
Greenwood
Ivyrock 1 & 2
Graignedd No. 3
Forest No. 1
Forest No. 2
Hebog
Ty'n-Wern
Blaengwrach
Cwmgwrach or Empire
Craig-y-Llyn
Craig-y-Pant
Llynfach
Venallt
Ivyrock 3
Upper Tyra
Lyn
Nant
Tyra No. 6
Lower Tyra
Rheola
Bryncwm
Graignedd No. 2
Graignedd No. 1
Pantygeifr
Sunnyside
Tyra No. 5
Tyra No. 4
Tweedle
Tynycwm
Tyra No. 2
Furnace
Tyra No. 3
Red Vein
Ladysmith
RESOLVEN
Pritchard
Morgan
No. 1 Level-y-Coed
Sunnyside
Level-y-Canddo
Blackband
Ynisarwed Drifts
Upper Ynisarwed ?
Tyra
Clydach Brook No. 1 Tunnel
Bryn Myrddin
Nant-y-Glo
Ynisarwed (2nd)
Resolven Upcast
Tynycwm Top
Ynisarwed Abergarwed (1st)
New Gored Merthyr
Glyn Merthyr
Lower Resolven
Tynycwm Middle
Lower Ynisarwed
MELINCOURT
Cwm Clydach
A Tunnel Mouth No. 2 (Clydach Brook)
B North Level
C Glyncastle Upcast
D -do- Downcast
E No. 3 Level (Clydach Brook)
F Ffaldydre Level
G Old South Level
Garth Merthyr No. 2
Lower Resolven
Garth Merthyr
Melincourt
Coedcae
Gored Merthyr
Coedcae
Ynysbyllog
CLYNE
Premier Merthyr
No. 6
Welsh Main or Corrwg Merthyr
Nantmelyn or Blaen Corrwg or East Rhondda No. 1
No. 2
MAP 13
North Rhondda No. 1
No. 2
No. 3
No. 5
No. 4
No. 3
No. 2
No. 1
Llwynyffynon No's 1-6
Corrwg Fechan or New Corrwg Fechan or Blaencorrwg
Clyne
Graig Merthyr
MAP 6
Old Clyne
Clyne Merthyr
Troed-y-Gwydd
Glyngwilim or Ystradowen or Dyfnant or Wenallt Merthyr
New Gored Merthyr
Cefn Mawr
Blaen-y-Cwm
Llwyn Coedwr
Hendregarreg No. 4
No. 3
No. 2
No. 1 or Glyn Gwilym
Corrwg Fechan or Corrwg Fach
Glyncorrwg North
Glyncorrwg No. 1 Level
Glyncorrwg South
Cwmcas
Blaennant Ddu
GLYNCORRWG
River Neath
Corrwg Fechan River
MAP 10
A B C D E F G H J K L M N
1 2 3 4 5 6 7 8 9 10

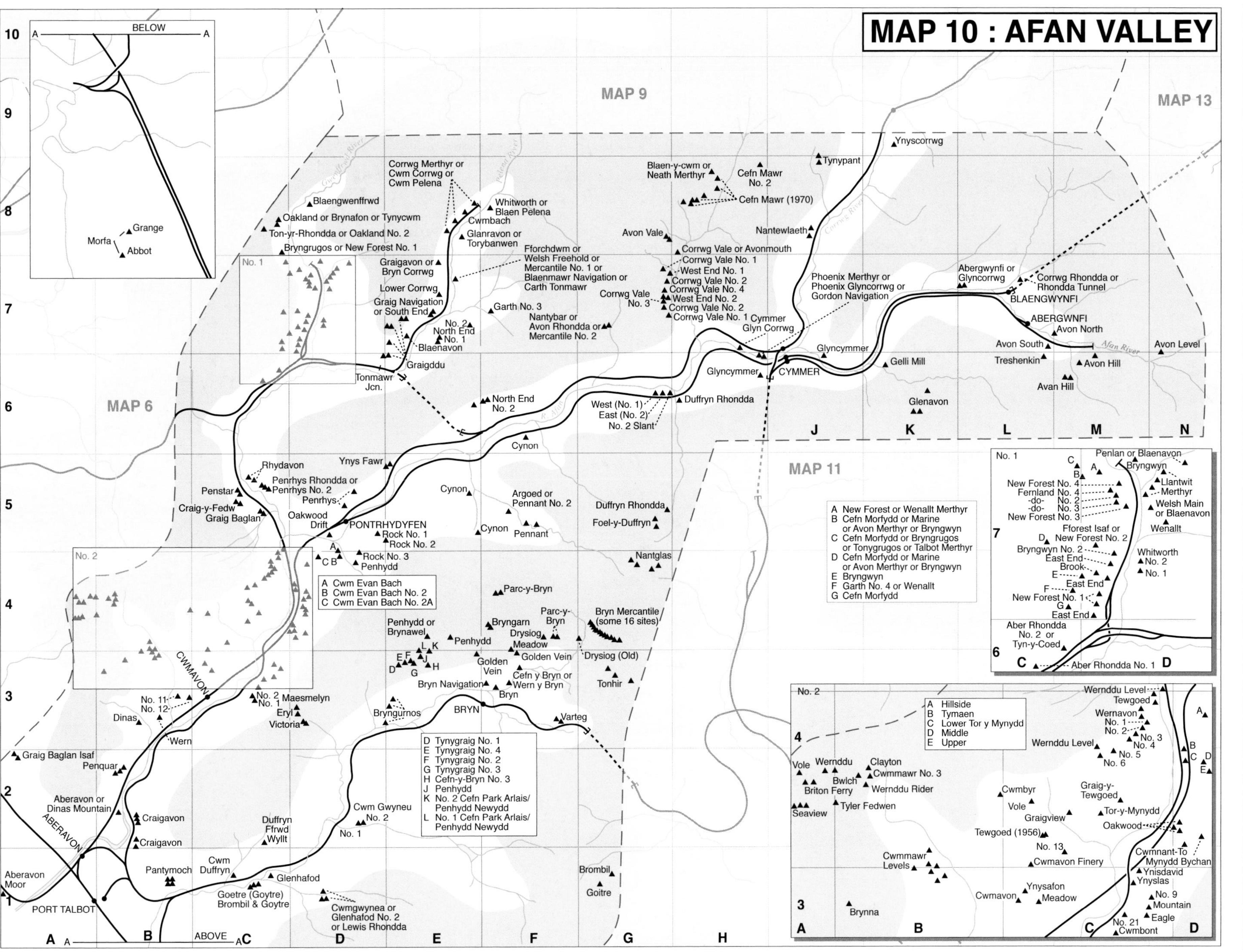
MAP 10 : AFAN VALLEY
MAP 9
MAP 13
MAP 6
MAP 11
BELOW
ABOVE
Morfa
Grange
Abbot
Blaengwenffrwd
Oakland or Brynafon or Tynycwm
Ton-yr-Rhondda or Oakland No. 2
Bryngrugos or New Forest No. 1
Corrwg Merthyr or Cwm Corrwg or Cwm Pelena
Whitworth or Blaen Pelena
Cwmbach
Glanravon or Torybanwen
Fforchdwm or Welsh Freehold or Mercantile No. 1 or Blaenmawr Navigation or Carth Tonmawr
Graigavon or Bryn Corrwg
Lower Corrwg
Graig Navigation or South End
No. 2 North End No. 1
Blaenavon
Graigddu
Tonmawr Jcn.
Garth No. 3
Nantybar or Avon Rhondda or Mercantile No. 2
Blaen-y-cwm or Neath Merthyr
Cefn Mawr No. 2
Cefn Mawr (1970)
Tynypant
Ynyscorrwg
Nantewlaeth
Avon Vale
Corrwg Vale or Avonmouth
Corrwg Vale No. 1
West End No. 1
Corrwg Vale No. 2
Corrwg Vale No. 4
West End No. 2
Corrwg Vale No. 3
Corrwg Vale No. 2
Corrwg Vale No. 1
Cymmer Glyn Corrwg
Phoenix Merthyr or Phoenix Glyncorrwg or Gordon Navigation
Abergwynfi or Glyncorrwg
Corrwg Rhondda or Rhondda Tunnel
BLAENGWYNFI
ABERGWNFI
Avon North
Avon South
Treshenkin
Avon Hill
Avan Hill
Avon Level
Afan River
Corrwg River
Glyncymmer
CYMMER
Gelli Mill
Glenavon
North End No. 2
West (No. 1)
East (No. 2)
No. 2 Slant
Duffryn Rhondda
Cynon
Rhydavon
Penrhys Rhondda or Penrhys No. 2
Penrhys
Penstar
Craig-y-Fedw
Graig Baglan
Ynys Fawr
Oakwood Drift
PONTRHYDYFEN
Rock No. 1
Rock No. 2
Rock No. 3
Penhydd
A Cwm Evan Bach
B Cwm Evan Bach No. 2
C Cwm Evan Bach No. 2A
Argoed or Pennant No. 2
Pennant
Duffryn Rhondda
Foel-y-Duffryn
Nantglas
Parc-y-Bryn
Penhydd or Brynawel
Bryngarn
Parc-y-Bryn
Drysiog Meadow
Bryn Mercantile (some 16 sites)
Golden Vein
Drysiog (Old)
Golden Vein
Cefn y Bryn or Wern y Bryn
Tonhir
Bryn Navigation
Bryn
BRYN
Varteg
Bryngurnos
D Tynygraig No. 1
E Tynygraig No. 4
F Tynygraig No. 2
G Tynygraig No. 3
H Cefn-y-Bryn No. 3
J Penhydd
K No. 2 Cefn Park Arlais/ Penhydd Newydd
L No. 1 Cefn Park Arlais/ Penhydd Newydd
CWMAVON
No. 11
No. 12
Wern
Dinas
No. 2 Maesmelyn
No. 1
Eryl
Victoria
Graig Baglan Isaf
Penquar
Aberavon or Dinas Mountain
ABERAVON
Aberavon Moor
PORT TALBOT
Craigavon
Craigavon
Pantymoch
Cwm Duffryn
Duffryn Ffrwd Wyllt
Cwm Gwyneu No. 2
No. 1
Glenhafod
Goetre (Goytre) Brombil & Goytre
Cwmgwynea or Glenhafod No. 2 or Lewis Rhondda
Brombil
Goitre
No. 1
Penlan or Blaenavon
Bryngwyn
Llantwit
Merthyr
Welsh Main or Blaenavon
Wenallt
New Forest No. 4
Fernland No. 4
-do- No. 2
-do- No. 3
New Forest No. 3
Fforest Isaf or New Forest No. 2
Bryngwyn No. 2
East End
Brook
East End
New Forest No. 1
East End
Whitworth No. 2
No. 1
Aber Rhondda No. 2 or Tyn-y-Coed
Aber Rhondda No. 1
A New Forest or Wenallt Merthyr
B Cefn Morfydd or Marine or Avon Merthyr or Bryngwyn
C Cefn Morfydd or Bryngrugos or Tonygrugos or Talbot Merthyr
D Cefn Morfydd or Marine or Avon Merthyr or Bryngwyn
E Bryngwyn
F Garth No. 4 or Wenallt
G Cefn Morfydd
No. 2
A Hillside
B Tymaen
C Lower Tor y Mynydd
D Middle
E Upper
Vole
Wernddu
Clayton
Bwlch
Cwmmawr No. 3
Briton Ferry
Wernddu Rider
Seaview
Tyler Fedwen
Wernddu Level
Tewgoed
Wernavon
No. 1
No. 2
No. 3
No. 4
Wernddu Level
No. 5
No. 6
Cwmbyr
Vole
Graigview
Graig-y-Tewgoed
Tor-y-Mynydd
Oakwood
Tewgoed (1956)
No. 13
Cwmavon Finery
Cwmmawr Levels
Cwmnant-To Mynydd Bychan
Ynisdavid
Ynyslas
Cwmavon
Ynysafon
Meadow
No. 9
Mountain
Eagle
Brynna
No. 21
Cwmbont

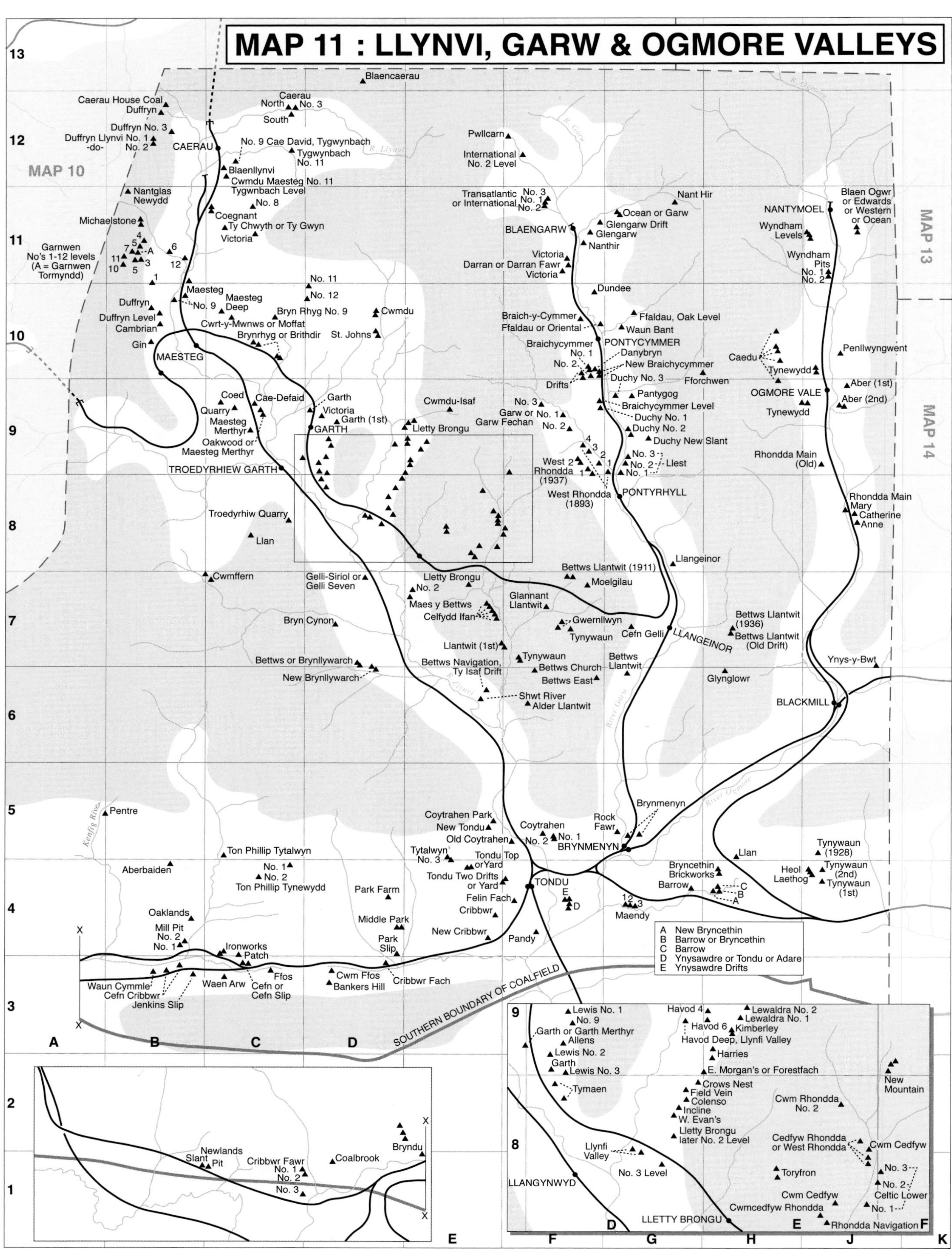
MAP 11 : LLYNVI, GARW & OGMORE VALLEYS
MAP 10
MAP 13
MAP 14
Blaencaerau
Caerau House Coal
Duffryn
Caerau
North
No. 3
South
Duffryn No. 3
Duffryn Llynvi No. 1
-do- No. 2
CAERAU
No. 9 Cae David, Tygwynbach
Tygwynbach
No. 11
R. Llynvi
Blaenllynvi
Cwmdu Maesteg No. 11
Tygwnbach Level
Nantglas
Newydd
No. 8
Coegnant
Michaelstone
Ty Chwyth or Ty Gwyn
Victoria
Garnwen
No's 1-12 levels
(A = Garnwen Tormyndd)
Duffryn
Duffryn Level
Cambrian
Gin
Maesteg
No. 9
Maesteg Deep
Cwrt-y-Mwnws or Moffat
No. 11
No. 12
Bryn Rhyg No. 9
Brynrhyg or Brithdir
Cwmdu
St. Johns
MAESTEG
Coed
Quarry
Maesteg Merthyr
Oakwood or Maesteg Merthyr
Cae-Defaid
Garth
Victoria
Garth (1st)
GARTH
Cwmdu-Isaf
Lletty Brongu
TROEDYRHIEW GARTH
Troedyrhiw Quarry
Llan
Cwmffern
Gelli-Siriol or Gelli Seven
Lletty Brongu
No. 2
Maes y Bettws
Celfydd Ifan
Bryn Cynon
Llantwit (1st)
Bettws or Brynllywarch
New Brynllywarch
Bettws Navigation, Ty Isaf Drift
R. Llynvi
Shwt River
Alder Llantwit
Pwllcarn
R. Garw
International No. 2 Level
Transatlantic or International
No. 3
No. 1
No. 2
Nant Hir
Ocean or Garw
Glengarw Drift
Glengarw
BLAENGARW
Nanthir
Victoria
Darran or Darran Fawr
Victoria
Dundee
Braich-y-Cymmer
Ffaldau or Oriental
Ffaldau, Oak Level
Waun Bant
Braichycymmer No. 1
PONTYCYMMER
Danybryn
No. 2
New Braichycymmer
Drifts
Duchy No. 3
Fforchwen
Pantygog
Braichycymmer Level
Duchy No. 1
No. 3
Garw or Garw Fechan
No. 1
No. 2
Duchy No. 2
Duchy New Slant
West Rhondda (1937)
West Rhondda (1893)
No. 3
No. 2
No. 1
Llest
PONTYRHYLL
Llangeinor
Bettws Llantwit (1911)
Moelgilau
Glannant Llantwit
Gwernllwyn
Tynywaun
Cefn Gelli
LLANGEINOR
Tynywaun
Bettws Church
Bettws East
Bettws Llantwit
River Garw
R. Ogmore
Blaen Ogwr or Edwards or Western or Ocean
NANTYMOEL
Wyndham Levels
Wyndham Pits No. 1 No. 2
Caedu
Tynewydd
Penllwyngwent
OGMORE VALE
Aber (1st)
Aber (2nd)
Tynewydd
Rhondda Main (Old)
Rhondda Main
Mary
Catherine
Anne
Bettws Llantwit (1936)
Bettws Llantwit (Old Drift)
Ynys-y-Bwt
Glynglowr
BLACKMILL
Kenfig River
Pentre
Aberbaiden
Ton Phillip Tytalwyn
No. 1
No. 2
Ton Phillip Tynewydd
Park Farm
Middle Park
Oaklands
Mill Pit
No. 2
No. 1
Ironworks
Patch
Park Slip
Waun Cymmle
Cefn Cribbwr
Jenkins Slip
Waen Arw
Cefn or Cefn Slip
Ffos
Cwm Ffos
Bankers Hill
Cribbwr Fach
Coytrahen Park
New Tondu
Old Coytrahen
Tytalwyn No. 3
Tondu Top or Yard
Tondu Two Drifts or Yard
Felin Fach
Cribbwr
New Cribbwr
Pandy
TONDU
Coytrahen
No. 2
No. 1
BRYNMENYN
Rock Fawr
Brynmenyn
River Ogmore
Maendy
Llan
Bryncethin Brickworks
Barrow
Heol Laethog
Tynywaun (1928)
Tynywaun (2nd)
Tynywaun (1st)
A New Bryncethin
B Barrow or Bryncethin
C Barrow
D Ynysawdre or Tondu or Adare
E Ynysawdre Drifts
SOUTHERN BOUNDARY OF COALFIELD
Newlands
Slant
Pit
Cribbwr Fawr
No. 1
No. 2
No. 3
Coalbrook
Bryndu
Lewis No. 1
No. 9
Garth or Garth Merthyr
Allens
Lewis No. 2
Garth
Lewis No. 3
Tymaen
Havod 4
Havod 6
Kimberley
Havod Deep, Llynfi Valley
Lewaldra No. 2
Lewaldra No. 1
Harries
E. Morgan's or Forestfach
Crows Nest
Field Vein
Colenso
Incline
W. Evan's
Lletty Brongu later No. 2 Level
New Mountain
Cwm Rhondda No. 2
Cedfyw Rhondda or West Rhondda
Cwm Cedfyw
Llynfi Valley
No. 3 Level
Toryfron
No. 3
No. 2
Celtic Lower
No. 1
Cwm Cedfyw
Cwmcedfyw Rhondda
Rhondda Navigation
LLANGYNWYD
LLETTY BRONGU
A B C D E F G H J K
1 2 3 4 5 6 7 8 9 10 11 12 13

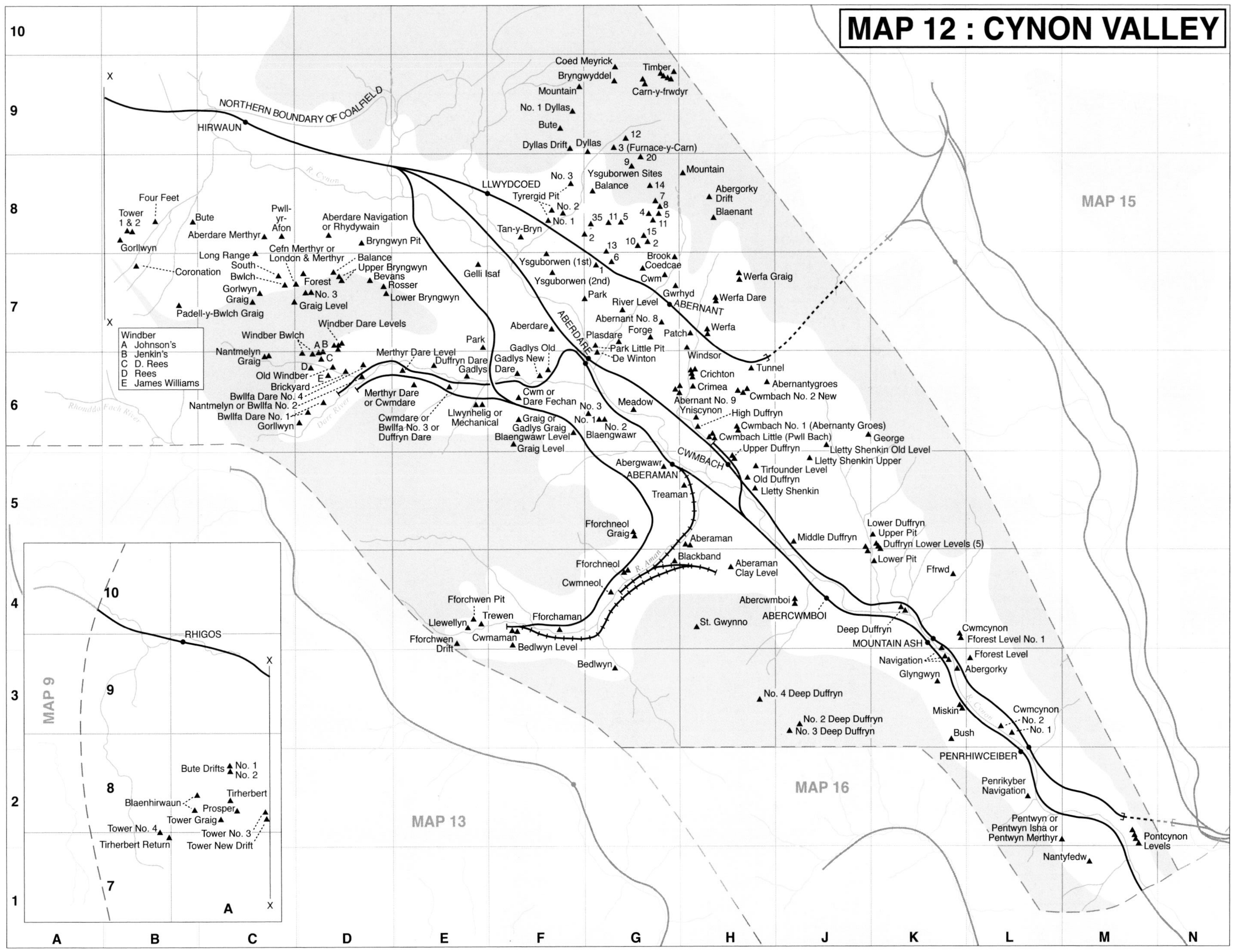

MAP 12 : CYNON VALLEY
NORTHERN BOUNDARY OF COALFIELD
HIRWAUN
LLWYDCOED
ABERDARE
ABERNANT
CWMBACH
ABERAMAN
ABERCWMBOI
MOUNTAIN ASH
PENRHIWCEIBER
R. Cynon
R. Aman
Dare River
Rhondda Fach River
MAP 15
MAP 16
MAP 13
MAP 9
Coed Meyrick
Bryngwyddel
Mountain
No. 1 Dyllas
Bute
Dyllas Drift
Dyllas
Timber
Carn-y-frwdyr
12
3 (Furnace-y-Carn)
20
9
Ysguborwen Sites
Balance
14
7
8
4
5
11
35
11
5
2
15
13
10
2
6
1
Mountain
Abergorky Drift
Blaenant
No. 3
Tyrergid Pit
No. 2
No. 1
Tan-y-Bryn
Ysguborwen (1st)
Ysguborwen (2nd)
Brook
Coedcae
Cwm
Gwrhyd
Werfa Graig
Werfa Dare
Werfa
Park
River Level
Abernant No. 8
Forge
Patch
Plasdare
Park Little Pit
De Winton
Windsor
Tunnel
Crichton
Crimea
Abernantygroes
Cwmbach No. 2 New
Abernant No. 9
Yniscynon
High Duffryn
Cwmbach No. 1 (Abernanty Groes)
Cwmbach Little (Pwll Bach)
George
Upper Duffryn
Lletty Shenkin Old Level
Lletty Shenkin Upper
Tirfounder Level
Old Duffryn
Lletty Shenkin
Meadow
Four Feet
Tower 1 & 2
Gorllwyn
Bute
Aberdare Merthyr
Pwll-yr-Afon
Aberdare Navigation or Rhydywain
Bryngwyn Pit
Long Range
South
Bwlch
Coronation
Cefn Merthyr or London & Merthyr
Balance
Upper Bryngwyn
Bevans
Rosser
Lower Bryngwyn
Forest
Gorlwyn Graig
No. 3
Graig Level
Padell-y-Bwlch Graig
Gelli Isaf
Windber Dare Levels
Windber Bwlch
A B
C
D
E
Nantmelyn Graig
Old Windber
Brickyard
Bwllfa Dare No. 4
Nantmelyn or Bwllfa No. 2
Bwllfa Dare No. 1
Gorllwyn
Windber
A Johnson's
B Jenkin's
C D. Rees
D Rees
E James Williams
Merthyr Dare Level
Duffryn Dare
Gadlys
Park
Aberdare
Gadlys Old
Gadlys New
Dare
Merthyr Dare or Cwmdare
Cwmdare or Bwllfa No. 3 or Duffryn Dare
Llwynhelig or Mechanical
Cwm or Dare Fechan
Graig or Gadlys Graig
Blaengwawr Level
Graig Level
No. 3
No. 1
No. 2
Blaengwawr
Abergwawr
Treaman
Fforchneol Graig
Fforchneol
Cwmneol
Aberaman
Blackband
Aberaman Clay Level
Fforchwen Pit
Llewellyn
Trewen
Fforchaman
Fforchwen Drift
Cwmaman
Bedlwyn Level
Bedlwyn
Abercwmboi
St. Gwynno
Middle Duffryn
Lower Duffryn
Upper Pit
Duffryn Lower Levels (5)
Lower Pit
Ffrwd
Deep Duffryn
Cwmcynon
Fforest Level No. 1
Fforest Level
Navigation
Glyngwyn
Abergorky
No. 4 Deep Duffryn
No. 2 Deep Duffryn
No. 3 Deep Duffryn
Miskin
Cwmcynon
No. 2
No. 1
Bush
Penrikyber Navigation
Pentwyn or Pentwyn Isha or Pentwyn Merthyr
Nantyfedw
Pontcynon Levels
RHIGOS
Bute Drifts
No. 1
No. 2
Tirherbert
Blaenhirwaun
Prosper
Tower Graig
Tower No. 4
Tirherbert Return
Tower No. 3
Tower New Drift
A
B
C
D
E
F
G
H
J
K
L
M
N
1
2
3
4
5
6
7
8
9
10
X

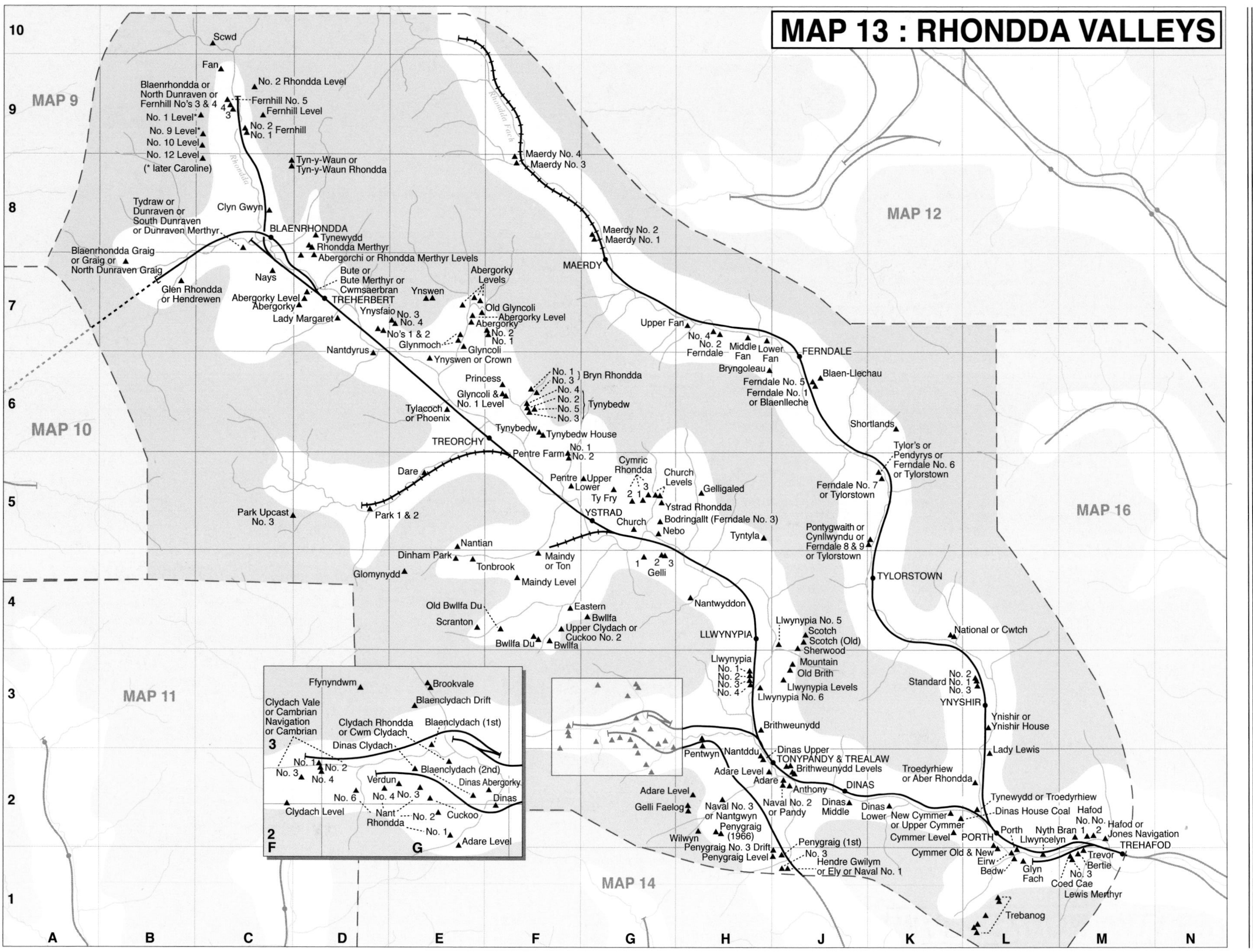
MAP 13 : RHONDDA VALLEYS
MAP 9
MAP 10
MAP 11
MAP 12
MAP 14
MAP 16
Scwd
Fan
No. 2 Rhondda Level
Blaenrhondda or North Dunraven or Fernhill No's 3 & 4
Fernhill No. 5
Fernhill Level
No. 1 Level*
No. 9 Level*
No. 10 Level
No. 12 Level
(* later Caroline)
No. 2
No. 1
Fernhill
Tyn-y-Waun or Tyn-y-Waun Rhondda
Rhondda
Rhondda Fach
Maerdy No. 4
Maerdy No. 3
Maerdy No. 2
Maerdy No. 1
MAERDY
Tydraw or Dunraven or South Dunraven or Dunraven Merthyr
Clyn Gwyn
BLAENRHONDDA
Tynewydd
Rhondda Merthyr
Abergorchi or Rhondda Merthyr Levels
Blaenrhondda Graig or Graig or North Dunraven Graig
Glen Rhondda or Hendrewen
Nays
Bute or Bute Merthyr or Cwmsaerbran
TREHERBERT
Abergorky Level
Abergorky
Lady Margaret
Ynswen
Abergorky Levels
Old Glyncoli
Abergorky Level
Abergorky
No. 2
No. 1
Ynysfaio
No. 3
No. 4
No's 1 & 2
Glynmoch
Glyncoli
Nantdyrus
Ynyswen or Crown
Upper Fan
No. 4
No. 2
Ferndale
Middle Fan
Lower Fan
FERNDALE
Bryngoleau
Blaen-Llechau
Ferndale No. 5
Ferndale No. 1
or Blaenlleche
Princess
Glyncoli & No. 1 Level
No. 1
No. 3
Bryn Rhondda
No. 4
No. 2
No. 5
No. 3
Tynybedw
Tylacoch or Phoenix
Tynybedw
Tynybedw House
TREORCHY
Pentre Farm
No. 1
No. 2
Shortlands
Tylor's or Pendyrys or Ferndale No. 6 or Tylorstown
Dare
Pentre
Upper
Lower
Ty Fry
Cymric Rhondda
2 1 3
Church Levels
Gelligaled
Ferndale No. 7 or Tylorstown
Park Upcast No. 3
Park 1 & 2
YSTRAD
Church
Ystrad Rhondda
Bodringallt (Ferndale No. 3)
Nebo
Tyntyla
Pontygwaith or Cynllwyndu or Ferndale 8 & 9 or Tylorstown
Nantian
Dinham Park
Tonbrook
Maindy or Ton
1 2 3
Gelli
TYLORSTOWN
Glomynydd
Maindy Level
Nantwyddon
Old Bwllfa Du
Scranton
Eastern
Bwllfa
Upper Clydach or Cuckoo No. 2
Bwllfa Du
Bwllfa
LLWYNYPIA
Llwynypia No. 5
Scotch
Scotch (Old)
Sherwood
Mountain
Old Brith
Llwynypia Levels
Llwynypia No. 6
Llwynypia
No. 1
No. 2
No. 3
No. 4
National or Cwtch
Standard
No. 2
No. 1
No. 3
YNYSHIR
Ynishir or Ynishir House
Brithweunydd
Lady Lewis
Ffynyndwm
Brookvale
Blaenclydach Drift
Clydach Vale or Cambrian Navigation or Cambrian
Clydach Rhondda or Cwm Clydach
Blaenclydach (1st)
Dinas Clydach
No. 1
No. 2
No. 3
No. 4
Blaenclydach (2nd)
Verdun
Dinas Abergorky
No. 6
No. 4
No. 3
Dinas
Clydach Level
Nant Rhondda
No. 2
Cuckoo
No. 1
Adare Level
Pentwyn
Nantddu
Dinas Upper
TONYPANDY & TREALAW
Brithweunydd Levels
Adare Level
Adare
Anthony
DINAS
Troedyrhiew or Aber Rhondda
Adare Level
Gelli Faelog
Naval No. 3 or Nantgwyn
Naval No. 2 or Pandy
Dinas Middle
Dinas Lower
New Cymmer or Upper Cymmer
Cymmer Level
Tynewydd or Troedyrhiew
Dinas House Coal
Hafod No. No. 1 2
Hafod or Jones Navigation
Wilwyn
Penygraig (1966)
Penygraig No. 3 Drift
Penygraig Level
Penygraig (1st)
No. 3
Hendre Gwilym or Ely or Naval No. 1
PORTH
Porth
Nyth Bran
Llwyncelyn
TREHAFOD
Cymmer Old & New
Eirw
Bedw
Glyn Fach
Trevor
Bertie
No. 3
Coed Cae
Lewis Merthyr
Trebanog
A B C D E F G H J K L M N
1 2 3 4 5 6 7 8 9 10

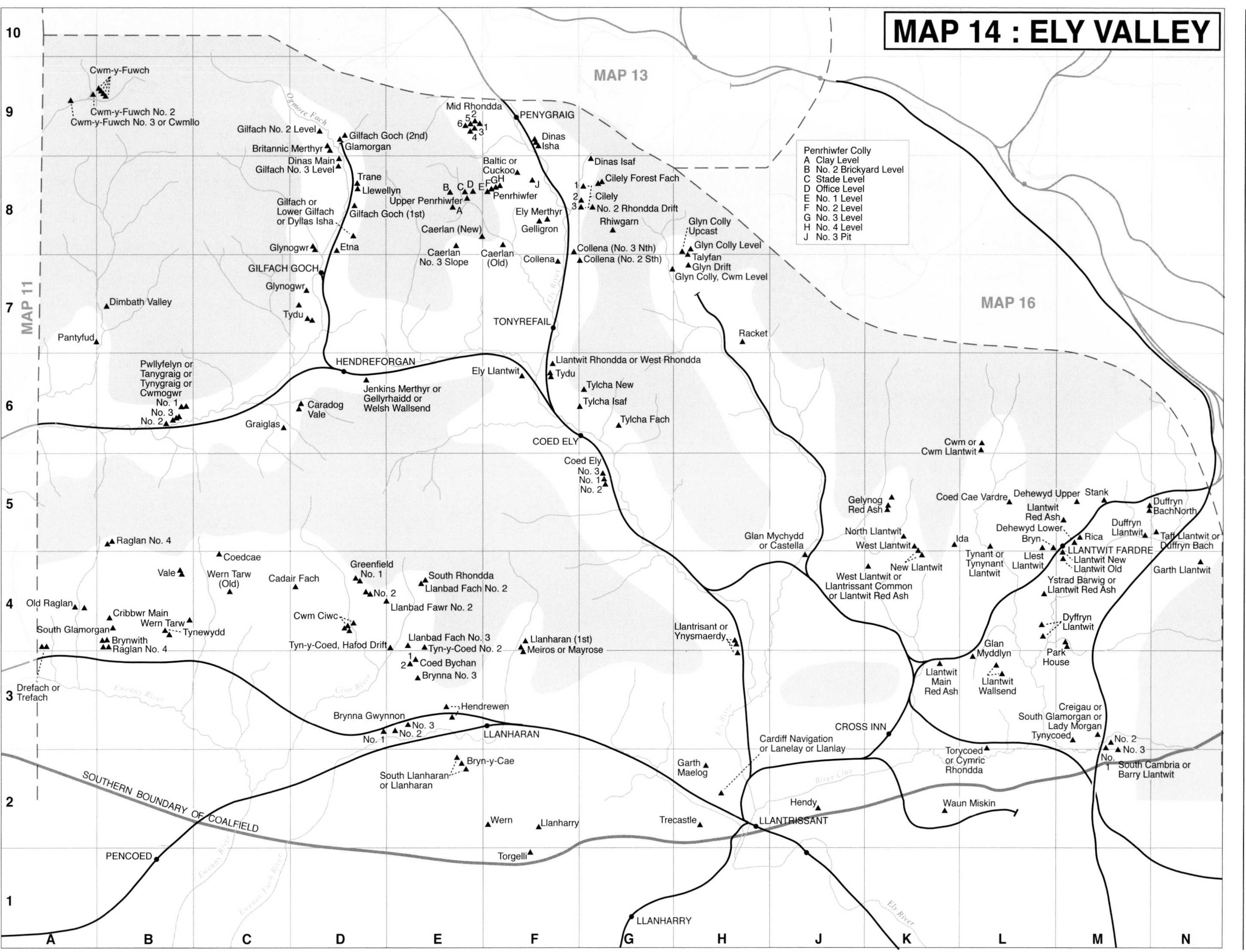

MAP 14 : ELY VALLEY
MAP 13
MAP 16
MAP 11
Penrhiwfer Colly
A Clay Level
B No. 2 Brickyard Level
C Stade Level
D Office Level
E No. 1 Level
F No. 2 Level
G No. 3 Level
H No. 4 Level
J No. 3 Pit
Cwm-y-Fuwch
Cwm-y-Fuwch No. 2
Cwm-y-Fuwch No. 3 or Cwmllo
Gilfach No. 2 Level
Gilfach Goch (2nd)
Glamorgan
Britannic Merthyr
Dinas Main
Gilfach No. 3 Level
Trane
Llewellyn
Gilfach or Lower Gilfach or Dyllas Isha
Gilfach Goch (1st)
Glynogwr
Etna
GILFACH GOCH
Glynogwr
Tydu
Dimbath Valley
Pantyfud
Mid Rhondda
PENYGRAIG
Dinas Isha
Baltic or Cuckoo
Upper Penrhiwfer
Penrhiwfer
Caerlan (New)
Caerlan No. 3 Slope
Caerlan (Old)
Ely Merthyr
Gelligron
Collena
Dinas Isaf
Cilely Forest Fach
Cilely
No. 2 Rhondda Drift
Rhiwgarn
Collena (No. 3 Nth)
Collena (No. 2 Sth)
Glyn Colly Upcast
Glyn Colly Level
Talyfan
Glyn Drift
Glyn Colly, Cwm Level
Racket
TONYREFAIL
HENDREFORGAN
Jenkins Merthyr or Gellyrhaidd or Welsh Wallsend
Ely Llantwit
Llantwit Rhondda or West Rhondda
Tydu
Tylcha New
Tylcha Isaf
Tylcha Fach
Pwllyfelyn or Tanygraig or Tynygraig or Cwmogwr
No. 1
No. 3
No. 2
Caradog Vale
Graiglas
COED ELY
Coed Ely
No. 3
No. 1
No. 2
Cwm or Cwm Llantwit
Gelynog Red Ash
Coed Cae Vardre
Dehewyd Upper
Stank
Duffryn BachNorth
Llantwit Red Ash
Dehewyd Lower
Bryn
Rica
Duffryn Llantwit
Taff Llantwit or Duffryn Bach
North Llantwit
West Llantwit
New Llantwit
Ida
Tynant or Tynynant Llantwit
Llest Llantwit
LLANTWIT FARDRE
Llantwit New
Llantwit Old
Garth Llantwit
Glan Mychydd or Castella
West Llantwit or Llantrissant Common or Llantwit Red Ash
Ystrad Barwig or Llantwit Red Ash
Raglan No. 4
Coedcae
Vale
Wern Tarw (Old)
Cadair Fach
Greenfield No. 1
No. 2
South Rhondda
Llanbad Fach No. 2
Llanbad Fawr No. 2
Old Raglan
Cribbwr Main
Wern Tarw
Tynewydd
South Glamorgan
Brynwith
Raglan No. 4
Cwm Ciwc
Tyn-y-Coed, Hafod Drift
Llanbad Fach No. 3
Tyn-y-Coed No. 2
Coed Bychan
Brynna No. 3
Llanharan (1st)
Meiros or Mayrose
Llantrisant or Ynysmaerdy
Dyffryn Llantwit
Park House
Glan Myddlyn
Llantwit Main Red Ash
Llantwit Wallsend
Drefach or Trefach
Hendrewen
Brynna Gwynnon
No. 3
No. 1
No. 2
LLANHARAN
CROSS INN
Creigau or South Glamorgan or Lady Morgan
Tynycoed
No. 2
No. 3
No. 1
South Cambria or Barry Llantwit
Cardiff Navigation or Lanelay or Llanlay
Torycoed or Cymric Rhondda
Bryn-y-Cae
South Llanharan or Llanharan
Garth Maelog
SOUTHERN BOUNDARY OF COALFIELD
Hendy
Waun Miskin
Wern
Llanharry
Trecastle
LLANTRISSANT
PENCOED
Torgelli
LLANHARRY
Ogmore Fach
Ely River
Ewenny River
Ewenny Fach River
Clun River
River Clun
A
B
C
D
E
F
G
H
J
K
L
M
N
1
2
3
4
5
6
7
8
9
10

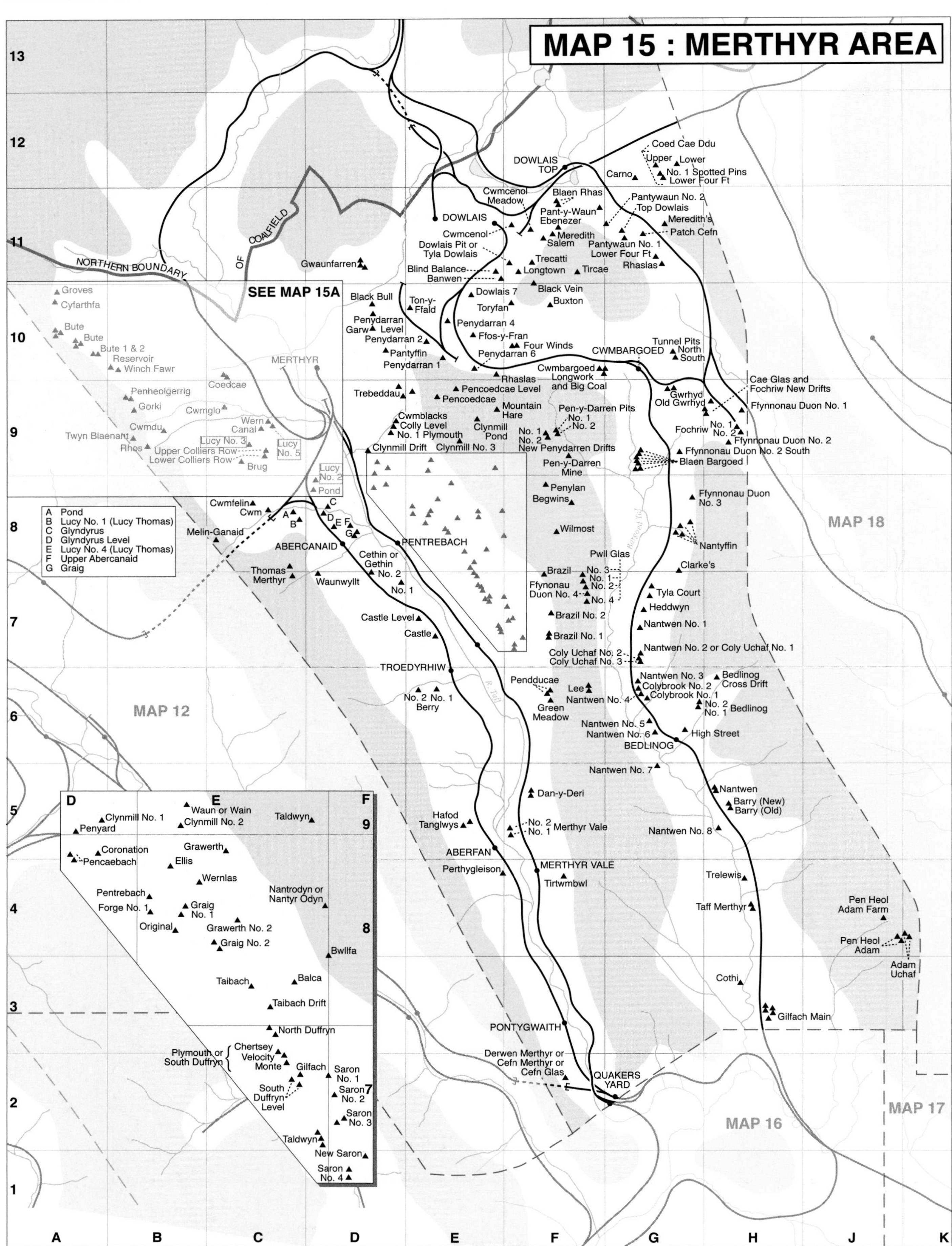
MAP 15 : MERTHYR AREA
SEE MAP 15A
NORTHERN BOUNDARY OF COALFIELD
MAP 12
MAP 16
MAP 17
MAP 18
DOWLAIS TOP
DOWLAIS
MERTHYR
ABERCANAID
PENTREBACH
TROEDYRHIW
ABERFAN
MERTHYR VALE
PONTYGWAITH
QUAKERS YARD
CWMBARGOED
BEDLINOG
A Pond
B Lucy No. 1 (Lucy Thomas)
C Glyndyrus
D Glyndyrus Level
E Lucy No. 4 (Lucy Thomas)
F Upper Abercanaid
G Graig

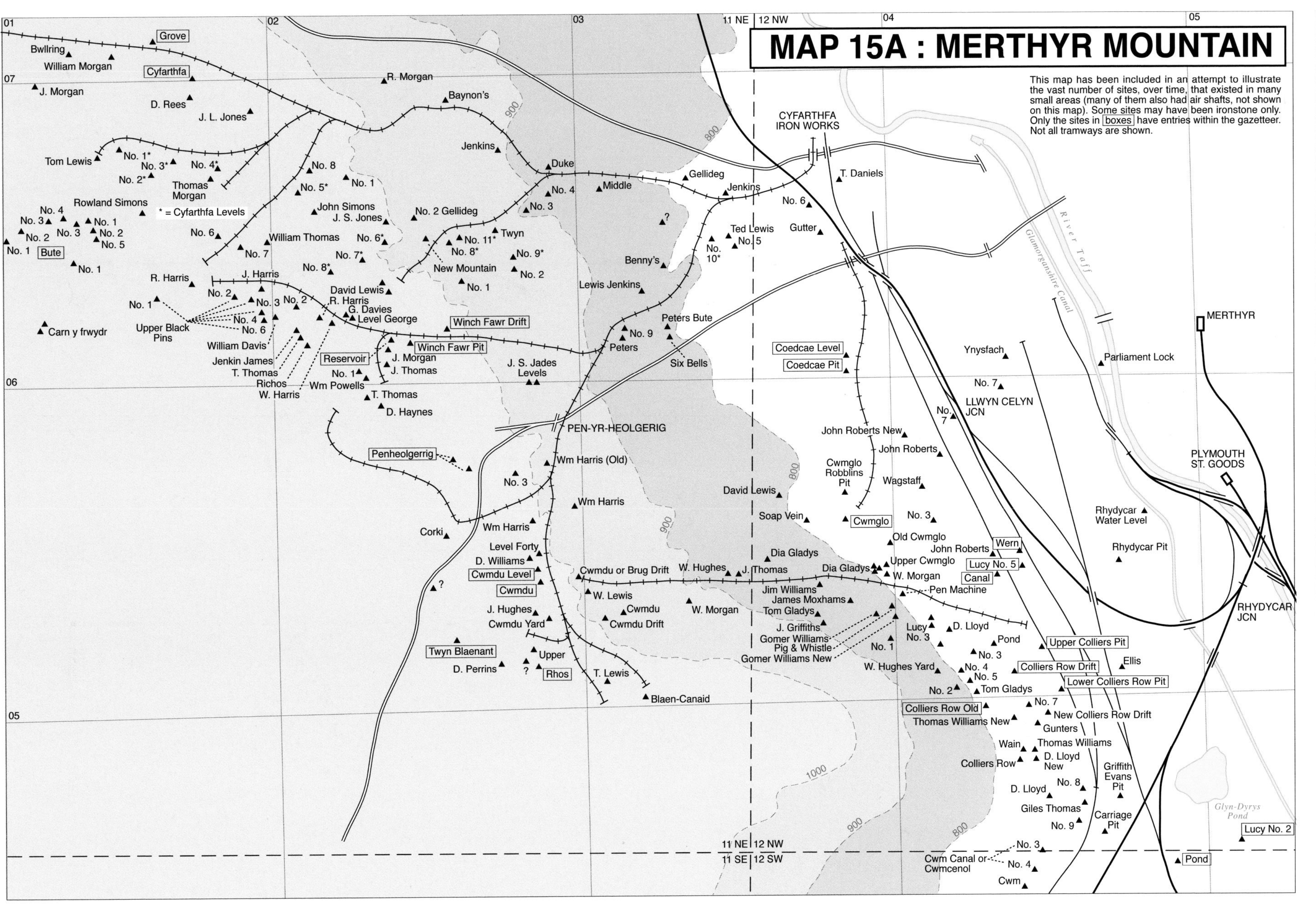
MAP 15A : MERTHYR MOUNTAIN
This map has been included in an attempt to illustrate the vast number of sites, over time, that existed in many small areas (many of them also had air shafts, not shown on this map). Some sites may have been ironstone only. Only the sites in boxes have entries within the gazetteer. Not all tramways are shown.
MERTHYR
PLYMOUTH ST. GOODS
RHYDYCAR JCN
CYFARTHFA IRON WORKS
LLWYN CELYN JCN
PEN-YR-HEOLGERIG
River Taff
Glamorganshire Canal
Glyn-Dyrys Pond
Parliament Lock
Rhydycar Water Level
Rhydycar Pit
Ynysfach
Lucy No. 2
Pond
Upper Colliers Pit
Colliers Row Drift
Lower Colliers Row Pit
Colliers Row Old
New Colliers Row Drift
Ellis
Griffith Evans Pit
Carriage Pit
Wern
Lucy No. 5
Canal
Pen Machine
Coedcae Level
Coedcae Pit
Cwmglo
Cwmglo Robblins Pit
John Roberts New
John Roberts
Wagstaff
Old Cwmglo
Upper Cwmglo
W. Morgan
Dia Gladys
Soap Vein
David Lewis
Jim Williams
James Moxhams
Tom Gladys
J. Griffiths
Gomer Williams
Pig & Whistle
Gomer Williams New
W. Hughes Yard
Thomas Williams New
Thomas Williams
Gunters
Wain
Colliers Row
D. Lloyd New
D. Lloyd
Giles Thomas
Cwm Canal or Cwmcenol
Cwm
W. Hughes
J. Thomas
Cwmdu or Brug Drift
W. Lewis
Cwmdu
Cwmdu Drift
Blaen-Canaid
T. Lewis
Rhos
Upper
Cwmdu Yard
J. Hughes
Cwmdu Level
D. Williams
Level Forty
Wm Harris
Wm Harris (Old)
Twyn Blaenant
D. Perrins
Corki
Penheolgerrig
Peters Bute
Six Bells
Peters
Lewis Jenkins
Benny's
Ted Lewis
Gutter
T. Daniels
Gellideg
Jenkins
Middle
Duke
Baynon's
R. Morgan
No. 2 Gellideg
New Mountain
Twyn
Winch Fawr Drift
Winch Fawr Pit
J. S. Jades Levels
J. Morgan
J. Thomas
T. Thomas
D. Haynes
Reservoir
Level George
G. Davies
R. Harris
David Lewis
Wm Powells
W. Harris
Richos
T. Thomas
Jenkin James
William Davis'
Upper Black Pins
J. Harris
R. Harris
William Thomas
John Simons
J. S. Jones
Grove
Cyfarthfa
D. Rees
J. L. Jones
Thomas Morgan
* = Cyfarthfa Levels
Tom Lewis
Rowland Simons
Bute
Carn y frwydr
Bwllring
William Morgan
J. Morgan
01
02
03
04
05
06
07
11 NE
12 NW
11 SE
12 SW
800
900
1000

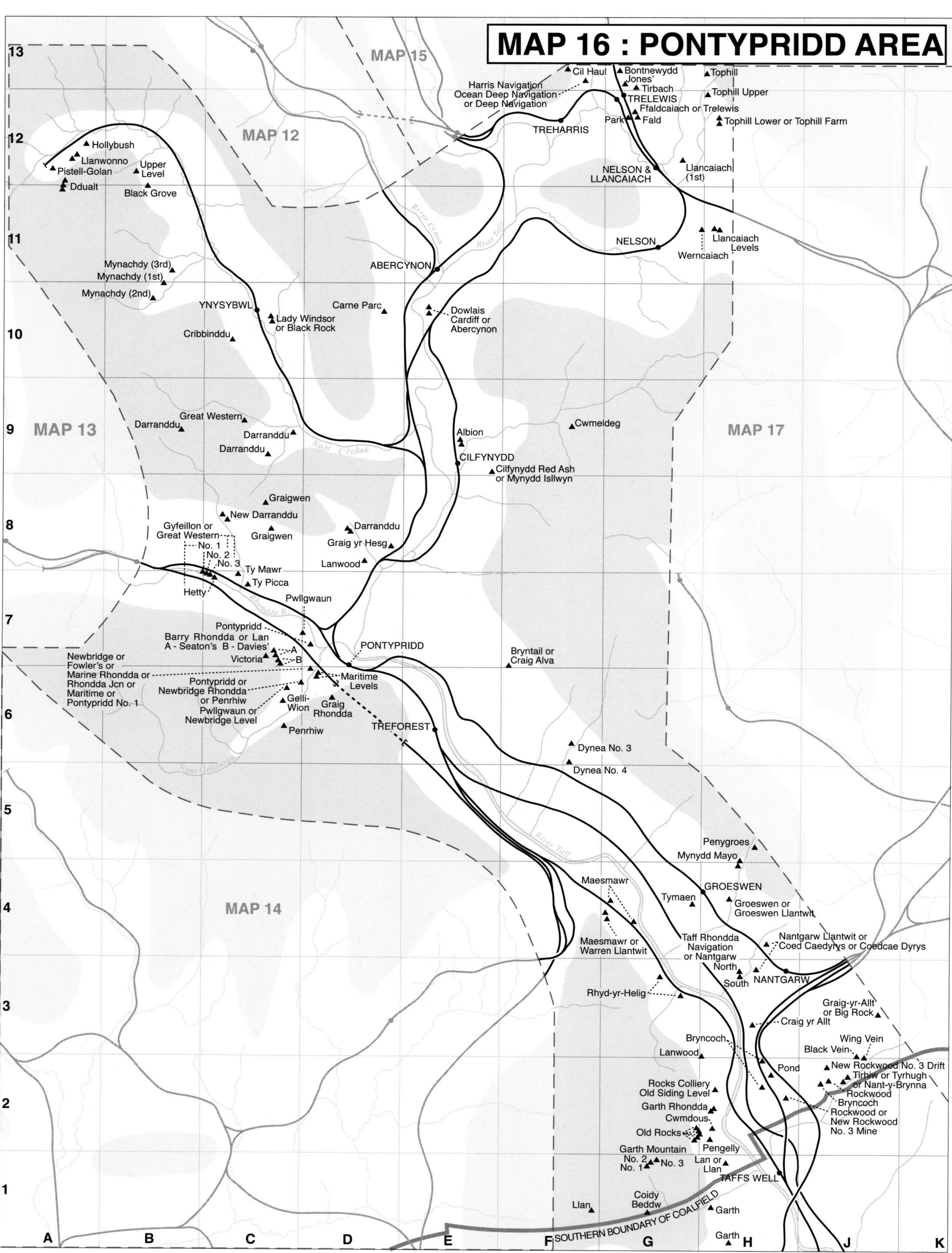
MAP 16 : PONTYPRIDD AREA
MAP 15
MAP 12
MAP 13
MAP 17
MAP 14
Cil Haul
Harris Navigation
Ocean Deep Navigation
or Deep Navigation
Bontnewydd
Jones'
Tirbach
TRELEWIS
Ffaldcaiach or Trelewis
Park
Fald
Tophill
Tophill Upper
Tophill Lower or Tophill Farm
TREHARRIS
NELSON &
LLANCAIACH
Llancaiach
(1st)
NELSON
Llancaiach
Levels
Werncaiach
Hollybush
Llanwonno
Pistell-Golan
Upper
Level
Dduallt
Black Grove
Mynachdy (3rd)
Mynachdy (1st)
Mynachdy (2nd)
YNYSYBWL
Lady Windsor
or Black Rock
Cribbinddu
Carne Parc
ABERCYNON
Dowlais
Cardiff or
Abercynon
River Cynon
River Taff
Great Western
Darranddu
Darranddu
Darranddu
Nant Clydach
Albion
CILFYNYDD
Cilfynydd Red Ash
or Mynydd Isllwyn
Cwmeldeg
Graigwen
New Darranddu
Graigwen
Darranddu
Graig yr Hesg
Lanwood
Gyfeillon or
Great Western
No. 1
No. 2
No. 3
Ty Mawr
Ty Picca
Hetty
Rhondda R.
Pwllgwaun
Pontypridd
Barry Rhondda or Lan
A - Seaton's B - Davies'
A
B
Victoria
Newbridge or
Fowler's or
Marine Rhondda or
Rhondda Jcn or
Maritime or
Pontypridd No. 1
Pontypridd or
Newbridge Rhondda
or Penrhiw
Pwllgwaun or
Newbridge Level
Maritime
Levels
Gelli-
Wion
Graig
Rhondda
Penrhiw
PONTYPRIDD
TREFOREST
Bryntail or
Craig Alva
Nant Gelliwion
Dynea No. 3
Dynea No. 4
River Taff
Penygroes
Mynydd Mayo
GROESWEN
Groeswen or
Groeswen Llantwit
Maesmawr
Tymaen
Maesmawr or
Warren Llantwit
Taff Rhondda
Navigation
or Nantgarw
North
South
NANTGARW
Nantgarw Llantwit or
Coed Caedyrys or Coedcae Dyrys
Rhyd-yr-Helig
Graig-yr-Allt
or Big Rock
Craig yr Allt
Bryncoch
Lanwood
Wing Vein
Black Vein
Pond
New Rockwood No. 3 Drift
Tirhiw or Tyrhugh
or Nant-y-Brynna
Rockwood
Bryncoch
Rockwood or
New Rockwood
No. 3 Mine
Rocks Colliery
Old Siding Level
Garth Rhondda
Cwmdous
Old Rocks
Pengelly
Garth Mountain
No. 2
No. 1
No. 3
Lan or
Llan
TAFFS WELL
Llan
Coidy
Beddw
SOUTHERN BOUNDARY OF COALFIELD
Garth
Garth
A
B
C
D
E
F
G
H
J
K
1
2
3
4
5
6
7
8
9
10
11
12
13

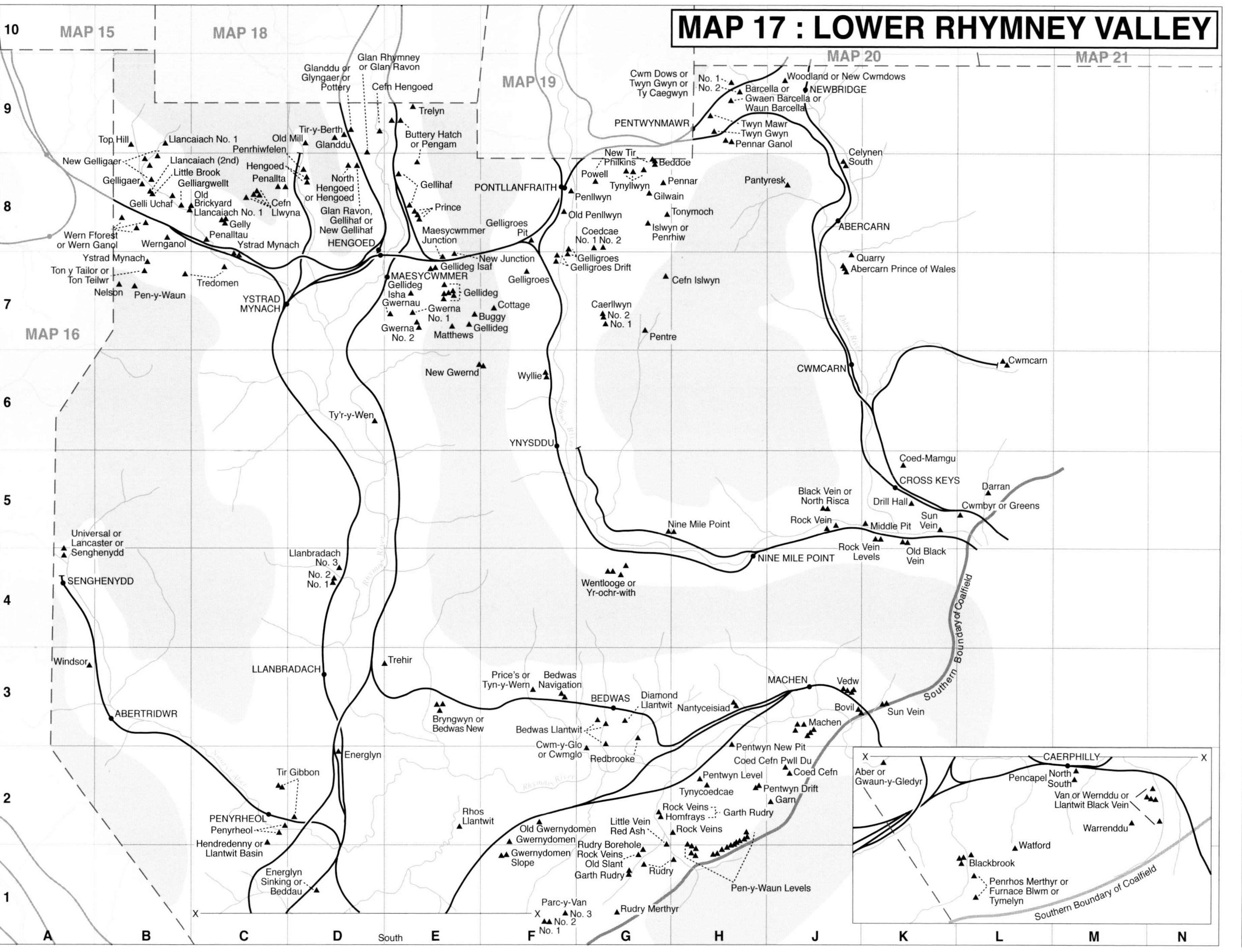
MAP 17 : LOWER RHYMNEY VALLEY
MAP 15
MAP 18
MAP 19
MAP 20
MAP 21
MAP 16
Glanddu or Glyngaer or Pottery
Glan Rhymney or Glan Ravon
Cefn Hengoed
Trelyn
Buttery Hatch or Pengam
Tir-y-Berth
Glanddu
Old Mill
Penrhiwfelen
Top Hill
Llancaiach No. 1
New Gelligaer
Llancaiach (2nd)
Little Brook
Gelligaer
Gelliargwellt
Hengoed
Penallta
North Hengoed or Hengoed
Gelli Uchaf
Old Brickyard
Llancaiach No. 1
Cefn Llwyna
Glan Ravon, Gellihaf or New Gellihaf
Gelly
Penalltau
Wern Fforest or Wern Ganol
Wernganol
Ystrad Mynach
HENGOED
Ystrad Mynach
Ton y Tailor or Ton Teilwr
Tredomen
Nelson
Pen-y-Waun
YSTRAD MYNACH
Gellihaf
Prince
Maesycwmmer Junction
PONTLLANFRAITH
Gelligroes Pit
New Junction
Gellideg Isaf
MAESYCWMMER
Gellideg Isha
Gwernau
Gellideg
Gwerna No. 1
Gwerna No. 2
Cottage
Buggy
Gellideg
Matthews
Gelligroes
New Gwernd
Wyllie
Cwm Dows or Twyn Gwyn or Ty Caegwyn
No. 1
No. 2
Barcella or Gwaen Barcella or Waun Barcella
Woodland or New Cwmdows
NEWBRIDGE
PENTWYNMAWR
Twyn Mawr
Twyn Gwyn
Pennar Ganol
New Tir Philkins
Beddoe
Powell
Tynyllwyn
Pennar
Penllwyn
Gilwain
Old Penllwyn
Tonymoch
Islwyn or Penrhiw
Coedcae No. 1 No. 2
Gelligroes
Gelligroes Drift
Cefn Islwyn
Caerllwyn No. 2 No. 1
Pentre
Pantyresk
Celynen South
ABERCARN
Quarry
Abercarn Prince of Wales
CWMCARN
Cwmcarn
Ty'r-y-Wen
YNYSDDU
Coed-Mamgu
CROSS KEYS
Darran
Black Vein or North Risca
Drill Hall
Cwmbyr or Greens
Sun Vein
Rock Vein
Middle Pit
Nine Mile Point
Rock Vein Levels
Old Black Vein
NINE MILE POINT
Universal or Lancaster or Senghenydd
SENGHENYDD
Llanbradach No. 3
No. 2
No. 1
Wentlooge or Yr-ochr-with
Windsor
LLANBRADACH
Trehir
Price's or Tyn-y-Wern
Bedwas Navigation
BEDWAS
Diamond Llantwit
Nantyceisiad
MACHEN
Vedw
Bovil
Sun Vein
Southern Boundary of Coalfield
ABERTRIDWR
Bryngwyn or Bedwas New
Bedwas Llantwit
Machen
Energlyn
Cwm-y-Glo or Cwmglo
Redbrooke
Pentwyn New Pit
Coed Cefn Pwll Du
Coed Cefn
Tir Gibbon
Pentwyn Level
Tynycoedcae
Pentwyn Drift
Garn
Rhos Llantwit
Rock Veins
Homfrays
Garth Rudry
PENYRHEOL
Penyrheol
Hendredenny or Llantwit Basin
Old Gwernydomen
Gwernydomen
Gwernydomen Slope
Little Vein
Red Ash
Rock Veins
Rudry Borehole
Rock Veins
Old Slant
Garth Rudry
Rudry
Energlyn Sinking or Beddau
Pen-y-Waun Levels
Parc-y-Van
No. 3
No. 2
No. 1
Rudry Merthyr
South
Rhymney River
Sirhowy River
Ebbw River
Nant yr Aber
X
Aber or Gwaun-y-Gledyr
CAERPHILLY
Pencapel
North
South
Van or Wernddu or Llantwit Black Vein
Warrenddu
Watford
Blackbrook
Penrhos Merthyr or Furnace Blwm or Tymelyn
Southern Boundary of Coalfield
A
B
C
D
E
F
G
H
J
K
L
M
N
1
2
3
4
5
6
7
8
9
10

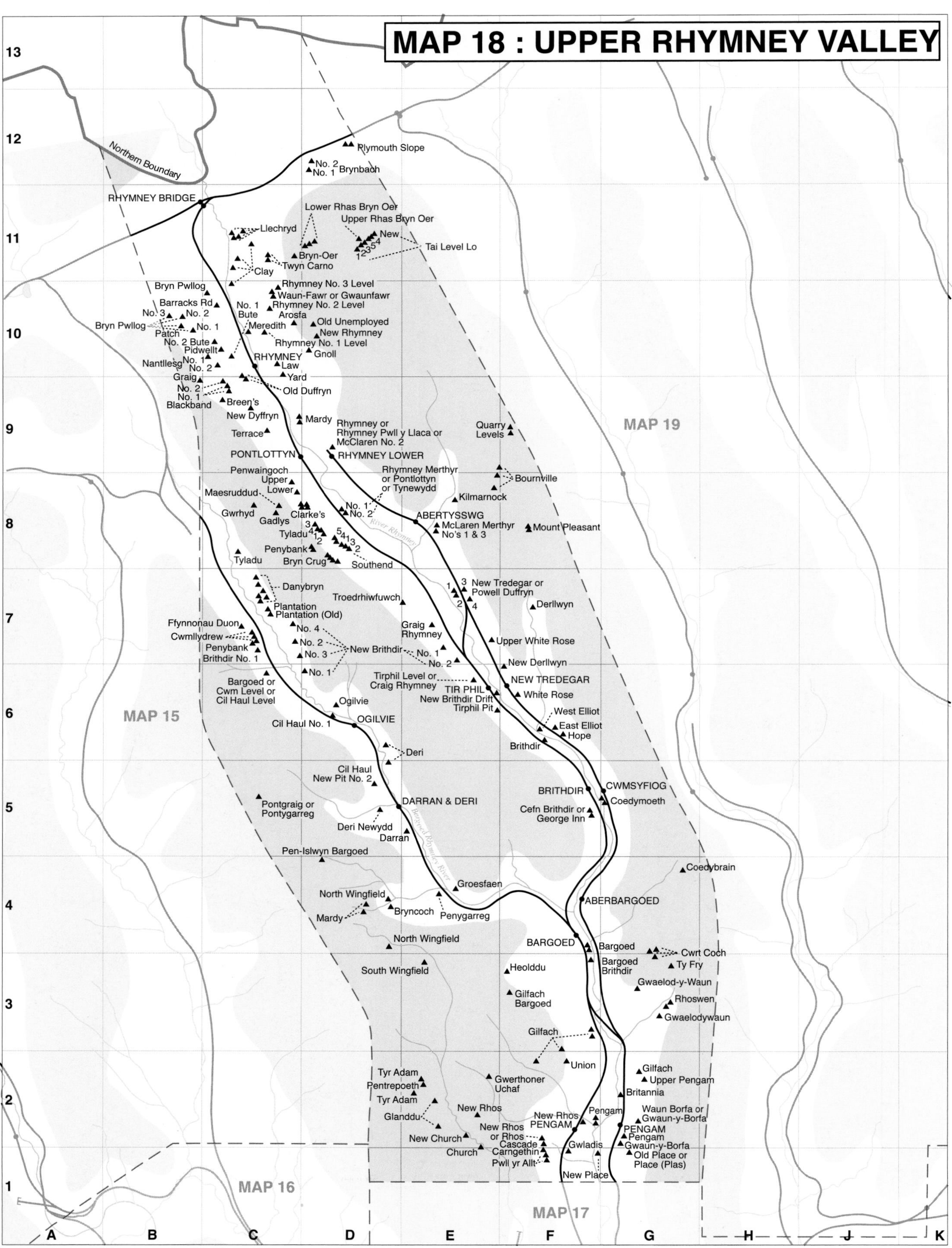
MAP 18 : UPPER RHYMNEY VALLEY
Northern Boundary
RHYMNEY BRIDGE
Plymouth Slope
No. 2
No. 1
Brynbach
Lower Rhas Bryn Oer
Upper Rhas Bryn Oer
New
Tai Level Lo
Llechryd
Bryn-Oer
Twyn Carno
Clay
Bryn Pwllog
Barracks Rd
No. 3
No. 2
Bryn Pwllog
No. 1
Patch
No. 2 Bute
Pidwellt
Nantllesg
No. 1
No. 2
Graig
No. 1
Bute
Meredith
Rhymney No. 3 Level
Waun-Fawr or Gwaunfawr
Rhymney No. 2 Level
Arosfa
Old Unemployed
New Rhymney
Rhymney No. 1 Level
Gnoll
RHYMNEY
Law
Yard
Old Duffryn
No. 2
No. 1
Blackband
Breen's
New Dyffryn
Terrace
Mardy
Rhymney or
Rhymney Pwll y Llaca or
McClaren No. 2
Quarry
Levels
MAP 19
PONTLOTTYN
RHYMNEY LOWER
Penwaingoch
Upper
Lower
Maesruddud
Gwrhyd
Gadlys
Clarke's
Rhymney Merthyr
or Pontlottyn
or Tynewydd
Bournville
Kilmarnock
No. 1
No. 2
ABERTYSSWG
McLaren Merthyr
No's 1 & 3
Mount Pleasant
Tyladu
Penybank
Bryn Crug
Southend
River Rhymney
Tyladu
Danybryn
Plantation
Plantation (Old)
Troedrhiwfuwch
New Tredegar or
Powell Duffryn
Derllwyn
Ffynnonau Duon
Cwmllydrew
Penybank
Brithdir No. 1
No. 4
No. 2
No. 3
No. 1
New Brithdir
Graig
Rhymney
No. 1
No. 2
Upper White Rose
New Derllwyn
Bargoed or
Cwm Level or
Cil Haul Level
Tirphil Level or
Craig Rhymney
TIR PHIL
New Brithdir Drift
Tirphil Pit
NEW TREDEGAR
White Rose
West Elliot
East Elliot
Hope
Brithdir
MAP 15
Ogilvie
Cil Haul No. 1
OGILVIE
Deri
Cil Haul
New Pit No. 2
BRITHDIR
CWMSYFIOG
Coedymoeth
Pontgraig or
Pontygarreg
DARRAN & DERI
Bargoed Rhymney River
Cefn Brithdir or
George Inn
Deri Newydd
Darran
Pen-Islwyn Bargoed
Coedybrain
Groesfaen
North Wingfield
ABERBARGOED
Mardy
Bryncoch
Penygarreg
North Wingfield
BARGOED
Bargoed
Bargoed
Brithdir
Cwrt Coch
Ty Fry
South Wingfield
Heolddu
Gwaelod-y-Waun
Gilfach
Bargoed
Rhoswen
Gwaelodywaun
Gilfach
Union
Tyr Adam
Pentrepoeth
Tyr Adam
Glanddu
Gwerthoner
Uchaf
New Rhos
New Rhos
PENGAM
Pengam
Gilfach
Upper Pengam
Britannia
Waun Borfa or
Gwaun-y-Borfa
PENGAM
Pengam
Gwaun-y-Borfa
New Church
New Rhos
or Rhos
Cascade
Carngethin
Pwll yr Allt
Church
Gwladis
Old Place or
Place (Plas)
New Place
MAP 16
MAP 17
13
12
11
10
9
8
7
6
5
4
3
2
1
A
B
C
D
E
F
G
H
J
K

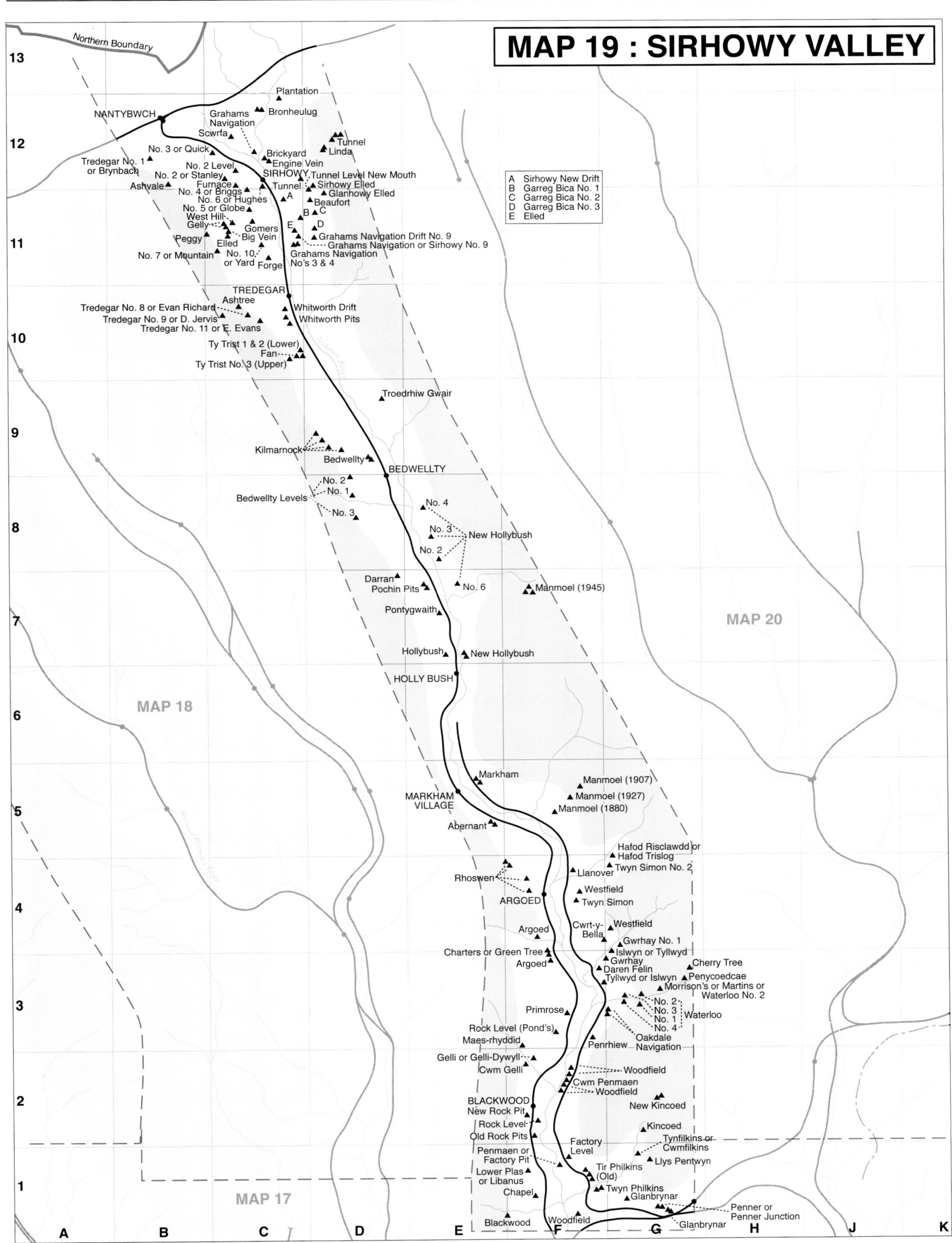

MAP 19 : SIRHOWY VALLEY
Northern Boundary
NANTYBWCH
Plantation
Bronheulug
Grahams Navigation
Scwrfa
Tunnel
Linda
No. 3 or Quick
Brickyard
Engine Vein
Tredegar No. 1 or Brynbach
No. 2 Level
SIRHOWY
Tunnel Level New Mouth
No. 2 or Stanley
Furnace
Sirhowy Elled
Ashvale
No. 4 or Briggs
Tunnel
Glanhowy Elled
No. 6 or Hughes
Beaufort
No. 5 or Globe
West Hill
Gelly
Gomers
Big Vein
Peggy
Elled
Grahams Navigation Drift No. 9
Grahams Navigation or Sirhowy No. 9
No. 7 or Mountain
No. 10 or Yard
Forge
Grahams Navigation No's 3 & 4
A Sirhowy New Drift
B Garreg Bica No. 1
C Garreg Bica No. 2
D Garreg Bica No. 3
E Elled
TREDEGAR
Ashtree
Tredegar No. 8 or Evan Richard
Whitworth Drift
Tredegar No. 9 or D. Jervis
Whitworth Pits
Tredegar No. 11 or E. Evans
Ty Trist 1 & 2 (Lower)
Fan
Ty Trist No. 3 (Upper)
Troedrhiw Gwair
Kilmarnock
Bedwellty
BEDWELLTY
No. 2
No. 1
Bedwellty Levels
No. 3
No. 4
No. 3
New Hollybush
No. 2
Darran
Pochin Pits
No. 6
Manmoel (1945)
Pontygwaith
MAP 20
Hollybush
New Hollybush
HOLLY BUSH
MAP 18
Markham
Manmoel (1907)
MARKHAM VILLAGE
Manmoel (1927)
Manmoel (1880)
Abernant
Hafod Risclawdd or Hafod Trislog
Twyn Simon No. 2
Llanover
Rhoswen
Westfield
ARGOED
Twyn Simon
Argoed
Cwrt-y-Bella
Westfield
Gwrhay No. 1
Charters or Green Tree
Islwyn or Tyllwyd
Argoed
Gwrhay
Cherry Tree
Daren Felin
Penycoedcae
Tyllwyd or Islwyn
Morrison's or Martins or Waterloo No. 2
No. 2
Primrose
No. 3
Waterloo
No. 1
No. 4
Rock Level (Pond's)
Oakdale Navigation
Maes-rhyddid
Penrhiew
Gelli or Gelli-Dywyll
Woodfield
Cwm Gelli
Cwm Penmaen
Woodfield
BLACKWOOD
New Kincoed
New Rock Pit
Rock Level
Kincoed
Old Rock Pits
Factory Level
Tynfilkins or Cwmfilkins
Penmaen or Factory Pit
Llys Pentwyn
Tir Philkins (Old)
Lower Plas or Libanus
Twyn Philkins
Chapel
Glanbrynar
MAP 17
Penner or Penner Junction
Blackwood
Woodfield
Glanbrynar
A
B
C
D
E
F
G
H
J
K
13
12
11
10
9
8
7
6
5
4
3
2
1

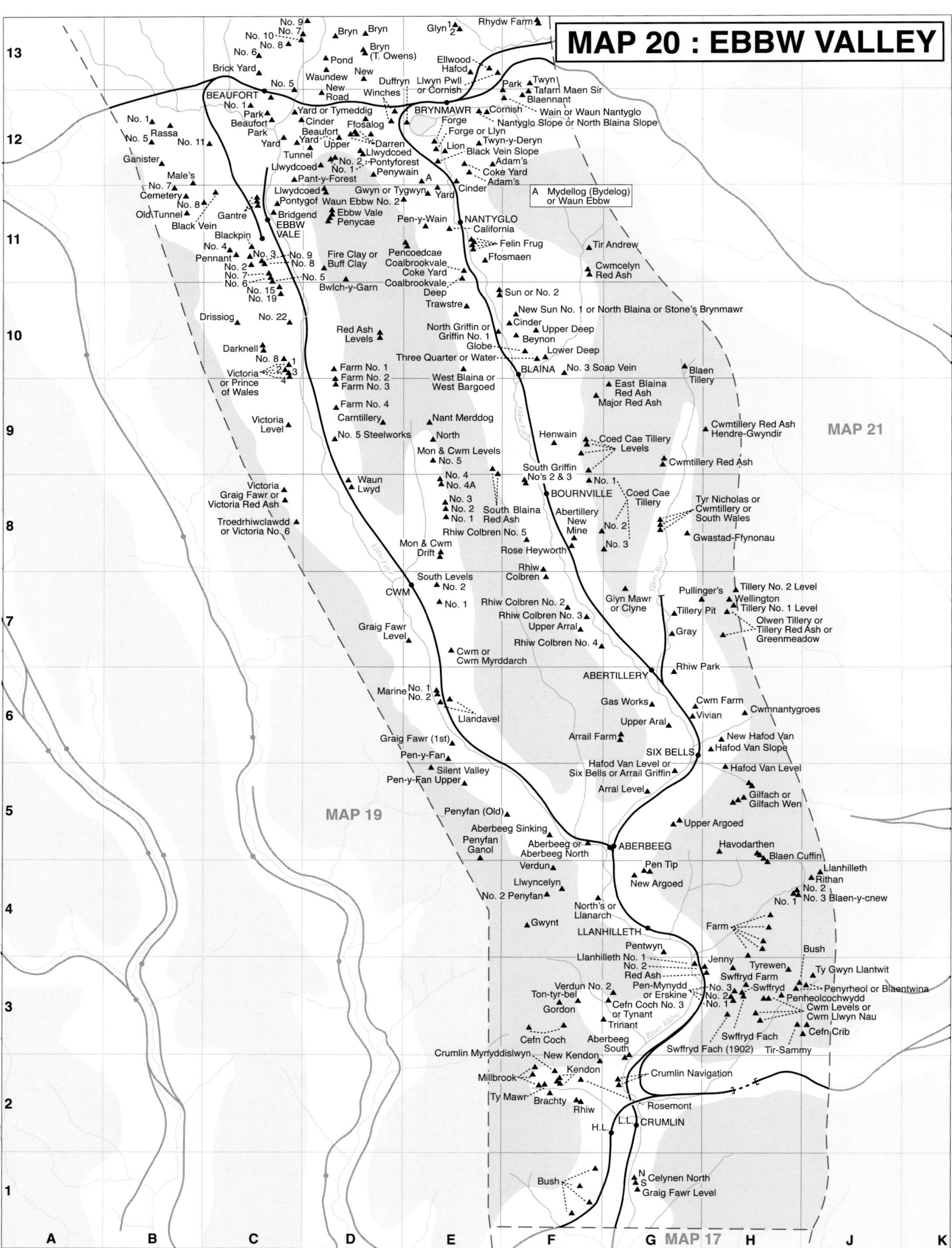
MAP 20 : EBBW VALLEY
MAP 19
MAP 21
MAP 17
A Mydellog (Bydelog) or Waun Ebbw
BEAUFORT
BRYNMAWR
NANTYGLO
EBBW VALE
BLAINA
BOURNVILLE
CWM
ABERTILLERY
SIX BELLS
ABERBEEG
LLANHILLETH
CRUMLIN
H.L.
L.L.
Ebbw Fach
Ebbw Fawr
Tillery River
River Ebbw
No. 9
No. 7
No. 10
No. 8
No. 6
Brick Yard
No. 5
Bryn
Bryn
Bryn (T. Owens)
Pond
New
Waundew
New Road
Duffryn
Winches
Llwyn Pwll or Cornish
Glyn 1 2
Rhydw Farm
Ellwood
Hafod
Park
Twyn
Tafarn Maen Sir
Blaennant
Cornish
Wain or Waun Nantyglo
Nantyglo Slope or North Blaina Slope
Forge
Forge or Llyn
Twyn-y-Deryn
Lion
Black Vein Slope
Adam's
Coke Yard
Adam's
Cinder
Yard
No. 1
Park
Beaufort Park
Yard or Tymeddig
Cinder
Ffosalog
Beaufort Yard
Yard
Upper
Darren
Tunnel
Llwydcoed
Llwydcoed
No. 2
No. 1
Pontyforest
Penywain
Pant-y-Forest
A
Gwyn or Tygwyn
No. 1
Rassa
No. 5
No. 11
Ganister
Male's
No. 7
Cemetery
No. 8
Old Tunnel
Gantre
Black Vein
Llwydcoed
Pontygof
Waun Ebbw No. 2
Bridgend
Ebbw Vale
Penycae
Pen-y-Wain
California
Felin Frug
Ffosmaen
Tir Andrew
Cwmcelyn Red Ash
Blackpin
No. 4
Pennant
No. 3
No. 9
No. 2
No. 8
No. 7
No. 5
No. 6
No. 15
No. 19
Fire Clay or Buff Clay
Pencoedcae
Coalbrookvale Coke Yard
Coalbrookvale Deep
Bwlch-y-Garn
Trawstre
Sun or No. 2
New Sun No. 1 or North Blaina or Stone's Brynmawr
Cinder
Upper Deep
Beynon
Lower Deep
Drissiog
No. 22
Red Ash Levels
North Griffin or Griffin No. 1
Globe
Three Quarter or Water
Darknell
No. 8
1
2
3
4
Victoria or Prince of Wales
Farm No. 1
Farm No. 2
Farm No. 3
Farm No. 4
West Blaina or West Bargoed
No. 3 Soap Vein
Blaen Tillery
East Blaina Red Ash
Major Red Ash
Carntillery
Nant Merddog
Victoria Level
No. 5 Steelworks
North
Henwain
Coed Cae Tillery Levels
Cwmtillery Red Ash
Hendre-Gwyndir
Mon & Cwm Levels
No. 5
Cwmtillery Red Ash
South Griffin No's 2 & 3
No. 4
No. 4A
No. 1
Coed Cae Tillery
Victoria
Graig Fawr or Victoria Red Ash
Waun Lwyd
No. 3
No. 2
No. 1
South Blaina Red Ash
Abertillery New Mine
No. 2
No. 3
Tyr Nicholas or Cwmtillery or South Wales
Troedrhiwclawdd or Victoria No. 6
Gwastad-Ffynonau
Rhiw Colbren No. 5
Mon & Cwm Drift
Rose Heyworth
Rhiw Colbren
South Levels
No. 2
No. 1
Pullinger's
Tillery No. 2 Level
Wellington
Tillery No. 1 Level
Glyn Mawr or Clyne
Tillery Pit
Rhiw Colbren No. 2
Rhiw Colbren No. 3
Upper Arral
Olwen Tillery or Tillery Red Ash or Greenmeadow
Gray
Graig Fawr Level
Rhiw Colbren No. 4
Cwm or Cwm Myrddarch
Rhiw Park
Marine No. 1
No. 2
Llandavel
Gas Works
Cwm Farm
Vivian
Cwmnantygroes
Upper Aral
Arrail Farm
Graig Fawr (1st)
New Hafod Van
Hafod Van Slope
Pen-y-Fan
Silent Valley
Pen-y-Fan Upper
Hafod Van Level or Six Bells or Arrail Griffin
Hafod Van Level
Arral Level
Gilfach or Gilfach Wen
Penyfan (Old)
Upper Argoed
Aberbeeg Sinking
Penyfan Ganol
Aberbeeg or Aberbeeg North
Havodarthen
Blaen Cuffin
Verdun
Pen Tip
New Argoed
Llanhilleth
Rithan
Llwyncelyn
No. 2
No. 1
No. 3 Blaen-y-cnew
No. 2 Penyfan
North's or Llanarch
Gwynt
Farm
Pentwyn
Bush
Llanhilleth No. 1
No. 2
Red Ash
Jenny
Tyrewen
Ty Gwyn Llantwit
Swffryd Farm
Verdun No. 2
Ton-tyr-bel
Pen-Mynydd or Erskine
No. 3
No. 2
No. 1
Swffryd
Penyrheol or Blaentwina
Penheolcochwydd
Gordon
Cefn Coch No. 3 or Tynant
Cwm Levels or Cwm Llwyn Nau
Trinant
Cefn Crib
Swffryd Fach
Cefn Coch
Aberbeeg South
Swffryd Fach (1902)
Tir-Sammy
Crumlin Mynyddislwyn
New Kendon
Kendon
Crumlin Navigation
Millbrook
Ty Mawr
Brachty
Rhiw
Rosemont
Bush
N
S
Celynen North
Graig Fawr Level
13
12
11
10
9
8
7
6
5
4
3
2
1
A
B
C
D
E
F
G
H
J
K

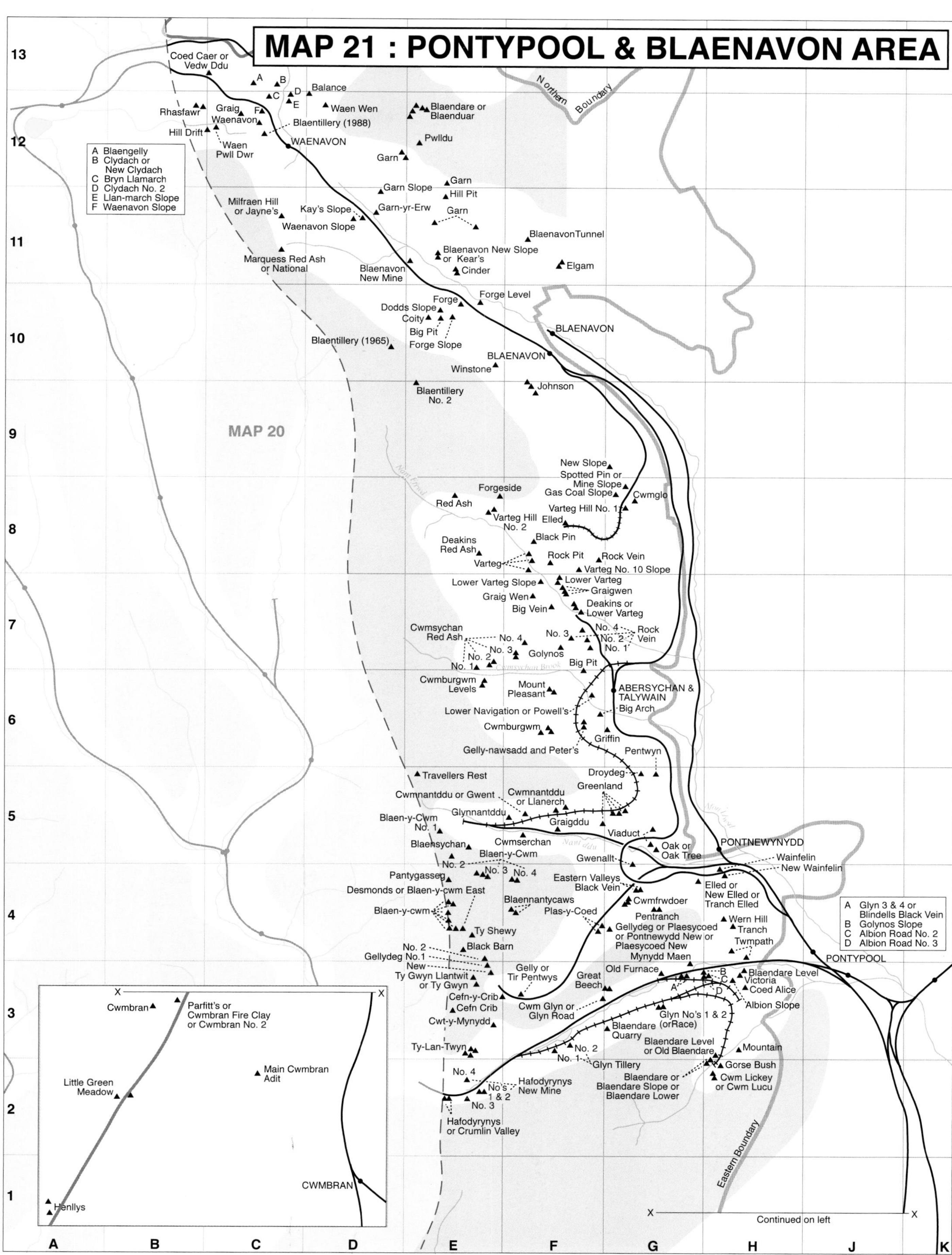

MAP 21 : PONTYPOOL & BLAENAVON AREA
Northern Boundary
Eastern Boundary
MAP 20
13
12
11
10
9
8
7
6
5
4
3
2
1
A
B
C
D
E
F
G
H
J
K
Coed Caer or Vedw Ddu
A
B
C
D
E
Balance
Rhasfawr
Graig
F
Waenavon
Waen Wen
Blaendare or Blaenduar
Hill Drift
Blaentillery (1988)
WAENAVON
Waen Pwll Dwr
Pwlldu
Garn
A Blaengelly
B Clydach or New Clydach
C Bryn Llamarch
D Clydach No. 2
E Llan-march Slope
F Waenavon Slope
Garn Slope
Garn
Hill Pit
Milfraen Hill or Jayne's
Kay's Slope
Garn-yr-Erw
Garn
Waenavon Slope
BlaenavonTunnel
Blaenavon New Slope or Kear's
Cinder
Elgam
Marquess Red Ash or National
Blaenavon New Mine
Forge Level
Forge
Dodds Slope
Coity
Big Pit
Forge Slope
BLAENAVON
Blaentillery (1965)
BLAENAVON
Winstone
Johnson
Blaentillery No. 2
New Slope
Spotted Pin or Mine Slope
Gas Coal Slope
Cwmglo
Forgeside
Red Ash
Varteg Hill No. 1
Varteg Hill No. 2
Elled
Black Pin
Deakins Red Ash
Rock Pit
Rock Vein
Varteg
Varteg No. 10 Slope
Lower Varteg Slope
Lower Varteg
Graigwen
Graig Wen
Deakins or Lower Varteg
Big Vein
Cwmsychan Red Ash
No. 4
No. 3
No. 4
Rock Vein
No. 2
No. 1
No. 3
Golynos
No. 2
No. 1
Big Pit
Cwmsychan Brook
Cwmburgwm Levels
Mount Pleasant
ABERSYCHAN & TALYWAIN
Lower Navigation or Powell's
Big Arch
Cwmburgwm
Griffin
Gelly-nawsadd and Peter's
Pentwyn
Travellers Rest
Droydeg
Greenland
Cwmnantddu or Gwent
Cwmnantddu or Llanerch
Blaen-y-Cwm No. 1
Glynnantddu
Graigddu
Viaduct
Cwmserchan
Blaensychan
Nant ddu
Oak or Oak Tree
PONTNEWYNYDD
Blaen-y-Cwm
No. 2
No. 3
No. 4
Gwenallt
Wainfelin
New Wainfelin
Pantygasseg
Eastern Valleys Black Vein
Elled or New Elled or Tranch Elled
Desmonds or Blaen-y-cwm East
Blaennantycaws
Cwmfrwdoer
Blaen-y-cwm
Plas-y-Coed
Pentranch
Wern Hill
Gellydeg or Plaesycoed or Pontnewydd New or Plaesycoed New
Tranch
Ty Shewy
Twmpath
Mynydd Maen
No. 2
Black Barn
Gellydeg No.1
New
Gelly or Tir Pentwys
Old Furnace
Ty Gwyn Llantwit or Ty Gwyn
Great Beech
PONTYPOOL
A Glyn 3 & 4 or Blindells Black Vein
B Golynos Slope
C Albion Road No. 2
D Albion Road No. 3
Blaendare Level
Victoria
Coed Alice
Cefn-y-Crib
Cefn Crib
Cwm Glyn or Glyn Road
Albion Slope
Glyn No's 1 & 2
Cwt-y-Mynydd
Blaendare (orRace) Quarry
Blaendare Level or Old Blaendare
Ty-Lan-Twyn
No. 2
No. 1
Glyn Tillery
Mountain
Gorse Bush
No. 4
Hafodyrynys New Mine
Blaendare or Blaendare Slope or Blaendare Lower
Cwm Lickey or Cwm Lucu
No's 1 & 2
No. 3
Hafodyrynys or Crumlin Valley
Cwmbran
Parfitt's or Cwmbran Fire Clay or Cwmbran No. 2
Main Cwmbran Adit
Little Green Meadow
CWMBRAN
Henllys
X
Continued on left

RESOLVEN. There were several sites in the Resolven area and this one has not been identified. [Map 9 E4]

A GLIMPSE OF THE COALFIELD

The photographs included in this publication contain very few close-up shots, none of specific equipment, none underground and none of the stalwarts who worked the mines. This has been a deliberate decision, as such photographs have appeared in many other publications and I wanted to portray, as far as possible, the collieries in the landscape and their relationship with the terrain and the railways, for without them the mines would not have prospered.

Regrettably, very few of the images were dated and some are of poor quality, but are included because of their rarity or interesting subject matter.

I have attempted to place informative captions, but not included ownership details as this often changed so frequently it is better referred to in the entry for that colliery. Any suggestions for expanding the descriptions would be very welcome, as of course would any corrections.

Regrettably, there is an imbalance of geographical cover, with much greater coverage of the central area than elsewhere. Should anyone have any photographs which they believe may be suitable for any possible future edition, then I would be extremely pleased to hear about them.

I am entirely grateful to Lightmoor Press for making their collection of photographs available and to Ian Pope for his advice and guidance. My special thanks as well to Robin Simmonds for permission to reproduce images from his two-volume history of the *Port Talbot Railway & Docks Co. and the South Wales Mineral Railway* and especially for offering several, previously unpublished, photographs. Also thanks are due to Paul Jackson for making his copies of various publications available from which images have been taken. Finally, but not least, my thanks again to John Mann, this time for the image of New Tredegar.

ABER (1). Opening in 1865 it survived until 1914. This view is looking north-east with the sidings to the left leading to the junction just north of Ogmore Vale station.

[Map 11 E9]

ABER (2). A closer and earlier view.

ABERAMAN. A view from the south-east with the wagons by the chimneys standing on the internal Powell Duffryn railway. The colliery was started in 1845 and survived until 1962. [Map 12 H5]

ABERBAIDEN COLLIERY, KENFIG HILL.

ABERBAIDEN. Started in 1900, it closed in 1959. This view, looking south, with the private line, three-quarters of a mile long, to the Ogmore Vale Extension line near Mill pit. The line, curving away to the right over a short bridge, led to Pentre Colliery over half a mile away. [Map 11 B4]

ABERBEEG COLLIERY. W.V.C.

ABERBEEG. The colliery was sunk on the north bank of the Ebbw Fawr river in the 1850s. This view is looking north. The Ebbw Vale Branch from Ebbw Vale (left) to Aberbeeg (right) ran the other side of the colliery, but is out of sight. It closed in 1965. [Map 20 F5]

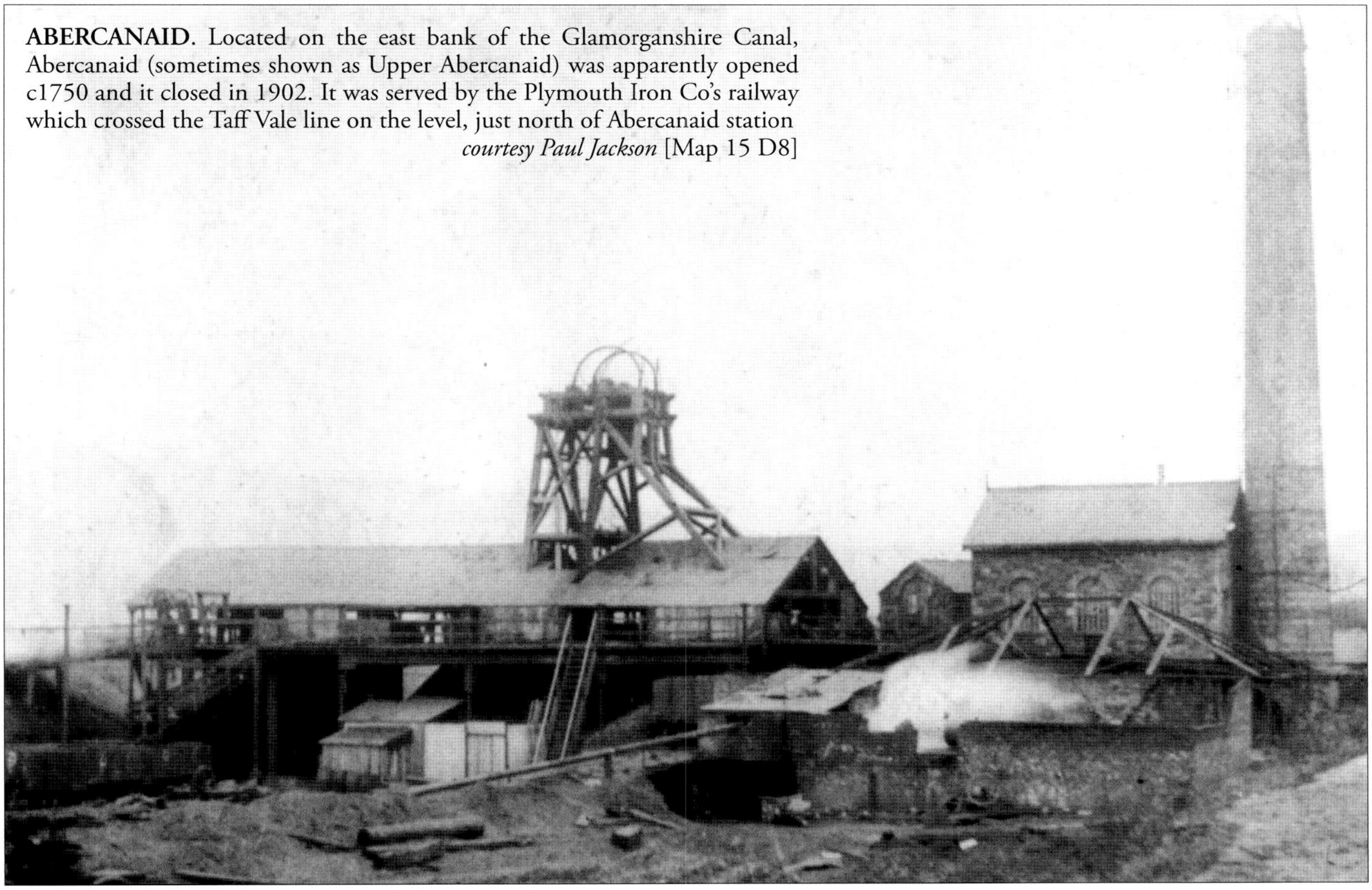

ABERCANAID. Located on the east bank of the Glamorganshire Canal, Abercanaid (sometimes shown as Upper Abercanaid) was apparently opened c1750 and it closed in 1902. It was served by the Plymouth Iron Co's railway which crossed the Taff Vale line on the level, just north of Abercanaid station *courtesy Paul Jackson* [Map 15 D8]

ABERCARN (1). Looking due east from the Western Valleys line, and across the Ebbw River (hidden from view), the sidings, bottom right, lead to Abercarn South Jcn. and those slightly further away (and in front of the first row of houses) led to the old coke ovens. The first pit was sunk in the 1830s and from 1863 the colliery was called Prince of Wales. It closed in 1931, but not abandoned until 1958. [Map 17 J7]

ABERCARN (2). A closer view looking north-east, with the colliery on the east side of the Ebbw river.

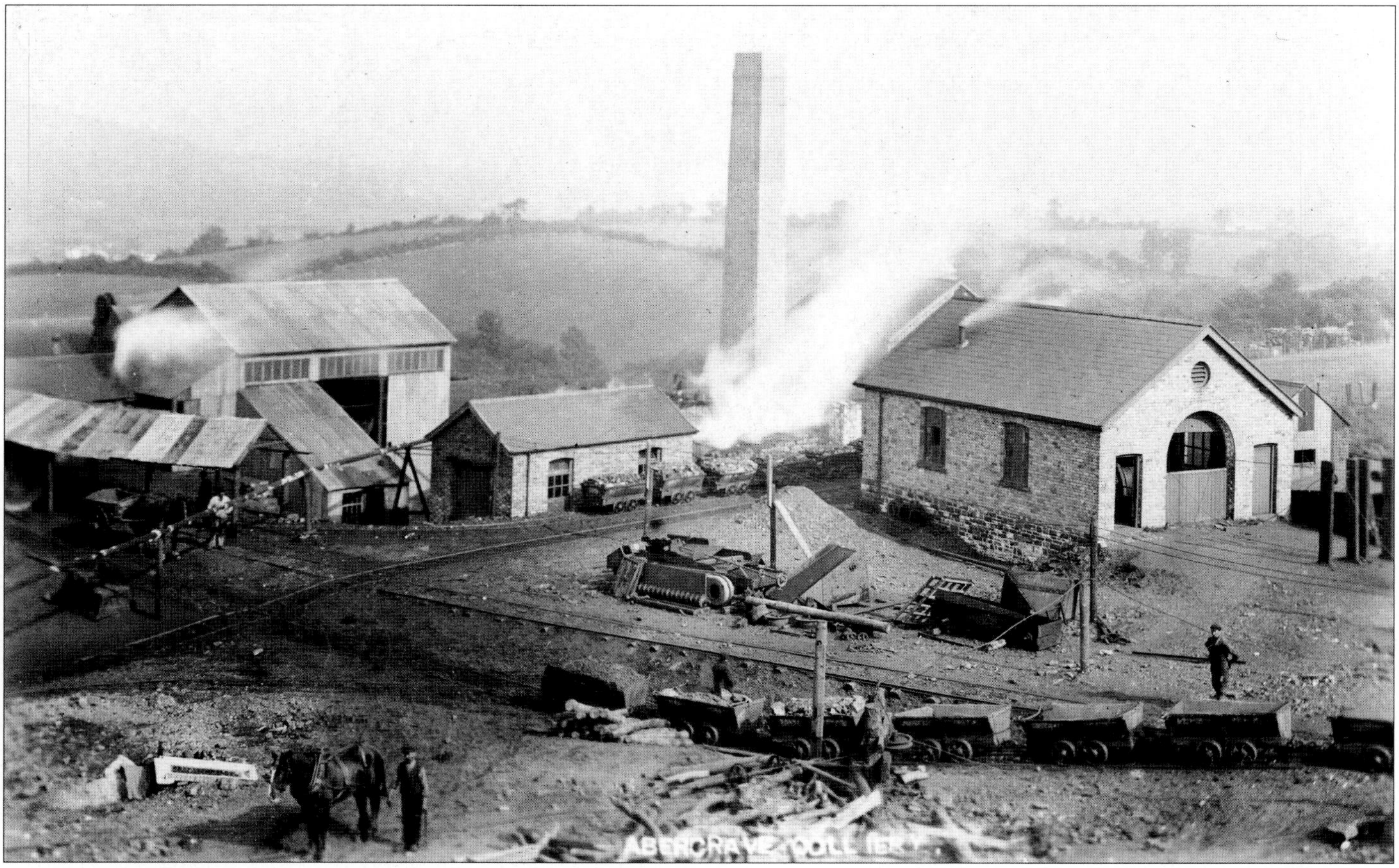

ABERCRAVE. A view taken looking north-east, a very early colliery (pre 1830) which was expanded and developed over time. The sidings on the N&B Rly., were the other side of the buildings and just east of Abercrave station. It did not close until 1967. [Map 8 K8]

The Colliery. Abercynon.

ABERCYNON. Looking north with the Glamorganshire Canal to the right. Sinking started in 1889 and it was more commonly known as Dowlais Cardiff Colliery. Located on the Dowlais Pits Branch, which connected with the Taff Vale's Nelson Branch north of Cilfynydd. In 1972 twin tunnels, nearly a mile long, linked it with Lady Windsor and the mine closed in 1975. [Map 16 E10]

ABERGORKY. This mine was at the end of a short branch from Treorchy and was first started as a level in 1859. The shafts followed from 1865 and the mine was abandoned in 1935. In this view, looking north, the tramway going up the mountain served Abergorchy Quarry. [Map 13 E7]

ABERNANT. Looking south-east down the Sirhowy Valley, with Abernant No. 2 Signal Box in the distance. Sunk in 1888 by the Bargoed Coal Co. Ltd, the colliery closed in 1932. [Map 19 E5]

ALBION. Sinking started in early 1885 and the mine survived until 1966 when it was closed. It was located at Cilfynydd, on the east side of the Taff Vale's Nelson Branch. This view is looking north, with the Glamorganshire Canal on the right. [Map 16 E9]

ALBION ROAD. Looking along the Taff Vale Extension line towards Pontypool, this colliery was located up the hill and connected to 'The Third Line' by an incline and operated from 1897 (?) to 1927 but then retained for pumping. The tramway in the foreground served Old Furnace Colliery (1912-24), out of sight off the page. [Map 21 H3]

AMMANFORD No. 2. Looking north-east, with the sidings behind the photographer joining into a single line and crossing the River Amman, then to split into lines forming both east and west facing junctions with the GWR Garnant Branch. The colliery existed from 1890 to 1976. [Map 7 M8]

AVON. Looking east over Abergwynfi, the colliery is prominent on the right with the GWR running lower right to bottom middle below the GW Hotel. The colliery was sunk in 1878 and closed in 1969. [Map 10 L7]

AVON (2). A closer view of the colliery looking north.

ABERBARGOED & RD. COLLIERIES.

BARGOED (1). Powell Duffryn took the decision to sink these pits in 1890 and work started in 1893. It closed in 1977. This view is looking north from the very south end. The two tracks on the left-hand side belonged to the Rhymney Rly and the two tracks to the right were the connecting line to the Brecon & Merthyr Rly which ran on the far side of the valley. [Map 18 F4]

BARGOED (2). This view is looking north with the Brecon & Merthyr's line towards New Tredegar going off right. The Rhymney's line, with a train on it, can be made out at top left.

BARGOED (3). This view is looking south down the Brecon & Merthyr's line towards Pengam and Hengoed. The Rhymney's line can be made out in the top right-hand corner. The remnant of a siding on the left is the remains of Lord Tredegar's quarry siding.

BARGOED (4). This view of Powell Duffryn's extensive loaded wagon sidings is looking south-east with the bridge over the Brecon & Merthyr railway being at Aberbargoed Jcn. The railway running out on the left is the connecting line to the Rhymney. The six sidings (constructed 1894) on the left, connect with the B&M and the four on the right (constructed 1904) curve round to join with the Rhymney to the right of the trees. At the other end, all the sidings join up and run through a short tunnel (part of retaining wall can be seen) and then half a mile north to the colliery and coke ovens.

BEDWAS. This view is looking south-east with the Brecon & Merthyr Railway beyond (not in sight). Bedwas or Bedwas Navigation was started in 1909 and closed in 1985. [Map 17 F3]

BEDWELLTY. Located on the west side of the Sirhowy Branch, just north of Bedwellty station. This view is looking south with the incline up to Bedwellty levels just visible behind the left-hand winding wheel. Known as New Bedwellty until 1873, it closed in 1942. [Map 19 D9]

BLAENAVON BIG PIT. A view looking south-east, of the pit sunk in 1860. Lasting one hundred years, it closed in 1960. [Map 21 E10]

BLAENANT COLLIERY, ABERDARE. Looking roughly north-east, this very early site was connected to the GWR's Merthyr Branch by the tramway shown bottom right, which ran in a straight line down a long incline to sidings west of Abernant station. The mine closed in 1927. [Map 12 H8]

BONVILLES COURT. Another early colliery, sunk in early 1840s and closed in 1930. [Map 1 L2]

BRITANNIC. Looking north-east at the top end of the valley at Gilfach Goch, Britannic Colliery, sunk in 1894, is in the foreground and the wagons on the floor of the valley (almost dead centre) are at Gilfach Goch Colliery. The top row of houses on the extreme left are Scotch Row. The colliery closed in 1960. [Map 14 D9]

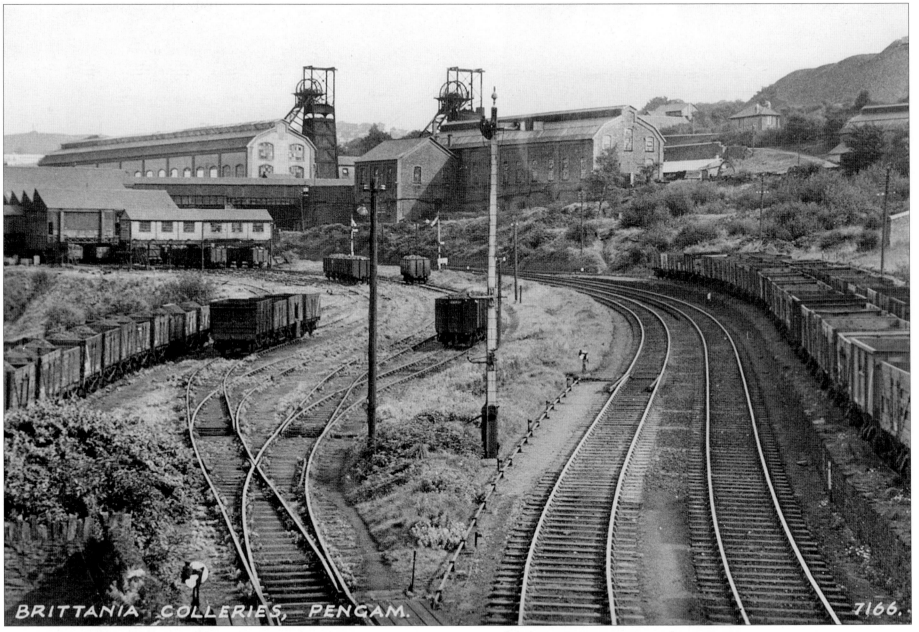

BRITTANIA. Looking slightly north-east up the Brecon & Merthyr line from Pengam station, the sinking of this colliery was started in 1910 and the mine survived until 1983. [Map 18 G2]

BRYNCETHIN. Located on the north side of the GWR's Pencoed Branch. This view is believed to be looking south. [Map 11 H4]

BRYNMENYN. This small colliery and brickworks lay just north of Brynmenyn station and junction (to the right), on the line up to Blaengarw (to the left). The river Garw lies just the other side of the three brick-kilns. The original Brynmenin level (1875-77) lay off the photograph to the left and the colliery, started in 1895, lay on the east bank of the river between it and the railway. Only operational between 1907 and 1910 when it closed with 150 men. An abortive attempt was made to reopen it 1925-28. *courtesy Robin Simmonds* [Map 11 G5]

BRYN NAVIGATION (1). This colliery was located on Baldwin's private lines and this view is looking south east where, beyond the screens, the line continues to a reversal for Bryn station (on the Port Talbot Railway) or on to Cefn-y-Bryn Colliery. The colliery was in operation at 1842 and closed around 1877, to reopen in 1896 and it continued until 1963. *courtesy Paul Jackson* [Map 10 F3]

BRYN NAVIGATION (2). A view looking back from the other side of the screens. *courtesy Paul Jackson*

BUTE. Located on the west side of the Taff Vale's Rhondda Branch, just north of Treherbert and looking west, the colliery was started as Cwmsaerbran in 1850. It seems to have closed in 1941 although it was not abandoned until 1960. [Map 13 D7]

BWLLFA. A smoky view looking north to Bwllfa or Bwllfa Dare No. 1 Colliery at the end of the Taff Vale Rly's Dare Valley Branch, and at the end of the GWR's Bwllfa Dare Branch (neither visible off to the right). It was sunk in the 1850s and survived until 1957 when it was merged with Mardy. [Map 12 D6]

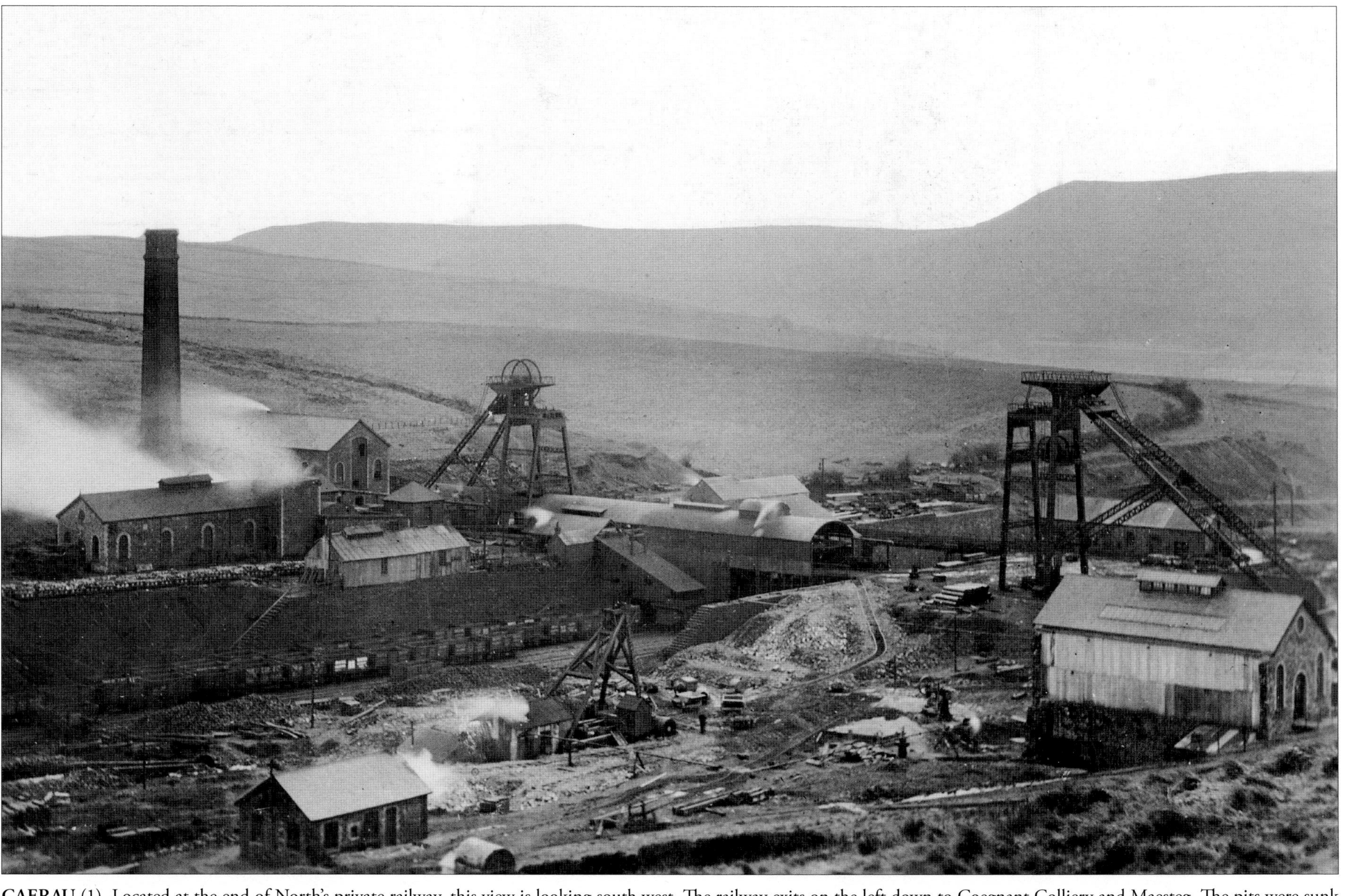

CAERAU (1). Located at the end of North's private railway, this view is looking south west. The railway exits on the left down to Coegnant Colliery and Maesteg. The pits were sunk in 1889 and the mine closed in 1977. [Map 11 C12]

CAERAU (2). The view looking north to Blaen-caerau.

CAMBRIAN NAVIGATION. Sinking started in 1872, No. 3 was sunk in 1889 and No. 4 in 1912. This view looking south-west shows No. 4, No. 2, No. 3 (in background) and No. 1 (on the right). The colliery closed in 1966. [Map 13 F3/G3]

CASTLE (Troedyrhiw). A view looking north over Castle Colliery, sunk 1866, which was connected to the GWR & Rhymney Joint line, with Merthyr to the left. To the east of this line ran the Glamorganshire Canal and the River Taff (neither in sight) and then the Taff Vale Railway whose sidings with a triangle led to South Duffryn Colliery to the right. Castle closed in 1935 but was retained for pumping until 1952. [Map 15 E7]

CAWDOR. This shows the loading point for Cawdor or New Cawdor or North Amman Colliery which lay over half a mile away to the south. It is looking south-west at the Cawdor branch with Gwaun cae Gurwen to the left and Garnant to the right. The colliery was opened in 1896 and closed in 1927 although not abandoned until 1941. The sidings had previously been used to serve Garnant level and Cwmdrisein Colliery. [Map 7 L6]

Near
Rhymney River, Aberbargoed. 1433.

CEFN BRITHDIR. Looking north-west from above the Brecon & Merthyr line, with the Rhymney Rly beyond the river. It operated from 1873 by the Rhymney Iron Co. Ltd until it was abandoned in 1910, only to be reopened in 1916 until it finally closed in 1921. [Map 18 F5]

Cefn Coed Pit, Crynant.

CEFN COED. This rural scene is looking north-west and includes the parking area for the workmen's buses. It was a much later colliery, being developed from 1920 on the Neath & Brecon line between Cilfrew and Crynant. It closed in 1968. [Map 6 G10]

CELYNEN SOUTH (1). Started in 1873, just Celynen until 1911 when the 'North' colliery was started, this view is looking north-east with the GWR's Western Valleys line bottom left. The colliery closed in 1985. [Map 17 J8]

CELYNEN SOUTH (2). A similar view taken slightly further south, looking north.

CETHIN. Cethin (or Gethin) dated from pre-1849 and this is believed to be No. 1 Colliery and looking north. It was connected to No. 2 colliery, which was alongside the GWR & Rhymney Joint line, by a short line off to the left. Between No. 2 and the signal, in the right middle distance, lay the Taff river and beyond the Taff Vale main line. The colliery closed in 1925. [Map 15 D7]

CILELY. This colliery, at the end of a short branch from the GWR's Ely Valley line, was opened in 1861 and survived until 1950. This view is taken from the north end looking back south-east. [Map 14 G8]

CLYDACH MERTHYR. Located on a private railway (a tramway until c1898) running alongside the Lower Clydach River, this view looks northwest, with Clydach down the line behind the photographer. The line continued north to Craig Merthyr Colliery serving several others on route. The colliery opened in 1863 as Nixon's Graigola, then became Western Merthyr, before adopting the Clydach Merthyr name and closed in 1961. *courtesy Paul Jackson* [Map 5 D9]

CLYDACH MERTHYR (2). These sidings are not at the colliery, but at the fuel works situated just north of Clydach on the north side of the Swansea canal. *courtesy Paul Jackson*

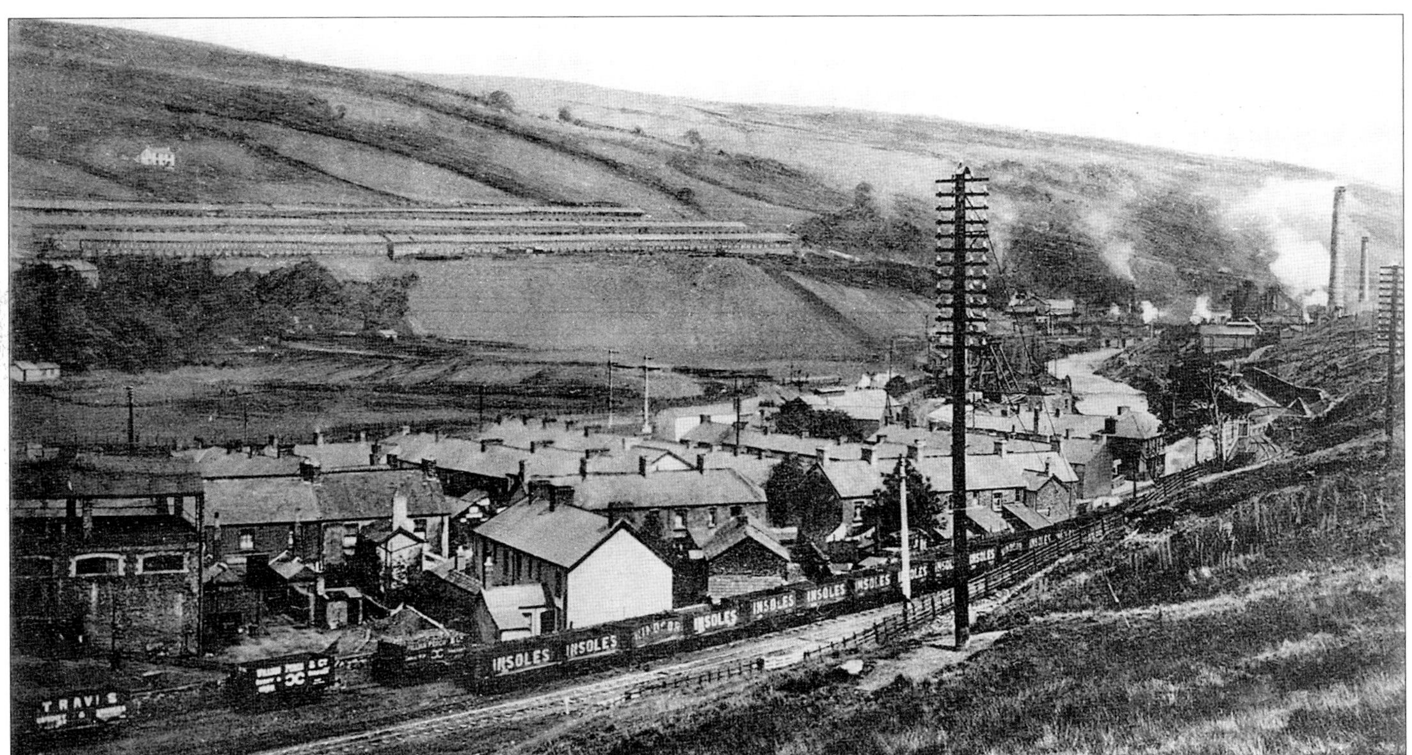

COEDCAE (1). This view looking east shows the Taff Vale Rly's Eirw Branch to Cymmer Colliery (to the left) with Coedcae Colliery top right (with the two tall chimneys). A level before 1847, the sinking started in 1857 and it survived until 1929. The sidings in the foreground served Porth Gas Works. Behind the telegraph pole is Llwyncelyn Colliery and behind the Taff river bridge is Hafod Colliery. [Map 13 M1]

COEDCAE (2). Looking south, the coal wagons in bottom right corner are standing in Hafod Colliery sidings. The three tracks are of the Taff Rly (so pre-1915) with Porth to the right and Trehafod to the left. Then on the far side of the Rhondda is the single line of the Eirw branch with the colliery and coke ovens beyond. *courtesy Paul Jackson*

COED ELY. Located on the west side of the GWR's Ely Valley Branch (out of view beyond the colliery) between Gellyrhaidd Jcn. and Llantrisant Common Jcn. This view is taken looking in a south-easterly direction. Started in 1906 it survived until 1977 when it was merged with Cwm Colliery. [Map 14 G5]

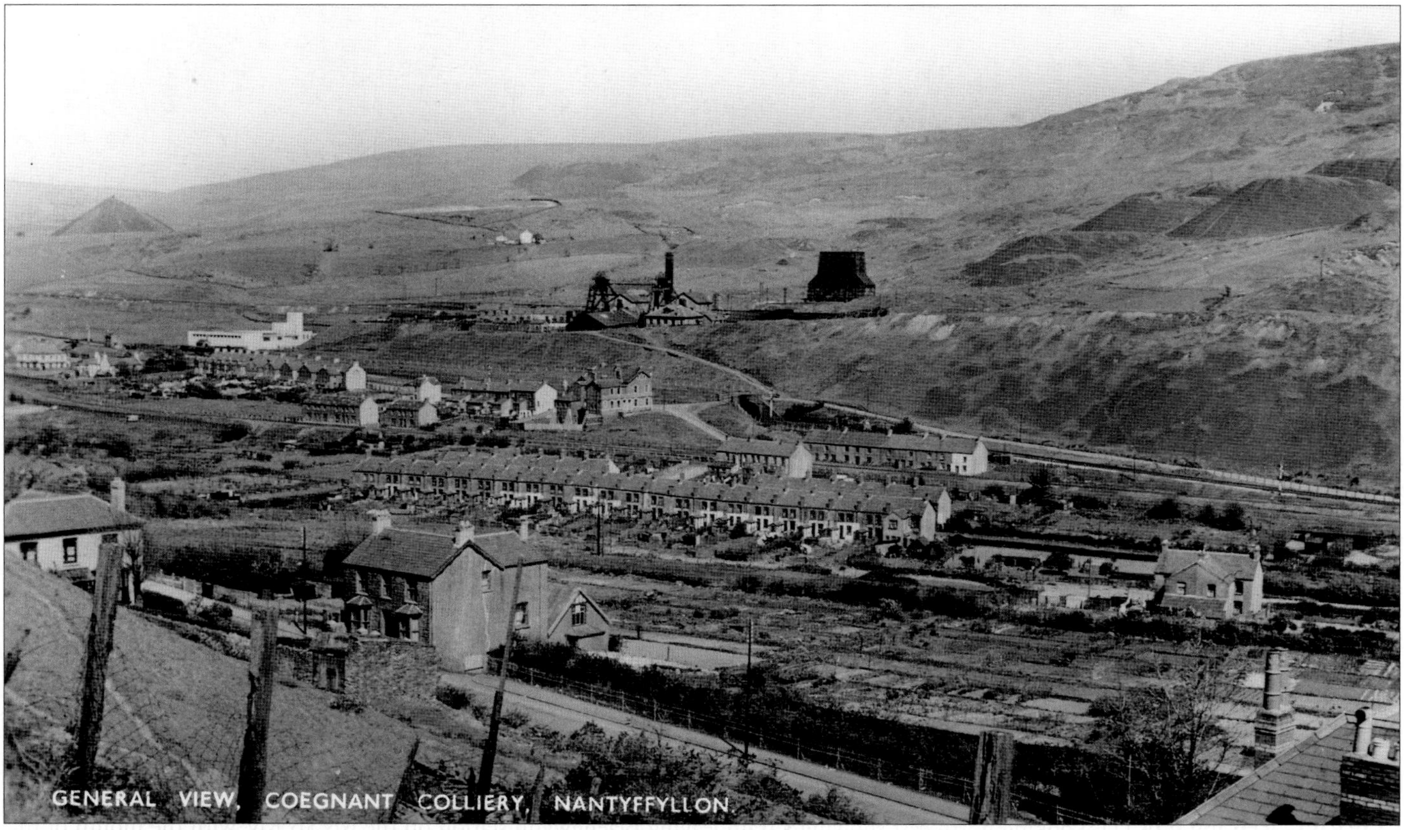

GENERAL VIEW, COEGNANT COLLIERY, NANTYFFYLLON.

COEGNANT (1). The colliery can be seen in the distance. The railway (with road overbridge and signal) running across from left to right, is the Bridgend to Abergwynfi line. The railway in front of it (this side of the row of cottages) is the Duffryn Branch, which joins with the B&A line at Nantyffyllon (just to the right). [Map 11 C11]

COEGNANT (2). Again looking north-east, this shows the colliery which was sunk in 1881 and closed in 1981. In the left far distance can be seen some wagons. These are on the North's private line to Caerau Colliery.

CORRWG RHONDDA (1). Looking north east showing a train leaving Blaengwynfi station on the R&SB Rly. with the mouth of the Rhondda tunnel just beyond. The colliery sidings branch off behind the signal box and the line this side of it is the GWR's branch to Abergwynfi and Avon Colliery. Corrwg Rhondda level, sometimes referred to as Rhondda Tunnel colliery, was high up and on the north side of the tunnel. *courtesy Robin Simmonds* [Map 10 L7]

CORRWG RHONDDA (2). A closer view of the colliery sidings, looking north. The Afan river runs just this side of the nearest siding and on this side of it (out of sight) lay the GWR line to Abergwynfi. The colliery opened in 1892 and closed in 1924. At the peak in 1908 479 men were employed, but this was reduced from 1908 and considerably more so from 1911. *courtesy Robin Simmonds*

COURT HERBERT. Looking east from inside the colliery sidings with the Vale of Neath line out of sight over to the right. The colliery operated from 1848 to 1928 and was at times called Dynevor or New Dynevor. [Map 6 C5]

COYTRAHEN PARK (1). Located north of Tondu, this view is believed to be looking north-east. The mine was started in 1904/5 and had closed in 1928. [Map 11 E5/F5]

COYTRAHEN (2). In this view looking east, the slant is located over by the chimney in the distance. The sidings exiting bottom left, lead to a connection at Tondu North Jcn. *courtesy Paul Jackson* [Map 11 E5]

CRIBBWR FAWR. The three slants of this colliery were served by sidings off the P. T. Rly's Ogmore Vale Extension Line and this view is looking north. The sidings beyond the screens led to a dead end. Initially called 'Coalbrook', development started in 1902, with No.3 slant opening in 1912. The colliery closed in 1930. [Map 11 D1]

CROSS HANDS (1). This colliery, at the top end of the Llanelly & Mynydd Mawr Railway, started by c1839 and did not close until 1962. This view looks broadly west, but I am unable to reconcile the line with two wagons to the left of the building with a large white roof. [Map 7 A7]

CROSS HANDS (2). A view looking east, in the opposite direction to the one previous. The colliery was listed as New Cross Hands between 1900 and 1913, and between 1932 and 1946.

CWMAMAN (1). Located at the end of the GWR's Dare Branch, this view is looking south-east. It must be pre-1897 when Powell Duffryn extended the line on, through the right-hand bottom corner, to Fforchwen Colly. [Map 12 F4]

CWMAMAN (2). A view looking west, taken from the end of Cwmaman Colliery Halt platform. The chimney in the right background is at Fforchwen Colliery. Cwmaman started in 1846 and closed in 1935. *courtesy Paul Jackson*

CWMBRAN. The colliery is in the middle distance, beyond the row of houses on the left, in this view looking north. Coal was worked at Cwmbran from (at least) 1837 and the mine closed in 1927. [Map 21 B3]

CWMCARN. A ventilation shaft for Abercarn Colliery was sunk here in 1873 but subsequently abandoned. The Cwmcarn pits were sunk from 1910 and connected by a new GWR branch from near Pontywain Jcn. This view looks north-west. The colliery closed in 1968. [Map 17 L6]

CWMCAS. This view looking north east up Afon Corrwg, of Cwmcas cottages, does not actually show the Cwmcas level, which was part of Glyncorrwg Colliery and located up the mountain to the right, 210 feet above the railway. The gable ended building, on the mountain is believed to be the engine house for Glyncorrwg No. 1 level, 155 feet above the railway. The S.W.M.R. to North Rhondda is on the left with Glyncorrwg South pit. Cwmcas opened in 1888 and closed in 1906. *courtesy Robin Simmonds* [Map 9 J2]

CWMCYNON. A view looking east from north of Penrhiwceiber with the Taff Vale's Aberdare Branch in the bottom right and the colliery on the other side of the River Cynon. It was connected to the GWR's Vale of Neath line and worked between 1889 and 1949. [Map 12 K4/L3]

CWMDARE (Bwllfa No. 3). Started in 1853 and known as Dare or Powell's pit, it was renamed Duffryn Dare in 1859 and Cwmdare in 1871. Closing in 1891, it reopened in 1907 as Bwllfa No. 3. This view is looking south-east along the GWR's Bwllfa Dare Branch towards Dare Jcn. It closed in 1936. *courtesy Paul Jackson* [Map 12 E6]

CWMGORSE. Looking north from the end of a short mineral line to Gwaun cae Gurwen, Cwmgorse (or New Cwmgorse) was started in 1887 and closed in 1964. [Map 7 M6]

CWMNEOL. Located on Powell Duffryn's private railway, which connected with sidings on the south side of the Taff Vale Rly. at Aberaman and to the south side of the GWR's Vale of Neath line, at Middle Duffryn. This view is looking north-east. The colliery dated from 1844 and closed in 1948. [Map 12 G4]

West Side Cwmtillery, from Crook Hill. 1377.

CWMTILLERY (1). Looking north-west at the end of the Cwmtillery Branch from Abertillery with Cwmtillery or South Wales No's 1 and 2 pits. Coal first worked in the early 1840s and it finally closed in 1960, when it was merged with Rose Heyworth. [Map 20 G8]

CWM TILLERY COLLIERIES. ABERTILLERY

CWMTILLERY (2). A closer view looking south-west. [Map 20 G8]

CYMMER (1). Looking west from the south bank of the Rhondda, with Porth over on the other bank. The colliery sidings are at the end of the Taff Vale's Eirw Branch from Trehafod and served the colliery from 1855 to 1939, although the colliery started in 1847. [Map 13 L1]

CYMMER (2). A closer view towards the end of the sidings. *courtesy Paul Jackson*

CYMMER GLYNCORRWG. Looking slightly south of east up the River Afan, the tramway from the drift can be seen crossing the river on its way to the screens and sidings on the upside of the R&SB line. Cymmer viaduct is in the background with, interestingly, some wagons standing on it, no doubt from Glyn Cymmer Colliery. Cymmer Glyncorrwg started in 1891 and in 1903 became Gordon's Navigation before being renamed Phoenix Glyncorrwg (sometimes known as Phoenix Merthyr) in 1904. It closed in 1908. *courtesy Robin Simmonds* [Map 10 H6]

DARE. This is Dare Colliery on the private Cwm-Parc Railway between Park Colliery (to the left) and Treorchy (to the right). Started in 1869 it was closed in 1955 when it was merged with Park. [Map 13 E5]

DARRAN FAWR. Another colliery with multiple names, located just south of Blaengarw. A Darren drift was working in 1877. From 1886 to 1894 it was Darran Fawr or Victoria. Then 1895-1901 Braich-y-Cymmer Darran and finally 1902-09 it was Darran. This view is looking west (Blaengarw to the right). It closed in 1909. [Map 11 F11]

DEEP DUFFRYN (1). Looking west with the GWR's Vale of Neath line disappearing towards Aberdare. The colliery was sunk in 1850 and remained in operation until 1979. [Map 12 K4]

DEEP DUFFRYN (2). A view taken from a little closer to the overbridge shown in the previous photograph.

Ocean Colliery, Treharris.

DEEP NAVIGATION (1). Looking north up the Bargoed Taf river with the Vale of Neath line crossing it by the 78 yard Treharris viaduct. Deep Navigation is on the left (started in 1872 as Harris Navigation) and it closed in 1991. In the far distance can just be made out the buildings of Taff Merthyr Colliery. [Map 16 F13]

DEEP NAVIGATION (2). A closer view from the east.

DINAS MAIN. Looking south from near the end of the Gilfach Branch towards Hendreforgan. The mine, started in 1864, ceased work in 1907. [Map 14 D8]

DUFFRYN RHONDDA PITS. Looking north, with the R&SB Railway at a lower level between the wagons and the fence. The faint horizontal line above the row of houses is the South Wales Mineral Railway. The pits were sunk in 1903 to replace the Duffryn Rhondda Colliery at Caerau. There was also a slant further east and on the opposite side of the railway line. The colliery closed in 1966. [Map 10 G6]

DULAIS. The colliery, just west of Onllwyn station, was named Drym until 1905 and closed in 1917. However, numerous slants had been opened and it finally closed in 1934. This view is looking north with the Neath & Brecon railway running in front of the sidings. [Map 8 K7]

EASTERN. Started in 1874 as Bwllfa, it was renamed in 1877 (but subsequently often referred to as Bwllfa) and was connected by a private line to Ystrad Rhondda (behind the photographer). This view looks south. It closed in 1939. *courtesy Paul Jackson* [Map 13 F4]

ELLIOT (1). The Rhymney river runs down bottom left in this view looking north-east. The West pit worked from 1883 to 1962 and the East from 1888 to 1967. [Map 18 F6]

ELLIOT (2). A similar view to that above.

Emlyn Colliery, Penygroes.

EMLYN. Looking north-west, the colliery was connected with the GWR's Mountain Branch from Tirydail. The line to the branch ran from the right-hand side of the photograph. The colliery was listed from 1892 having previously been the site of Glanlash Colliery and it closed in 1939. [Map 7 B8]

Nos 1 and 5 Pits, Ferndale.

FERNDALE 1 & 5. Looking north-east over the Rhondda Fach river with Ferndale station a little distance further left. The colliery operated between 1857 and 1959. [Map 13 J6]

FERNDALE 2 & 4. These two pits were started in 1868 and lasted until 1932. The view is looking west with the Taff Vale's Maerdy Branch to the right. Maerdy station is about a mile further on and Ferndale station half a mile to the right. The signal box was Maerdy Sidings box. [Map 13 H7]

FERNDALE 2 & 4 (2). A view of the loaded wagon sidings looking east (the pits were to the left) with the Taff Vale's Maerdy branch being crossed by a footbridge. To the right of this can been seen the twin gable ends of Ferndale engine shed and out of sight behind these the line led to Ferndale station.

FERNDALE No's 6 & 7. This colliery, originally known as Pendyrys or Tylor's, was started in 1873 and was located on the Maerdy Branch between Ferndale and Tylorstown. It was closed in 1935. This view is looking north-east. [Map 13 K5]

FERNDALE No's 8 & 9. A view looking south-east of Cynllwyndu Colliery (or No's 8 & 9) on the Taff Vale's Maerdy Branch. A pit was started in 1856 but abandoned. No. 8 was sunk 1891, closed 1934 and No. 9 in 1904, closed in 1960. [Map 13 K5]

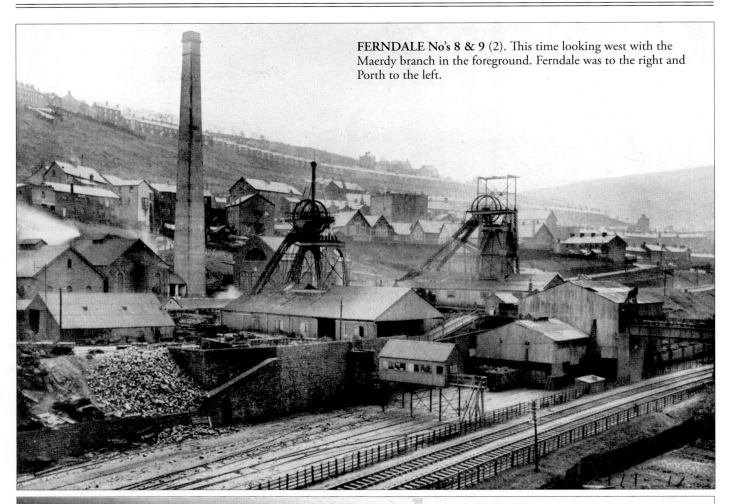

FERNDALE No's 8 & 9 (2). This time looking west with the Maerdy branch in the foreground. Ferndale was to the right and Porth to the left.

General View of Tylorstown. With 8 & 9 Pits 408

FERNDALE No's 8 & 9. This view looks due west over the Maerdy Branch. Ferndale to the left.

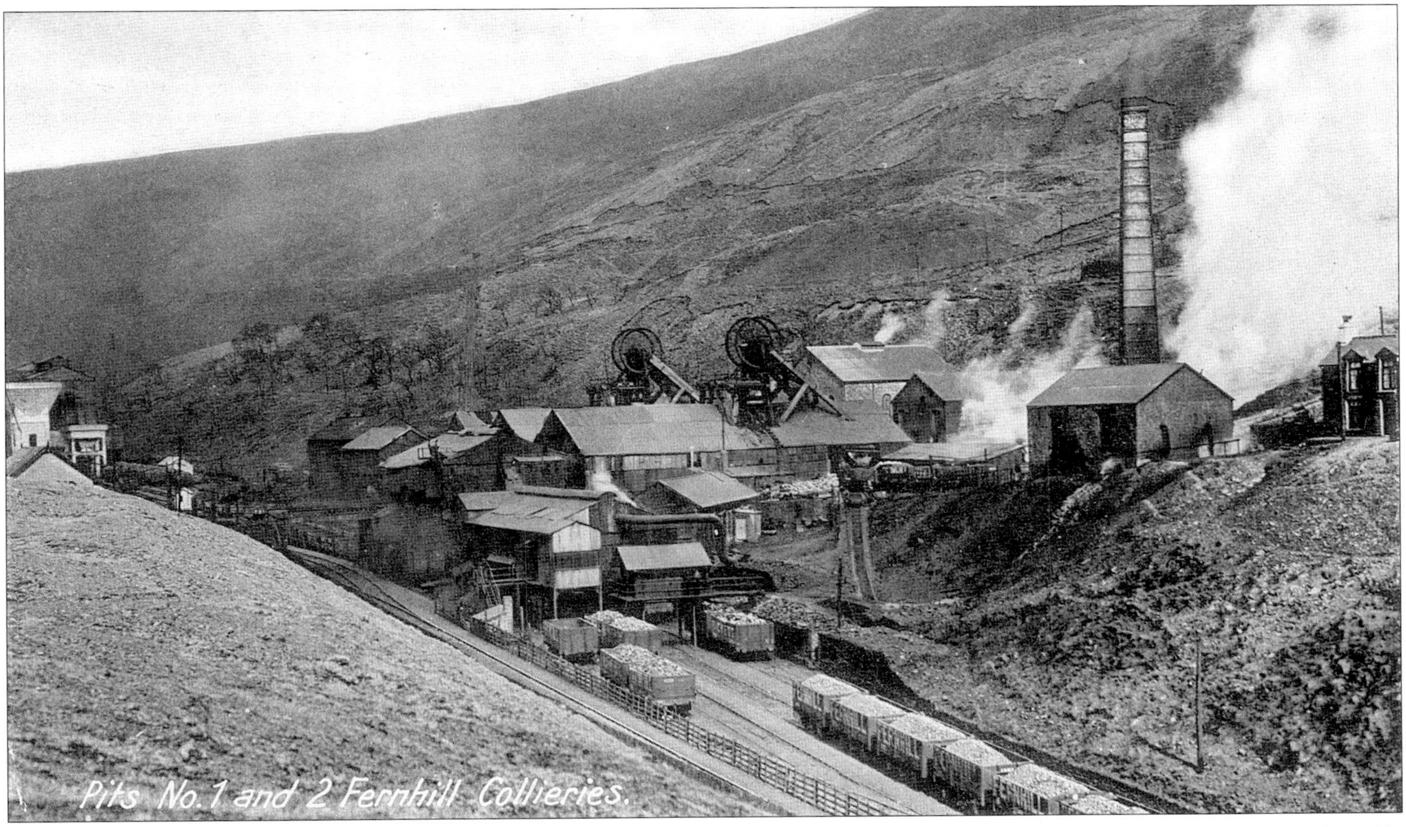

FERNHILL 1 & 2. Looking north up the Taff Vale's Blaenrhondda Branch, from Treherbert, towards the terminus. Blaen Rhondda Colliery (No's 3 & 4) is further on to the left. Fernhill started in 1866 and closed in 1966 when it was merged with Tower. [Map 13 C9]

FFALDAU. Looking north-east over the southbound platform of Pontycymmer station on the GWR's Garw Branch. A little further on, opposite Ffaldau was Victoria Colliery. Ffaldau started in 1877 and closed in 1975 when it was merged with Garw Colliery. [Map 11 F10]

FFORCHAMAN (1). To what 'Brighteye' refers to is not known, but the colliery is Fforchaman, sunk in 1850. It lies alongside the Dare Branch and the line continues to the left to terminate at Cwmaman Colliery. [Map 12 D4]

FFORCHAMAN (2). A closer look at Fforchaman, sunk by Burnyeat & Brown, and referred to locally as 'Brown's Pit'.

FFORCHWEN. This colliery and the Trewen shaft (just visible in top right) lie just beyond Cwmaman Colliery (further to the right) and the view is looking north. Fforchwen was sunk in 1897 and Trewen in 1906. Both closed down in 1935 but were retained for ventilation. [Map 12 E4]

GARTH MERTHYR. Looking north-east with Garth station on the Llynvi Valley Rly behind the photographer. Started in 1864 it closed in 1930. [Map 11 F9]

GARTH TONMAWR. This 1961 view is looking north up the Whitworth Branch from Tonmawr Jcn. At that time, the colliery was known as Garth Tonmawr (since 1948), having previously been Fforch Dwm in the 1830s, Welsh Freehold (from 1872), Mercantile (from 1893), Blaenmawr (from 1914) and then Garth (from 1929). It had several spells of being closed, but survived until 1964. [Map 10 E7]

GARW. Looking northwest, this colliery was often referred to as Blaengarw or Ocean. The community of Blaengarw is off to the left. The pits were started in 1883 and the colliery survived until 1985. *courtesy Paul Jackson* [Map 11 G11]

GELLI (Ystrad) (1). Located south of Ystrad Rhondda on the Taff Vale's Rhondda Branch, this view is looking east. The sidings terminate just to the right and continue to the left to join the main line. Note the tramway incline up to a quarry. The colliery operated from pre 1868 to 1962. [Map 13 G4]

GELLI (Ystrad) (2). Looking down from the mountain with the Taff Vale's Rhondda Branch in the background.

Gellyceidrim Colliery Glanamman.

GELLYCEIDRIM. Looking south east, this is probably the No. 2 Slant, started in 1923. The trams are on an incline down to sidings on the south side of the Garnant Branch east of Glanamman station. It closed in 1957. [Map 7 J8]

GILFACH. Located between Pengam (left) and Bargoed (right) on the Rhymney Rly. this view is looking south. After protracted sinking from 1886, coal was worked from 1893 until it closed in 1931. *courtesy Paul Jackson* [Map 18 F3]

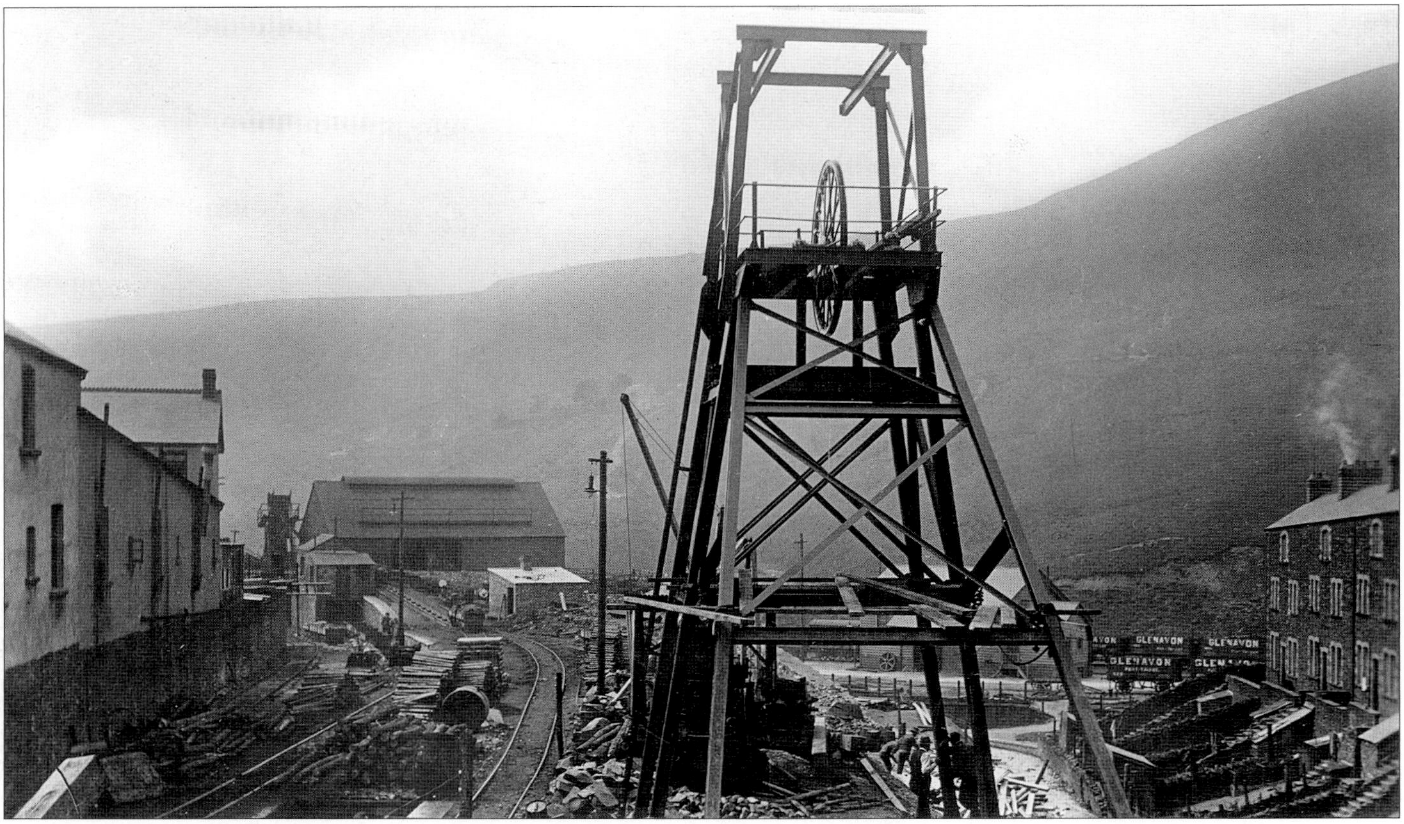

GLENGARW. A 1919 view looking south west, with Blaengarw station out of sight behind the row of houses. Opened pre 1875 as Nanthir levels, renamed Victoria in 1889 (also known as Blaengarw) and Glengarw in 1907 (for a time New Blaengarw), it closed in 1959. It was also sometimes referred to as Ballarat Colliery. The pits were sunk 1914-1919. [Map F11/G11]

GLYNCASTLE. Looking down the Vale of Neath line, towards Neath, with Resolven East S.B. in view. The colliery, which operated in some form or other between 1874 and 1965, is behind the photographer and between the sidings and the main line. [Map 9 E4/F4]

GLYNCORRWG (Blaengwynfi) (1). Located on the R&SB line just west of Blaengwynfi (Treherbert to the right), this view is looking north. Immediately below the colliery screens and sidings is the River Afan and the R&SB Rly and sidings. At a higher level, this side of the fence (and out of shot) was the GWR's line to Abergwynfi. The colliery was known as Abergwynfi from 1890, as Abergwynfi or Glyncorrwg from 1895 and just Glyncorrwg from 1903 until it closed in 1925 (Not to be confused with the Glyncorrwg Colliery at Glyncorrwg). It was also referred to as Perch's pit or Blaengwynfi Colliery. *courtesy Robin Simmonds* [Map 10 L7]

GLYNCORRWG (Blaengwynfi) (2). A similar, but closer, view to the above. *courtesy Robin Simmonds*

GLYNCORRWG SOUTH PIT. Looking east across the SWMR (North Rhondda to the left) is the South pit being sunk 1903-05. The building, high up on the mountain, is the disused engine house of the original Glyncorrwg Colliery level and the route of the tramway can be seen descending to the sidings. The colliery started in 1861 and survived until 1970. [Map 9 J2]

GLYN CYMMER. This lovely photograph is looking east over Cymmer, with the colliery, with its connections to both the GWR and the R&SB lines, prominent in the foreground. The tramway serving the colliery curves around from middle bottom, going behind the one large building to the entrance of the level just off the page on the lower right. Working into and out of the colliery from the GWR line involved shunting on the 110 yard long Cymmer viaduct. The SWMR to Glyncorrwg is on the extreme left, with Cymmer Corrwg sidings. The R&SB from Duffryn Rhondda enters lower left and curves round through Cymmer Afan station on its way to Blaengwynfi and the GWR enters lower right out of the 1,595 yard Cymmer tunnel to curve round via Cymmer General station on its way alongside the R&SB to Abergwynfi. The colliery started in 1894 and closed as early as 1928. [Map 10 H6/J6]

GRAHAM'S No. 9. This small colliery, also known as Sirhowy No. 9, was started pre 1873 and closed in 1924. It was located north-east of Tredegar station on the ironworks private lines. Between 1925 and 1939 a No. 9 Drift was listed. [Map 19 D11]

GRAIG MERTHYR. This view looking north-west at the end of a lengthy private line (disappearing into the distance and a tramway until c1900) from the Birchrock Sidings, on the east side of the L&NW Rly., between Swansea and Pontardulais. From 1913, connected to Graig Merthyr Colliery sidings west of Pont Lliw station on the GWR's Swansea District line. The colliery was started c1870 as Birchrock and lasted until 1978. [Map 5 A10]

GRAY. Looking north up the Cwmtillery Branch, Gray Colliery was the first pit to be encountered. Just around the corner on the left was Tillery pit. Gray was sunk in 1889 and closed in 1927 but retained for ventilation until 1950. [Map 20 G7]

GREAT MOUNTAIN No's 1 & 2. Looking south with the Llanelly & Mynydd Mawr Railway heading south to Llanelly in the distance. No. 1 slant was started in 1887 (No. 2 in 1906) and they closed in 1962. [Map 2 M8]

GREAT WESTERN. A view looking south west with Hetty (left), No. 3 and No. 2 shafts shown. The colliery was started in 1849 as Gyfeillon, renamed in 1871 and closed in 1929. [Map 16 C7]

SOUTH GRIFFIN COLLIERY. BLAINA, MON. I.

GRIFFIN, SOUTH (1). Located on a mile and a quarter private loop line between Abertillery and Blaina, to the west of the Western Valleys Branch, this colliery was in existence from 1881 to 1921. This view looking west. [Map 20 F8]

SOUTH GRIFFIN PIT. BLAINA W.W.&C.

GRIFFIN, SOUTH (2). A shot taken a little further north. Note the carriages bottom right.

GROESFAEN. This early view looking north-east towards Bargoed, shows Groesfaen to the left and its sister pit Penygarreg to the right. Sinking from 1903 they lasted until 1968. [Map 18 E4]

GWAUN-CAE-GURWEN EAST PIT. A latter development, being started in 1910, it survived until 1962. This view, looking east, shows the massive screens and extensive sidings. *courtesy Paul Jackson* [Map 8 B8]

GWENALT. This view looking north-west from above Branches Fork Jcn. S.B. (at the right-hand end of the row of houses) shows the long siding from the south side of the GWR's Cwmnantddu Branch to Gwenallt Colliery (1900-1949). Immediately above is Llanerch Colliery (the white smudge below the skyline). Towards the bottom right, with three chimneys, is the Oak Brickworks and beyond it, but out of site, Viaduct Colliery. The railway that enters bottom right and disappears bottom left, then reappears slightly higher up and runs across, exiting middle right, having crossed Cwmnantddu Viaduct (centre of photo), is the Talywain Branch to Abersychan. [Map 21 G4]

HAFOD. Looking slightly south of west up the Rhondda, Coedcae Colliery is on the left and Hafod (at times, Jones' Navigation) on the right. It was sunk in 1848 and closed in 1934. [Map 13 M2]

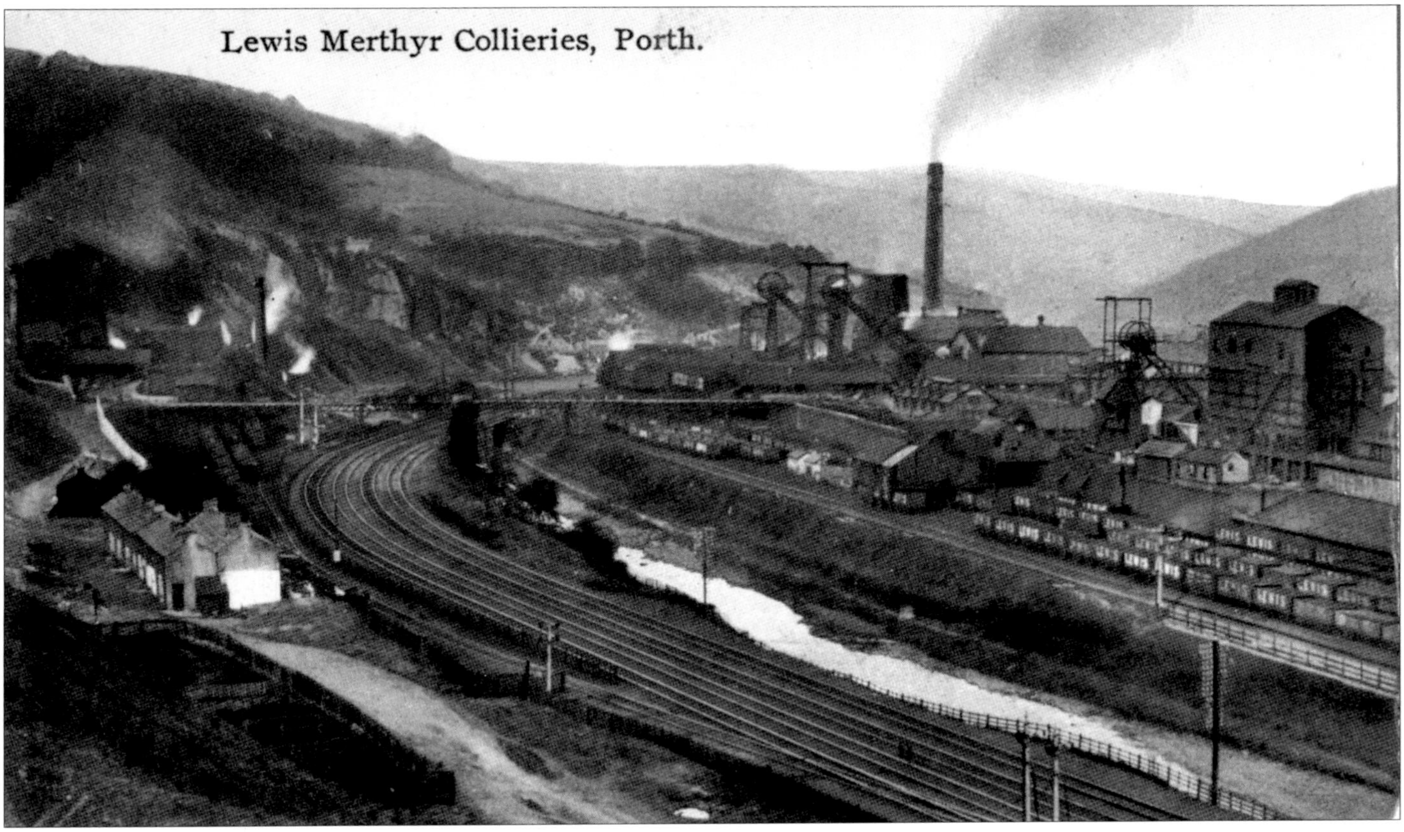

Lewis Merthyr Collieries, Porth.

HAFOD & COEDCAE (1). Hafod Colliery is on the left (a poor view) and Coedcae on the right in this view looking down the Rhondda towards Trehafod. More detail can be seen under the Coedcae photographs. [Map 13 M1]

HAFOD & COEDCAE (2). This view looks north over Coedcae Colliery to Hafod Colliery, which was sunk in 1848 and closed in 1934.

INTERNATIONAL (Blaengarw). This is Pwllcarn, started in 1875, renamed Transatlantic in 1884 and International in 1886. This view looks north-west with all three shafts in evidence. The colliery closed in 1967. Blaengarw station is out of site down bottom left. The difficulties of accessing some collieries is well illustrated here. [Map 11 F11/F12]

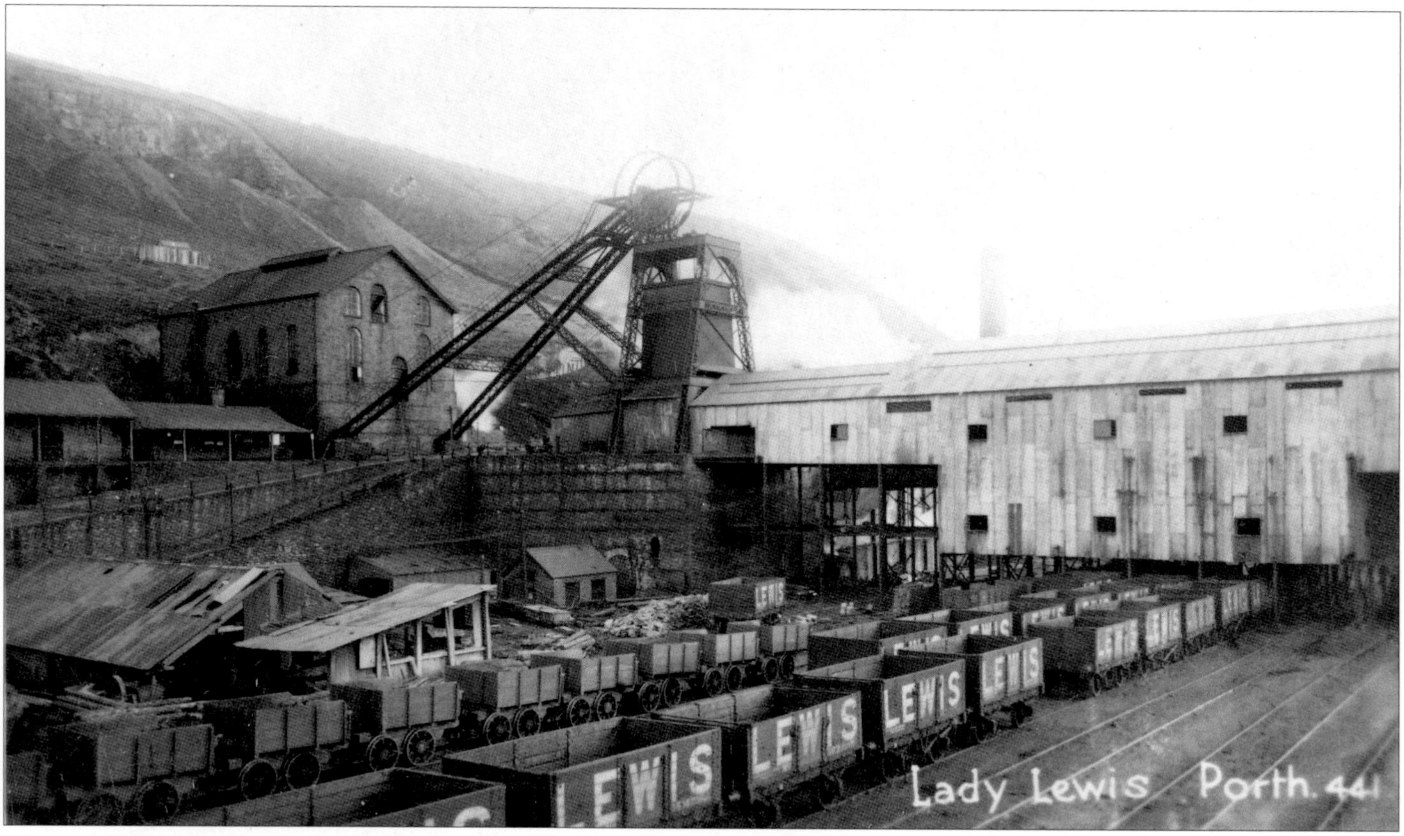

LADY LEWIS. This comparatively late colliery, sunk 1903, was on the east bank of the river and the Taff Vale's Maerdy Branch. This view is looking south-east. The mine closed in 1925 and was retained for ventilation. [Map 13 L2]

LADY MARGARET (1). At Treherbert, with the Taff Vale Railway station and carriage shed (so pre-1913) on the right, this view is looking north-west. The colliery functioned from 1877 to 1944. [Map 13 D7]

LADY MARGARET (2) Looking south east at the screens with the Taff Vale Railway over to the left (out of sight).

LLANBRADACH. Looking slightly north-west, with the Rhymney Railway between Caerphilly (left) and Ystrad Mynach (right) running just in front of the screens (but out of sight at a lower level). The colliery was sunk in 1887 and closed in 1961. [Map 17 D4]

LLANHARAN. Over time there were several Llanharan sites and it is uncertain to which one this photograph relates. [Map 14 E2]

LLANHILLETH (1). Looking north on the Western Valleys line showing work to divert the Ebbw river in order to provide for extensive additional colliery sidings. The House Coal (Red Ash) Colliery on the right operated from pre 1834 to 1946 and the Steam Coal Colliery from 1889 to 1969. [Map 20 G3/H3]

Llanhilleth. Colliery

LLANHILLETH (2). A similar but later view with Llanhilleth Middle S.B. in the centre.

Llanover Colliery Argoed. Nr Blackwood. 409

LLANOVER. Looking north-east across the Sirhowy river, with Llanover Colliery on the east side of the GWR's Pennar Branch. It did not start until 1908 and after a short life, closed in 1929, but was retained for pumping. [Map 19 F4]

P.D. COLLIERY. LLANTRISANT

LLANTRISANT. This colliery, sometimes referred to as Ynysmaerdy, was not opened until 1921 and closed in 1933. It reopened from 1936 to 1941. This view is looking west with the Ely Valley line running in front of it. Llantrisant to the left and Coed Ely to the right. [Map 14 H4]

LLETTY SHENKIN. Looking north at the Upper Colliery which was connected by a tramway to the Lower Colliery alongside the Taff Vale Rly south of Aberaman station. Later connected to sidings alongside the GWR line.. Opened in 1843, it closed in 1922. [Map 12 J5]

LLWYNHELIG. Looking south west, this colliery was connected to the GWR's Bwllfa Dare branch, just west of Dare Jcn. It started in 1906 and lasted until 1946.
courtesy Paul Jackson [Map 12 E6]

LLWYNYPIA (1). Looking north-west over the Taff Vale's Rhondda Branch north of Tonypandy. The sidings on the right lead to No. 6 pit and on the other side of the Rhondda river lie No's 4 to 1 pits (not all in view). The colliery started in 1863 closed in 1945. [Map 13 H3]

LLWYNYPIA (2). Looking east at No. 6 pit with the by-products plant to the left.

LLWYNYPIA (3). Looking south-west from the east side of the Rhondda branch with pits No's 1 to 3.

LOWER DUFFRYN. This colliery, also known as Lower Cwmpennar, was located on the private railway from Mountain Ash (Taff Vale) to the George Colliery and operated between 1850 and 1927. This view looks north towards George. [Map 12 K4/K5]

LOWER VARTEG SLOPE. Quite how this photograph relates to the site has not been established. The slope, also known as Deakins Slope, was driven in 1899 and closed in 1957. [Map 21 F7]

MAESMELYN. This is a view of the colliery sidings at Cwmavon looking west. The small colliery was located several hundred yards to the south and was served by the tramway seen on the left, with the trams being lowered by the hoist. The railway is the PTR Co.'s line from Port Talbot (to the left) to Tonmawr Jcn. and behind the covered van, is the short miners' platform. Just beyond the tall chimney, the R&SB Rly's line (also running from left to right) with Cwmavon station, can just be made out. The bridge over the River Avon originally carried the Bryn Tramroad from the collieries there to Cwmavon Works. Maesmelyn Colliery operated between 1912 and 1928 and 1929 and 1932. The large building under construction (so taken c1921) was to be the wagon shops of H. Hudson, the colliery owner and the siding beyond it was Cwmavon mileage siding. *courtesy Robin Simmonds* [Map 10 C3]

MAESTEG DEEP. This view is looking north east with Maesteg over to the left. The colliery opened c1868 and ended its life in 1931 as two drifts, 1,600 yards long. It was then retained for pumping. [Map 11 C10]

MAIN No. 1. Located on the Main Colliery Co.'s private line between Bryncoch Colliery and Neath Abbey wharves, this view is looking north-east. The colliery was started in 1891 and known as Duffryn Main until 1901. It closed in 1929. [Map 6 C7]

MAIN No's 3 & 4. Started in 1900, it had a very short life being closed in 1925. This view looks north and the colliery was connected only with the private lines of the Main Colliery Co. [Map 6 B5]

MAIN COLLIERY Co.'s INCLINE. This view from near the GWR South Wales main line east of Skewen, looks north-west at No. 3 & 4 pits, over the incline that linked their network with Neath Abbey wharves. The steam, centre right, is from the winding engine house. [Map 6 B5]

MAINDY. Looking north-west, the colliery was at the end of a short private line from the Taff Vale near Ystrad. It was sunk in 1864 and closed 1948. [Map 13 F4]

MARDY 1 & 2. Started in 1875 on a private railway above Maerdy, this view is looking west. The tramway on the hillside served a quarry. The colliery closed in 1948. [Map 13 G8]

Maerdy. No. 3. Pit.

MARDY No. 3. Located in a very remote spot, one mile above Maerdy on a private mineral line, this view is looking west. It was started in 1892 (and No. 4 in 1913) and lasted until 1986, when it was merged with Tower Colliery. It was the last pit in the Rhondda. [Map 13 F8]

MARINE COLLIERY, NEAR EBBW VALE. W.4644.

MARINE (1). Looking north-west up the GWR's Ebbw Vale branch towards Ebbw Vale. The pits were started in 1887 and the colliery survived until 1989. [Map 20 E6]

MARINE (2). A view from the rear of the colliery looking east, with the coke ovens. Note the wagons endorsed with 'Coke Marine-Victoria only.' A rather short distance journey.

MARITIME. Started in 1841 as Newbridge, it changed to Fowler's Pontypridd, then to Marine Rhondda, then Rhondda Jcn., before adopting the name Maritime in 1884. This view looks north-east towards the town and the signal box, just to the left of the chimney, is Pontypridd Graig on the Barry Rly. Co.'s line. The mine closed in 1961. [Map 16 D6]

MARKHAM (1). Looking due north with the L&NWR's Sirhowy Branch (towards Holly Bush) on the left and Markham Colliery at the terminus of the GWR's Penar branch. [Map 19 E5]

MARKHAM (2). This close up view shows the two pits sunk in 1910. The colliery closed in 1985.

McLAREN No. 1. Taken looking slightly north-east, the B&M Rly line is just this side of the fence shown in the bottom left corner. The pit was sunk in 1897 (with No. 3 following in 1906) and lasted until 1958. *courtesy Paul Jackson* [Map 18 E8]

McLaren Colliery, Abertysswg. Mon.

McLAREN No's 1 & 3. Looking north from the Brecon & Merthyr's Rhymney Branch, the two pits were sunk from 1897 and survived until 1958. [Map 18 E8]

McLAREN No. 2. This mine (referred to locally as Pwll-y-llaca) was located right at the end of the B. & M. Co.'s Rhymney branch and was sunk in 1878 and abandoned in 1899. [Map 18 D9]

MEIROS. Located at the end of a half mile long private branch from Llanharan, this view looks east (Llanharan to the right) The mine was sunk in 1886 and closed in 1931. [Map 14 F3]

MERTHYR VALE (1). Looking east. In the middle (between the two pit frames) is a footbridge. This crosses the Taff Vale main line between Merthyr (left) and Quakers Yard (right). The colliery, sunk from 1869, was served by both the Taff Vale and GW & Rhymney Joint lines by connections a considerable distance to the right. The Colliery closed in 1989. [Map 15 F5]

MERTHYR VALE (2). Looking north from the south end of the complex. River Taff on the left passing the gas works.

MILL PIT CEFNCRIBBWR 1316

MILL PIT. Started in 1907, this colliery lasted less than five years and despite employing 275 men in 1912, it was closed in February of that year. This view is looking east with the sidings on the right being connected to the Cefn Low Level siding at Aberbaiden on the Port Talbot's O.V.E. line. Beyond the colliery the sidings were also connected to the private line serving Ty-Talwyn and Ton Phillip Collieries.
courtesy Robin Simmonds [Map 11 B4]

Morfa Colliery Port Talbot 874.

MORFA. This view is looking south at the Grange pit. The Abbot pit, out of sight, was a little further on. The branch railway, originally to the GWR at Margam, and to Morfa Copper Works, ran from bottom right behind the photographer. Opened pre-1839 and originally called Margam Colliery, it closed in 1913, after an unhappy history of major explosions in 1863, 1870 and 1890 killing 39, 30 and 87 men.
courtesy Robin Simmonds [Map 10 B8]

NANTEWLAETH. Looking west, the colliery started as a drift mine in 1913 and the two pits were sunk from 1920. Located on the SWMR, which ran between the shafts and the screens, Cymmer is to the left and Glyncorrwg to the right. It closed in 1948.

[Map 10 J8]

NANTGWYN, Also known as Naval No. 3, it was connected to both the Ely Valley line and the Taff Vale at Pandy pit, off to the right of the picture, in this view looking west. It was opened in 1891 and closed in 1924. [Map 13 H2]

NANTMELYN (BWLLFA No. 2). At middle left can just be made out part of a reservoir and the string of wagons in front of it are on the TV Rlys Dare Valley Branch. The GWR's Bwllfa Dare Branch is behind the photographer. The view is thus looking west and the colliery was started in 1860 and closed in 1957 when it was linked to Mardy. [Map 12 D6]

NATIONAL. This view looking north shows the streets thronged with people following an explosion at the pit on the 11th July 1905. The colliery, also often referred to as Cwtch, was started in 1880 and it survived until 1968. [Map 13 K4]

NAVAL (ELY). Located half a mile south of Penygraig, this is looking north-west with the Ely Valley line out of sight to the right. It opened in 1875 and closed in 1928. [Map 13 H1]

NAVAL (PANDY). Looking south-east from Tonypandy & Trealaw station at Pandy Colliery. [Map 13 H1]

NAVIGATION (CRUMLIN) (1). Could not resist this one of the famous viaduct, especially as it shows two trains on it. The colliery is in clear view and work started in 1906 and it worked on until 1967. [Map 20 G2]

NAVIGATION (Crumlin) (2). A close-up looking west with a south bound coal train on the GWR's Western Valleys line.

NAVIGATION (Mountain Ash). Looking south-east with the GWR line and Cardiff Road station on the left, the north end of Navigation Colliery sidings, the river Taff and the Taff Vale's Oxford Street station. The sinking was carried out in 1855 and colliery closed in 1932, although it was retained for ventilation. [Map 12 K3]

NEW TREDEGAR (1). Looking west at the colliery started in 1853, located on the B&M Rly's Rhymney branch (entering bottom middle, exiting right middle, but not distinct) and also served by a short branch from the Rhymney Rly. It closed in 1930. [Map 18 E7]

NEW TREDEGAR (2). This view along the B&M Rly is looking north and was taken on the 11th February 1930, a matter of weeks before a mountain landslide overwhelmed the colliery on the 13th April and completely blocked the railway which never reopened. Most of the surface buildings were wrecked and two of the shafts were very seriously damaged and coal raising ceased. The colliery had closed in 1927, but reopened in 1929. In 1905 there was a major landslide that did serious damage to the colliery. Note the colliers' platforms, the north bound one is just around the curve.

courtesy John Mann

NINE MILE POINT (1). Quite why this card is titled 'Coronation Colliery' is not known, but it was never listed by that name. This early view of the colliery sunk in 1901, is looking north-east. It closed in 1964. [Map 17 H5]

NINE MILE POINT (2). A later view taken from more or less the same position. The colliery was on the north bank of the Sirhowy river and the sidings joined up further to the right, crossed over the river, and were connected to the L&NWR by a short branch.

STONES. COLLIERY. BLAINA.

NORTH BLAINA (STONE'S). Located within the Blaina Works complex, this view is looking south-west with the tinplate works on the left. The GWR's Western Valleys line ran across in front of the rows of house (not discernible) with Blaina to the left and Nantyglo to the right. The colliery was started in 1879 as New Sun and closed in 1923. [Map 20 F10]

NORTH RHONDDA. Not yet a colliery, but work is underway to provide facilities for the two drifts that would become North Rhondda. Right at the top end of the S.W.M. Rly, beyond Glyncorrwg, it was started in 1908 and lasted until 1960. [Map 9 J3]

OAKDALE. Looking south, this colliery was developed from 1907 on the site of the earlier Waterloo levels. In the bottom right corner are three sidings and the two unoccupied lines alongside are the GWR's Pennar Branch down (out of the right-hand side) to Pennar Jcn. on the Vale of Neath line. [Map 19 G3]

OAKWOOD. Started in 1868 as Oakwood, it later became Maesteg Merthyr. This (post 1900) view over the Llynvi & Ogmore line (Maesteg to the left) is looking south-east. It closed in 1927. [Map 11 C9]

PARK (1). Looking north-east towards Treorchy, Park pits 1-3 were located at the bottom of the tramway in the foreground. Further along the private railway was Dare Colliery (with the tall chimney). Park operated between 1865 and 1966. [Map 13 C5/D5]

CWMPARC, RHONDDA VALLEY W 5497

PARK (2). Looking west from alongside Dare Colliery towards Park Colliery.

General View of Colliery, Ystrad Mynach.

PENALLTA (1). This distant view of the colliery is looking north-west with the Cylla Branch, from above Ystrad Mynach, just in view beyond the trees in the lower front. The colliery was started in 1904 and survived until 1991. [Map 17 C8]

PENALLTA (2). A closer view looking almost due north.

PENGAM. Located on the B&M Rly. just south of Pengam station, this view is looking north-east with Pengam station to the left. The colliery lasted from 1902 to 1956. [Map 18 F2]

Cary's Collieries Gas Plant, Ogmore Vale

PENLLWYNGWENT. Looking east across the GWR's Ogmore branch and the Ogwr Fawr river. Ogmore Vale station is to the right and the line runs down to Blackmill and Tondu. To the left, the line continued to Nantymoel. The drift mine here was started in 1906 and remained in operation until it closed in 1969. [Map 11 J10]

PENRIKYBER COLLIERY PENRHIWCEIBER.

PENRHIWCEIBER. Looking slightly south-east, the Taff Vale Rly lies further over to the left with Penrhiwceiber station well behind the photographer. The colliery was started in 1872 and closed in 1985. [Map 12 L2]

PENTRE (Aberbaiden). Looking north-west from the tramway to Aberbaiden Colliery, this slant was driven in 1907 and closed in 1959, with Aberbaiden Colliery. *courtesy Paul Jackson* [Map 11B5]

PENTRE (Rhondda). Looking north over the loaded wagon sidings. These were connected to the Taff Vale's Rhondda Branch, north of Ystrad (behind the photographer). [Map 13 F5/G5]

PENTRE (Swansea). Callands was part of Pentre Colliery near Landore, which was opened pre 1815. This view is looking north-west (?) shows wagons on the private line which ran via an incline to a siding on north side of the GWR at Landore station and also to the Swansea Canal. The colliery closed in 1925. [Map 5 D4]

PENYBONT. A view looking north-east with the incline (between the houses) up to Pullinger's Level. The colliery was started in 1850 as Cwmtillery, then became Price's Tillery, Tillery and, from 1890, Penybont. It closed in 1930. [Map 20 G7]

POCHIN. Located on the west side of the L&NWR south of Bedwellty, this view is looking north-west. The colliery was started in 1876 and closed in 1964. [Map 19 E7]

PONTYCLERC. Located north of Pantyffynnon, this is a view looking north. There were several sites and several periods of operation. First in use c1849, the colliery closed in 1934. [Map 7 E6]

RHIW. If this is Rhiw, then it was located on the hillside west of Crumlin, and situated opposite the Millbrook and Kendon Collieries. It was in operation from 1923 to 1974. [Map 20 F2]

RHONDDA MAIN. Located on the east side of the Ogmore branch, south of Ogmore Vale. Catherine pit (left) and Anne pit (right) were started in 1909, but the colliery closed in 1924. In 1923 a third pit was started (Anne) on the left bank of the river. [Map 11 J8]

RHYMNEY MERTHYR. Lying just south of Pontlottyn, this view looks south-east. The colliery was often referred to as Pontlottyn or Tynewydd. Started in 1890, it closed in 1924. *courtesy Paul Jackson* [Map 18 D8]

RISCA BLACK VEIN (1). A view looking north-west, of the sidings at Rock Vein Siding South signal box, with the colliery beyond, on the other side of the Sirhowy river (out of sight at a lower level between the contractor's hut and the road). The railway here, between Nine Mile Point (to the left) and Risca, was GWR. The colliery was sunk from 1873 and closed in 1966. The sidings to the left with a rake of wagons, were on the site of Rock Vein Colliery. [Map 17 J5]

RISCA BLACK VEIN (2). A closer and earlier view of the colliery itself.

RIVER LEVEL. A very old pit, dating from the 1820s, looking north with the remains of Abernant ironworks. The colliery closed down in 1940. [Map 12 G7]

ROSE HEYWORTH. Located on the eastern side of the Western Valleys line, north of Abertillery. The mine was started in 1872 and closed in 1960 when it became part of Abertillery New mine. [Map 20 F8]

SENGHENYDD (1). The fateful colliery, where on the 14th October 1913 439 were killed in Britain's worst mining disaster, is clearly seen looking north above Senghenydd, with the station and goods yard at the end of the branch line from Caerphilly. The colliery was started in 1891 and resumed after the explosion, to close in 1928. [Map 17 A4]

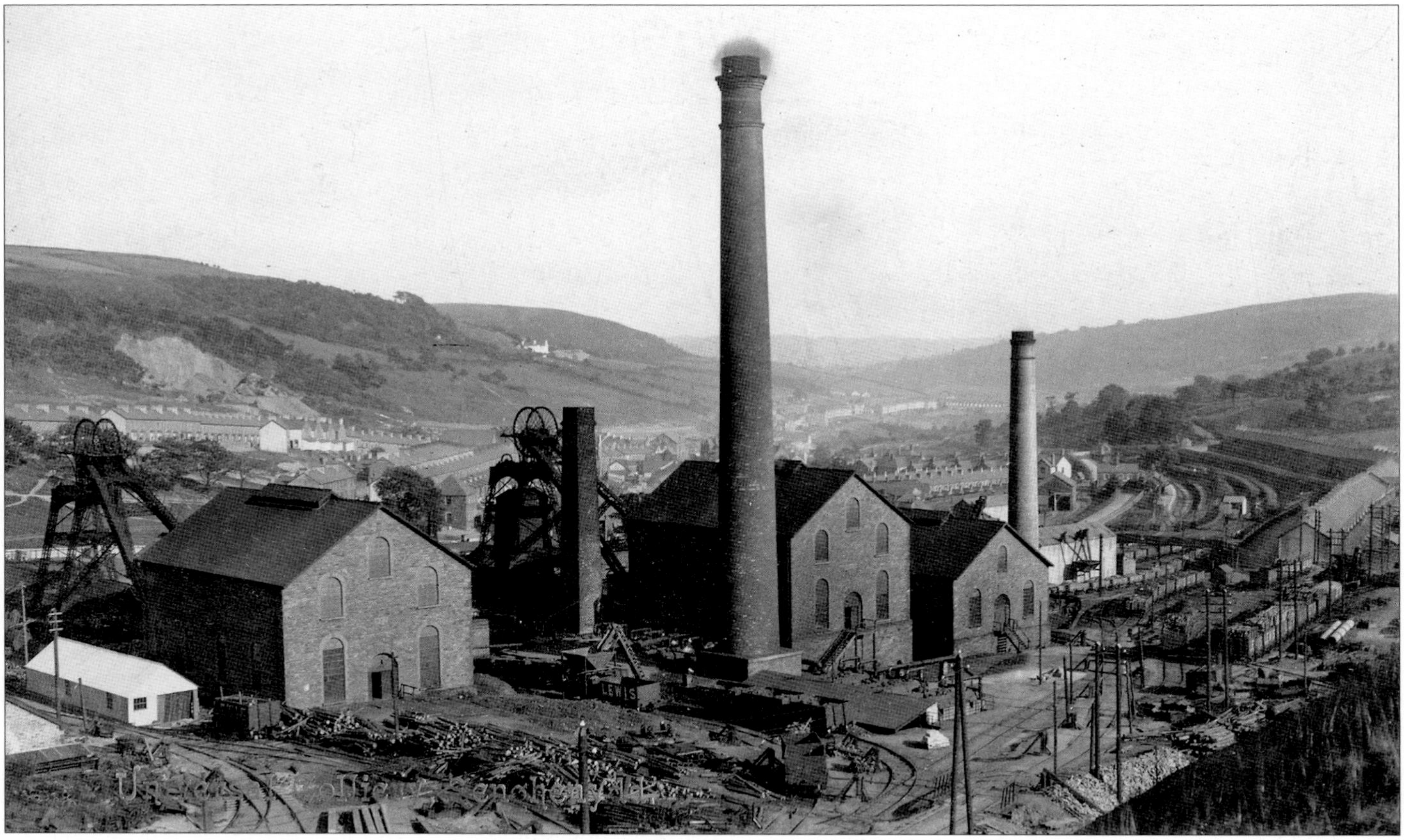

SENGHENYDD (2). This time from the north end looking south, with the station and goods yard to the right. The colliery was also referred to as Universal.

SEVEN SISTERS. This shot, looking north, was taken from the station footbridge on the N. & B. Rly. The colliery was commenced in 1872 and closed in 1963. [Map 8 J6]

SIX BELLS (1). Looking north-east across the Ebbw Fach river, with the Monmouthshire Rly. out of sight behind the photographer. The shafts were sunk from 1891, although a colliery existed here at least back to 1865. It became listed as Aral Griffin Nos. 4 & 5 from 1920 and renamed Six Bells again on 15.6.1954. It merged with Marine in 1980 and Blaenserchan merged with it in 1984. It was abandoned in 1987. (Note there were many spellings of Aral Griffin) [Map 20 G5]

SIX BELLS (2). A similar view to that above.

SOUTH RHONDDA. Started in 1889, it was located at the end of a mile and a quarter private branch from the Cardiff & Ogmore Rly. This view is looking north and the colliery closed in 1927. [Map 14 E4]

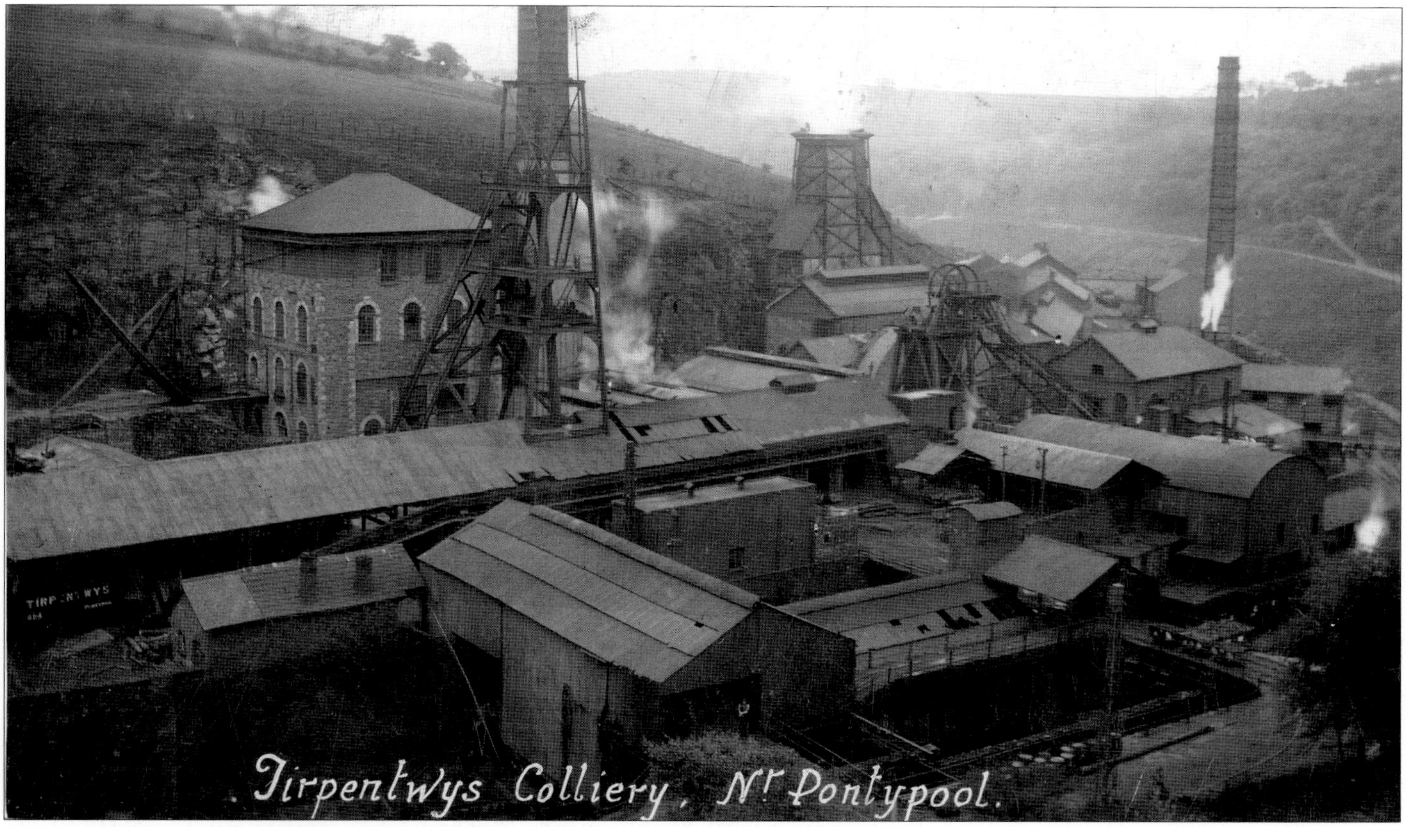

Tirpentwys Colliery, Nr Pontypool.

TIRPENTWYS. It was located at the end of the Cwmffrwdoer Branch from Branches Fork Jcn. The pits were commenced in 1878 and it closed in 1969. This view is looking north. [Map 21 F3]

TOR Y COED. Connected by a tramway to a siding on the south side of the TVR's Llantrisant No. 1 Branch, between Common Branch Jcn. & Waterhall Jcn. Started in 1897 and closed in 1932. [Map 14 L2]

TOWER (1). Tower colliery comprised numerous sites over time and this one has not been identified. [Map 12 B8]

TOWER (2). Likewise this site has also not been identified.

TY TRIST. With the L&NWR's Sirhowy branch running through the picture, with Tredegar to the left and Newport to the right, this view looks south-east. The colliery opened 1823 (unconfirmed), it closed in 1959. [Map 19 C10]

TYDRAW (1). Looking east with Treherbert behind the colliery, in the middle left distance can be made out the platform of Blaenrhondda station on the R.&S.B. Rly. The colliery started in 1856 as Dunraven, then became South Dunraven, Dunraven Merthyr, Dunraven again and in 1898 Tydraw. It closed in 1959. [Map 13 C8]

TYDRAW (2). A further east view and higher up than the one above. The R&SB Rly. sweeps across from lower left to middle right, with Blaenrhondda station to the right of the Tydraw chimney. To the left of the chimney there is an opening in the R&SB embankment, where the Blaenrhondda branch crosses underneath.

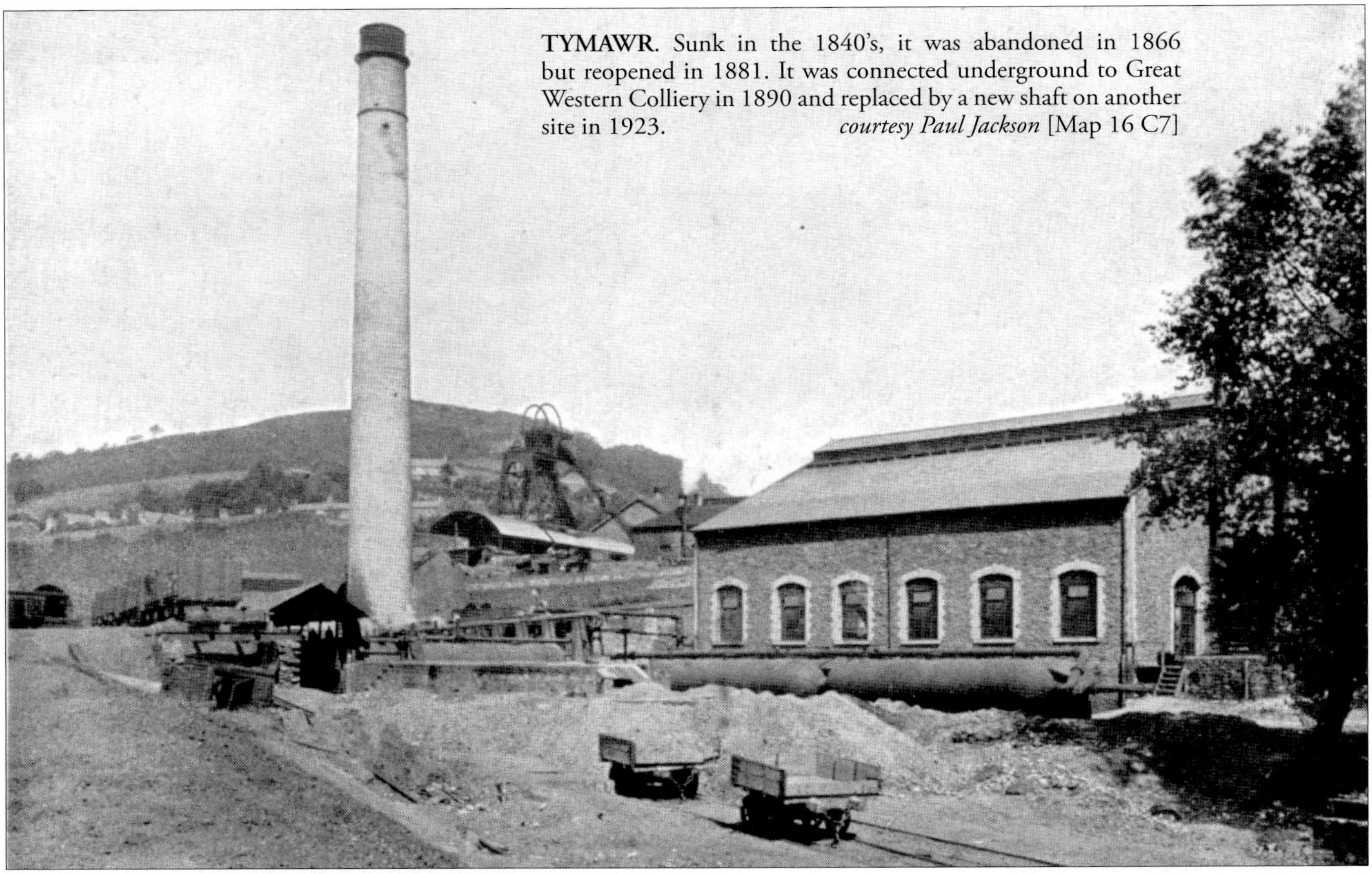

TYMAWR. Sunk in the 1840's, it was abandoned in 1866 but reopened in 1881. It was connected underground to Great Western Colliery in 1890 and replaced by a new shaft on another site in 1923. *courtesy Paul Jackson* [Map 16 C7]

TYNYBEDW. Looking west with the Taff Vale's line to Treherbert in the top left. The colliery was sunk in 1874 and closed in 1931. [Map 13 F6]

TYTALWYN. Looking east, this colliery was connected by a private line to the Port Talbot Rly on the Ogmore Vale Extension line at Mill pit. It operated from 1903 to 1928. *courtesy Robin Simmonds* [Map 11 C5]

UPPER CYMMER. Sunk in 1851 and closed in 1915. This view, looking north shows the Taff Vale line (Treherbert to the left and Porth to the right) and between it and the colliery lay the Rhondda river. [Map 13 K2]

VICTORIA No. 1 (1). Located on the Ebbw Vale Co.'s private lines, the colliery was sunk in 1846 and closed in 1914? This view is looking south south-east. [Map 20 C10]

VICTORIA No. 1 (2). This view is looking in the opposite direction, north-westwards.

VICTORIA No. 5. There was a No. 5 pit in operation pre 1857, but it was abandoned in 1893. A new No. 5 was sunk in 1913, becoming part of Prince of Wales Colliery. This was closed in 1930. [Map 20 C10]

VIVIAN. A view looking north-west towards Abertillery with the Ebbw Fach river and Western Valleys railway prominent. The colliery was started in 1889, at the same time as the Gray pit, and closed in 1958 when it merged with Six Bells. [Map 20 G6]

WAUNLLWYD. This view is looking south-east down the Ebbw Vale branch towards Aberbeeg. The colliery was started in 1874 and closed in 1964 when it was merged with Marine. [Map 20 D8]

WERNOS. Located on the Rhos Colliery mineral line, this view is facing south, with the line from Pantyffynnon to the left and to the right it continues on to Rhos and Nantyci Collieries. It worked from 1905 to 1965. [Map 7 D6]

WESTERN. Looking north-west at what was originally 'Edward's', then 'Western' then 'Ocean Western.' The line curving around to the left leads to Nant-y-moel, whilst the one on the right emerges at Wyndham. The colliery was started in 1873 and was merged with Wyndham in 1964. [Map 11 J11]

WHITWORTH. Located on the Tredegar Iron & Coal Co. Ltd.'s lines on the west side of the Sirhowy line south of Tredegar, this is a view looking south with Ty Trist Colliery immediately adjacent to the left (but out of sight) and Tredegar behind the photographer. The colliery, started in 1874, was closed in 1921. [Map 19 C10]

WINDBER (1). This colliery comprised some ten sites over time and this poor view looking north-east, shows the screens. The sidings (just seen beyond the reservoir) were connected to the Taff Vale's Dare Valley Branch. Started in 1905 the final site was closed in 1935. *courtesy Paul Jackson* [Map 12 D6/7]

WINDBER (2). One of the ten sites looking north. Not established which one this is. *courtesy Paul Jackson*

WINDSOR. Sinking started in 1896 and the colliery survived until March 1975 when it was merged with Nantgarw. This view is looking north with the Rhymney Rly's Aber Branch on the right of the fence. *courtesy Paul Jackson* [Map 17 A3]

WYLLIE. Another colliery in the Sirhowy valley, between Pontllanfraith and Nine Mile Point, looking west. A late colliery, it was started in 1923 and lasted until 1968. [Map 17 F6]

WYNDHAM. Looking north-west with the Ogmore branch from Blackmill entering from the left and running out on the right to Nantymoel. The colliery started from c1865 and closed in 1983. [Map 11 J11]

YNISCEDWYN. Located at the end of a private lengthy line from Clayphon, itself on a branch from Gurnos. The colliery dates from 1871 and closed in 1968. [Map 8 G7]

YNYSARWED. A splendid view looking south with the Vale of Neath line from Resolven entering top left and exiting top right down to Neath. On this line, top left, the wagons are standing at New Gored Merthyr Colliery. To the right of that can be made out a signal box and this side of it is Glyn Merthyr Colliery. These sidings join to cross the River Neath and swing round to the sidings and screens of Ynisarwed. From the screens, a tramway emerges on the right to cross the Neath Canal and run a straight line to levels, out of view to the right. Ynisarwed, with numerous sites, operated pre-1841 to 1893, 1903 to 1925 and 1929 to 1955. [Map 9 C4/D4]

YNYSHIR STANDARD (1). A north-west view of the Rhondda Fach valley looking towards Ferndale. Ynyshir station is located just to the left of the church on the left. The colliery was started in 1875 and closed in 1927, although retained for ventilation. [Map 13 L3]

YNYSHIR STANDARD (2). A closer view looking west with the railway to Ferndale going off lower right.

APPENDIX A – ABBREVIATIONS

AC	Anthracite Committee
AGM	Annual General Meeting
aka	also known as
AL	*Aberdare Leader*
ANDR	Alexandra (Newport & South Wales) Docks & Rly. Co.
AR	Annual Report
AT	*Aberdare Times*
AVC	*Amman Valley Chronicle*
Bd Min	Board minute
B&M	Brecon & Merthyr Rly
B&RE	*Brecon & Radnor Express*
B.C.T.	*Brecon County Times*
BDN	*Barry Dock News*
BoT	Board of Trade
BGS	British Geological Survey
BLN	*Branch Line News*
BM	Board Meeting
BOI	*Burdett's Official Intelligence*
BR	British Railways
BT31	Company Registration Files at NA Kew
BWJ	*Berrow's Worcester Journal*
c	Circa
C & I	*Coal and Iron*
C & M G	*Cardiff & Merthyr Guardian*
CA	Coal Authority reference
Cam	Cambrian
Car	Company Annual Report
CCM	Chief Commercial Manager
CCN	*Coal & Colliery News*
CCND	Coal & Colliery News Digest
CDL	*Cambrian Daily Leader*
C.E.C.	Children's Employment Commission
CG	*Colliery Guardian*
Ch	Chairman
CJ	*Carmarthen Journal*
CMD	Command Paper [No.]
c/o	Care of
CO&MCA	*County Observer & Monmouthshire Central Advertiser*
COD	Court Order to Dissolve
COWU	Court Order to Wind Up
C.P.P.	Coal preparation plant
CRO	County Records Office (now usually Archives)
CSSW	Collier's Strike in South Wales
CT	*Cardiff Times*
CWR	*Carmarthen Weekly Reporter*
CYBCTD	*Colliery Year Book & Coal Trades Directory*
DA	Descriptive Article
Dirs	Directors
EE	*Evening Express*
EDOS	Established by Deed of Settlement
Eng.	*The Engineer*
FAL	Fatal Accident Lists
Fin. Com.	Finance Committee
G&AC	Glamorganshire & Aberdare Canals
GFP	*Glamorgan Free Press*
GG	*Glamorgan Gazette*
GGAT	Glamorgan-Gwent Archaeological Trust
GL	Guildhall Library
GM	General Manager
GM&BG	*Glamorgan, Monmouthshire &Brecon Gazette*
GW FJ & PS	Great Western Foreign Jcns & Private Sidings Committee
GWO	Gloucester C. & W. Co. records
GWR	Great Western Railway
HBL	History of Bynea & Llwynhendy
HMIM	H. M. Inspector of Mines *Annual Report.*
HMS	*Hunt's Mineral Statistics*
HoS	RCH *Handbook of Stations*
HoW	*Herald of Wales*
H.&M.H.T.	*Haverfordwest & Milford Haven Telegraph*
ICTR	*Iron & Coal Trades Review*
i.c.w.	In connection with
IMHLBP	*Industrial & Maritime History of Llanelly & Burry Port*
IRS	Industrial Railway Society Bulletin
Jcn	Junction
L.d.	Letter dated
L. & C. G.	*Llanelly & County Guardian*
L&O	Llynvi & Ogmore Railway
LG	*Labour Gazette*
Llan. G.	*Llanelli Guardian*
LM	*Llanelly Mercury*
LM Survey	Licenced Mines Survey
LM&SR	London Midland & Scottish Railway
L&NWR	London & North Western Railway
LoM	List of Mines
LS	*Llanelli Star*
MD	Managing Director
ME	*Merthyr Express*
Lon.G	*London Gazette*
MGR	Merry-go-round
Mid	Midland Railway
Min.	Minute
MJ	*Mining Journal*
MM	*Monmouthshire Merlin*
MRCP	M. R. Connop Price
MT	*Merthyr Telegraph*
N&B	Neath & Brecon Railway
NA	National Archives (formerly PRO)
NAS	Neath Antiquarian Society, Transactions of
NCB	National Coal Board
nd	no data
NGR	National Grid Reference
OCIN	O'Connell's Coal & Iron News
OS	Ordnance Survey
PC	Pontypridd Chronicle
PCG	Pembroke County Guardian
PDSC	Powell Duffryn Steam Coal Co. Ltd.
PFC	*Pembrokeshire the Forgotten Coalfield*
PFP	*Pontypool Free Press*
PH	*Pembrokeshire Herald*
PPL	Parish Production Lists
Potts	Potts' *Mining Register & Directory*
PRO	Public Record Office (now National Archives)
PSA	Private Siding Agreement
PSA papers	PSA records in the author's collection
PTHS	Port Talbot History Society, Transactions of
PTR	Port Talbot Railway
P.W.	Permanent Way
RA	Receiver appointed
RCH	Railway Clearing House
RCOA	Records of the Coal Owners' Associations
RDC	Register of Defunct Companies
Reg.	Registered
RGT BP	R. G. Thomas, Burry Port
Rhy	Rhymney Railway

RL	*Rhondda Leader*	SWP	*South Wales Press*
RN	Renamed	SWS	*South Wales Star*
RO	*Railway Observer*	SWWN	*South Wales Weekly News*
RPJ NMW	Robert Protheroe Jones, National Museum of Wales	SWWP	*South Wales Weekly Post*
RSB	Rhondda & Swansea Bay Railway	t.a.	trading as
S & S	*Syren & Shipping*	Tfc Com	Traffic Committee
SEOI	*Stock Exchange Official Intelligence*	TVR	Taff Vale Railway
SEOYB	*Stock Exchange Official Year Book*	VL	Voluntary Liquidation
SEYB	*Stock Exchange Year Book*	VoN	Vale of Neath Rly
SMSW	*Small Mines of South Wales* (Booth)	VWU	Voluntary Winding Up
Star	*Star of Gwent*	WCF	*Welsh Coal Fields*
s.t.s.c.	Some time since constructed	WCIR	*World Coal Industry Report & Directory*
SWCA	*South Wales Coal Annual*	w.e.f.	With effect from
SWCF	*South Wales Coal Field*	WGRO	West Glamorgan Records Office, Swansea
SWCT	*South Wales Coal Trade*	WM	*Western Mail*
SWD	South Western Division (of the N. C. B.)	WMail	*Weekly Mail*
SWDN	*South Wales Daily News*	WMS	Welsh Mines Soc.
SWE	*South Wales Echo*	WU	Wound Up
SWIE	South Wales Institute of Engineers	WUM	Winding Up meeting
SWMF	South Wales Miners' Federation	WWO	Western Wagon Co. records
SWMR	South Wales Mineral Railway	y.e.	year ending
SWN	*South Wales News*		

APPENDIX B – TERMINOLOGY

PART ONE – MEASURES (appearing in the text of this volume)

Inch	–	2.54cm	Twelve to a foot
Foot (feet)	12 inches	30.48cm	Three to a yard
Yard	3 feet	91.44cm	Twenty-two to a chain or 1,760 to a mile
Rod, pole or Perch	16.5 feet	5.03m	Four to a chain
Chain	22 yards	20.12m	Ten to a furlong or eighty to a mile
Furlong	220 yards	201.17m	Eight to a mile
Mile	1,760 yards	1.61km	
Fathom	6 feet	1.83m	
Acre	4,840 sq. yards	= 0.4 hectares	
Pence (d)	–	= 0.42p	
Shilling (s)	12 pence	= 5p	
Pound (£)	20 shillings	= £1	
Guinea	21 shillings	= £1.05p	

PART TWO – MINING TERMS (Kindly supplied by Robert Protheroe Jones)

Adit — A walkable mine entry, driven either in-seam or cross-measure. Floor inclination may vary from effectively horizontal (though usually slightly inclined outwards to facilitate drainage) to steeply inclined (including more steeply than full dip of the seam). Near-horizontal adits were termed 'levels'; distinctly inclined adits were termed 'drifts', 'slants', and 'slopes'.

Bank, The — The area around the mine entrance where the coal was unloaded.

Cross Measure — A walkable tunnel which cuts across strata from one horizon to another; may be effectively horizontal (though usually slightly inclined to facilitate drainage) or inclined. The frequently used term 'cross measure drift' encompassed both horizontal and inclined tunnels.

Day level — Near-horizontal entry that enabled walkable access to and from a mine; often applied to entries wholly or substantially reserved for the ingress and egress of workmen.

Declivity	Inclined walkable tunnel driven down from one horizon to another.
Downcast	The entry by which fresh air enters a mine: may be an adit or a shaft.
Drift	(i) Synonym for a walkable entry (see adit); usually applying to a distinctly inclined entry and thus a synonym for slant or slope. (ii) A walkable tunnel which cuts across strata from one horizon to another within a mine; may be effectively horizontal (though usually slightly inclined to facilitate drainage) or inclined. The frequently used term 'cross measure drift'(which see) encompassed both horizontal and inclined tunnels.
Fathom	A measure of depth equal to six feet or 1.8288 metres.
Free level	Seldom used term apparently meaning a walkable near-horizontal mine entry inclined slightly outwards for the drainage of water; compare 'level'.
Gob fire	Spontaneous heating of waste coal underground leading to combustion. 'Gob' is the inaccessible, partly or wholly collapsed zone to the rear of an advancing area of working, into which waste rock and small coal was filled.
Hard heading	A walkable tunnel driven in, or through, strata of sandstone.
Level	(i) A mine entrance which is effectively horizontal (though usually slightly inclined outwards to facilitate drainage). (ii) A near-horizontal tunnel within a mine; if driven within a seam, a level followed the strike or 'level course' of the seam, this being at right angles to the 'full dip' (maximum gradient) of the seam. Levels were often used for water-drainage. In this case they would normally have a slight gradient (1 in 100 to 1 in 300) to allow the water to flow out steadily. Less than that, the water would not flow freely and be prone to silting up; if steeper than that, the increased water velocity would tend to erode gullies in the tunnel floor.
'Mine' pit	A mine ('pit' implies a shaft) primarily or entirely working iron ore. 'Mine' is the South Wales term for sedimentary ironstone that occurs within the Coal Measures.
Rider	A thinner seam of coal occurring a short distance above a major seam of coal.
Slant	A distinctly inclined walkable mine entry. May be driven within a coal seam or, more usually, as a cross measure drift (which see) that may be steeper, or less steeply inclined than the coal seam. Term particularly used in west Wales.
Slope	Synonym for slant (which see). Term particularly used in Monmouthshire coal field.
Staple pit	Wholly underground shaft connecting two coal seams – it does not extend to surface; usually relatively small compared to shafts from surface.
Stone Coal	Archaic term for anthracite, being a direct translation of the Welsh term for this coal – 'glo carreg'
Take	The area of minerals leased to a mining concern.
Upcast	The entry by which stale air leaves a mine: may be an adit or a shaft.

APPENDIX C – SOUTH WALES LIST OF MINES
GIVING INSPECTORS DISTRICT & ORDER OF LISTING

	BRECON		CARMARTHEN	GLAMORGAN		MONMOUTH	PEMBROKE
	WEST	EAST		WEST	EAST		
1873-74	South Wales OWNER	South West RANDOM	South Wales OWNER	South Wales OWNER	South West RANDOM	South West RANDOM	South Wales OWNER
1875-79	South Wales OWNER	South West **MINE**	South Wales OWNER	South Wales OWNER	South West **MINE**	South West **MINE**	South Wales OWNER
1880-86	South Wales OWNER	South West **MINE**	South Wales OWNER	South Wales OWNER	South West **MINE**	South West **MINE**	South Wales OWNER
1887-88	South Wales OWNER	South West OWNER	South Wales OWNER	South Wales OWNER	South West OWNER	South West OWNER	South Wales OWNER
1889-93	South Wales **MINE**	South West OWNER	South Wales **MINE**	South Wales **MINE**	South West OWNER	South West OWNER	South Wales **MINE**
1894-1900	South Wales **MINE**	South West **MINE**	South Wales **MINE**	South Wales **MINE**	South West **MINE**	South West **MINE**	South Wales **MINE**
1901-02	Swansea **MINE**	Cardiff **MINE**	Swansea **MINE**	Swansea **MINE**	Cardiff **MINE**	Southern **MINE**	Swansea **MINE**
1903-09	Swansea OWNER	Cardiff OWNER	Swansea OWNER	Swansea OWNER	Cardiff OWNER	Southern OWNER	Swansea OWNER
1910-23	South Wales OWNER	South Wales OWNER	South Wales OWNER	South Wales OWNER	South Wales OWNER	South Wales OWNER	South Wales OWNER
1924-45	Swansea OWNER	Cardiff & Npt* OWNER	Swansea OWNER	Swansea OWNER	Cardiff & Npt* OWNER	Cardiff & Npt* OWNER	Swansea OWNER

* Cardiff & Forest of Dean from 1929, Cardiff at 1945

APPENDIX D – MULTIPLE OWNERS USING A COMMON ENTRANCE

1. GENERAL DUPLICATION

I had long been perplexed by the number of sites in the early days which had two entries with differing owners for a mine or mines with the same name. Quite how these should be interpreted is to my mind full of doubt. Were some errors, in that change of ownership resulted in duplicate entries with the old ones languishing in the lists for some time or were they (a) two distinct and separate sites, (b) two levels worked within a site with common forwarding facilities or (c) even just a single hole in the ground.

Some evidence came to light from the Star of Gwent, which for October 1853 and from April to November 1854, published a table headed 'Coal brought into Newport for the month of xxxx'. These figures must have come from railway sources. From these tables a total of nine sites appear with apparently duplicate owners.

Joseph Latch was shown as forwarding from two sites in his own right, Barcilla and Cilvach. The interesting point is that the forwardings from Barcilla show over 400 tons per month up to September when they drop dramatically and even more so for October and November. This period ties in with the forwardings from Price's sites and I speculate that Barcilla ran into some difficulty in September and Latch arranged with Price to purchase his coal 'ex-pit' (if that is the correct term) to make up the shortfall. Latch would therefore be paying the carriage charges and would be shown as the consignor in railway sourced statistics. If this is correct, and I think it must be plausible, it shows the pitfall of using or trying to interpret such material.

Whilst this may well explain these particular duplications, many others currently remain unresolved.

		1853	1854							
Coal brought into Newport for the month of		Oct	Apl	May	June	July	Aug	Sept	Oct	Nov
	Source, *Star of Gwent* dated	11.11.53	06.05.54	10.06.54	08.07.54	12.08.54	09.09.54	14.10.54	11.11.54	09.12.54
Cilvach	Joseph Latch & Co.	1094.12	912.05	861.05	982.07	867.03	864.11	841.03	721.08	678.10
Barcilla	Joseph Latch & Co.	942.06	462.14	547.17	677.03	408.05	579.05	167.06	20.18	57.04
Cwm Nant Groes	Joseph Latch & Co.							195.02	186.13	131.11
	T. P. & D. Price	1080.12	880.13	1445.13	1172.08	1595.14	1565.11	1692.03	1144.18	1371.17
Rhiw Park	Joseph Latch & Co.							179.17	137.16	170.15
	T. P. & D. Price	617.06		(a)	130.12	405.12	405.12	312.18	464.03	429.00
Tellery	Joseph Latch & Co.							257.11	195.12	107.19
	T. P. & D. Price	1838.03	618.14	1985.14	2102.17	2766.14	2712.00	2316.11	2427.10	2013.02

(a) Rhiw Park figure included in 'Tellery.'

2. EXAMPLES

GELLY HAF

The Lists of Mines for 1894-1904 give two sites by the name of Gelly Haf, one owned by T. H. Jones and the other by David Treasure. The interesting point is that the entries are endorsed 'two owners working through the same level.'

GLANDDU

In May 1875 there was an accident which was briefly reported in the press as follows:

> Inquest on two men killed at Glanddu Colliery. Witness stated that '*He worked at Pottery Colliery, which is the same road as Glanddu.*' Richard Evans stated '*He was proprietor of Pottery Colliery, coming out of Glanddu Level, employing eight men.*' The Inspector stated '*The portion of the level where the accident occurred is used by* ***three or four separate*** *coal owners to bring out the produce of their mines.*'

The following month it was reported that:

> *Further accident at Glanddu Colliery, collier in employ of Davies, Williams & James* [See under 'Glyngaer' entry], *one of the parties that worked* ***a section of this colliery****. Work is now suspended at this colliery altogether.*

The above examples go some way to illustrate the difficulties in interpreting data and in trying to pinpoint the exact entrance to a named mine.

APPENDIX E – THE TERRIBLE TOLL – COLLIERY DISASTERS 1851-1997

With five or more persons killed

(Disasters with Special Inquiry Reports are shown as *– see note at end)

Date	Mine	No. killed	Cause	Owner
04.09.1851	WERFA	14	Shaft	John Nixon & Co.
10.05.1852	GWENDRAETH	26	Quicksand	Alfred Watney
10.05.1852	MIDDLE DUFFRYN	65	Explosion	Thomas Powell
12.03.1853	RISCA ROCK VEIN	10	Explosion	John Russell
23.12.1853	BRYNDU	5	Explosion	G. S. Ford & Son
18.04.1855	ABERAMAN	5	Explosion	Crawshay Bailey
28.11.1855	CWM NEOL	8	Shaft	Carr & Morrison
24.05.1856	CWMAVON	12	Explosion	Gov. & Company of Copper Miners
03.07.1856	COALBROOKVALE OLD COAL	11	Explosion	Coalbrook Vale Co.
15.07.1856	CYMMER	114	Explosion	George Insole & Son
27.05.1857	TYR NICHOLAS	13	Explosion	Russell, John
25.02.1858	LOWER DUFFRYN	19	Explosion	Thomas Powell & Son
28.05.1858	BRYNDU	12	Explosion	Ford & Son
11.08.1858	CYFING	6	Explosion	Thomas Walters
13.10.1858	PRIMROSE	10	Explosion	G. Lewis & Co.
04.11.1858	CAE	10	Inundation	Francis Davies & Co.
06.04.1859	MAIN	26	Inundation	Neath Abbey Coal Co.
06.11.1860	LOWER DUFFRYN	12	Explosion	Thomas Powell & Son
01.12.1860	RISCA BLACK VEIN	142	Explosion	Risca Coal & Iron Co.
08.03.1861	BLAENGWAWR	13	Explosion	David Davis
19.02.1862	CETHIN *	47	Explosion	William Crawshay
03.07.1862	OLD CASTLE	6	Inundation	Sims, Willyams, Nevill, Druce & Co.
26.06.1863	PARK (Briton Ferry)	6	Explosion	Thomas & Co.
17.10.1863	MORFA	39	Explosion	Vivian & Sons
26.12.1863	LLYNVI	15	Explosion	Llynvi Vale Iron Co. Ltd.
16.06.1865	BEDWELLTY	26	Explosion	Tredegar Iron Co.
20.12.1865	CETHIN	34	Explosion	William Crawshay
08.11.1867	FERNDALE	178	Explosion	David Davis & Sons
27.12.1867	BWLLFA	5	Explosion	Bwllfa Coal Co.
25.05.1869	CWMNANTDDU	7	Explosion	Ebbw Vale Iron Co.
10.06.1869	FERNDALE	53	Explosion	David Davis & Sons
11.11.1869	HENDREFORGAN	6	Explosion	Alexander Bain
08.01.1870	FOCHRIW NO. 1	5	Shaft	Dowlais Iron Co.
14.02.1870	MORFA	30	Explosion	Vivian & Sons
23.07.1870	CHARLES	19	Explosion	C. H. Smith
08.10.1870	ABERCWMBOY	5	Explosion	David Davies & Sons
24.02.1871	PENTRE	38	Explosion	Church & Pentre Coal Co.
02.03.1871	VICTORIA	19	Explosion	Ebbw Vale Iron Co.
22.01.1872	LIBANUS	5	Shaft	Protheroe Bros.
14.02.1872	MAESTEG MERTHYR	11	Explosion	William Davis
05.04.1873	TILLERY	6	Explosion	John Jayne & Co.
07.12.1874	WESTERN (OGMORE SINKING)	5	Explosion	David Davies & Co.
04.12.1875	NEW TREDEGAR	23	Explosion	Powell Duffryn Steam Coal Co. Ltd.
06.12.1875	LLAN	16	Explosion	T. W. Booker & Co. Ltd.
18.12.1876	SOUTH WALES	23	Explosion	South Wales Colliery Co. Ltd.
10.03.1877	WEIGFACH	18	Explosion	Landore Siemens Steel Co. Ltd.
11.04.1877	TYNEWYDD	5	Inundation	Llynvi, Tondu & Ogmore Coal & Iron Co. Ltd.
11.09.1878	ABERCARN *	268	Explosion	Ebbw Vale Iron Co.
13.01.1879	DINAS MIDDLE PIT	63	Explosion	Coffin & Co.
02.04.1879	BEDWELLTY	6	Explosion	Tredegar Iron Co.
26.04.1879	MEADOW (CWMAVON)	6	Shaft	Gov. & Co.'s successors
10.03.1880	BEDWELLTY	6	Explosion	Tredegar Iron & Coal Co.
07.07.1880	GARNGOCH	6	Explosion	John Glasbrook

Date	Mine	No. killed	Cause	Owner
15.07.1880	RISCA BLACK VEIN *	120	Explosion	London & South Wales Coal Co. Ltd.
10.12.1880	PENYGRAIG *	101	Explosion	Naval Steam Coal Co.
27.02.1882	HENWAIN	5	Explosion	John Lancaster & Co.
25.06.1883	NEW DUFFRYN	6	Explosion	Rhymney Iron Co. Ltd.
21.08.1883	GELLI	5	Explosion	Thomas & Griffiths
16.01.1884	GARNANT	10	Shaft	Garnant Colliery Co.
27.01.1884	NAVAL *	11	Explosion	Naval Steam Coal Co.
08.11.1884	POCHIN *	14	Explosion	Tredegar Iron & Coal Co.
23.12.1885	MARDY *	81	Explosion	Lockett's Merthyr Steam Coal Co.
09.12.1886	GEORGE	5	On incline	Powell Duffryn Steam Coal Co. Ltd.
18.02.1887	NATIONAL *	39	Explosion	National Steam Coal Co. Ltd.
14.05.1888	ABER	5	Explosion	Aber Colliery Co.
22.01.1890	GLYN	5	Explosion	Ebbw Vale Steel, Iron & Coal Co. Ltd.
06.02.1890	LLANERCH *	176	Explosion	Partridge, Jones & Co. Ltd.
10.03.1890	MORFA *	87	Explosion	Vivian & Sons
30.09.1891	BLAENGWYNFI	8	Shaft	William Perch & Co.
24.08.1892	YNYSCEDWYN	6	Shaft	Yniscedwyn Colliery Co.
26.08.1892	PARK SLIP *	112	Explosion	North's Navigation Collieries (1889) Ltd.
23.01.1893	DOWLAIS CARDIFF	8	Shaft	Dowlais Iron Co.
11.04.1893	GREAT WESTERN *	63	Fire	Great Western Colliery Co. Ltd.
23.06.1894	ALBION *	290	Explosion	Albion Steam Coal Co. Ltd.
09.09.1895	DOWLAIS CARDIFF	6	Shaft	Dowlais Iron Co.
09.09.1895	TYNYBEDW	6	Shaft	Cory Bros. Ltd.
27.01.1896	FERNDALE 7 & 8 *	57	Explosion	David Davis & Sons
04.08.1896	MAIN (BRYNCOCH) *	7	Explosion	Main Colliery Co. Ltd.
09.12.1896	RIVER LEVEL *	6	Inundation	Aberdare Works & Collieries Co.
05.01.1897	BROADOAK	5	Explosion	Thomas, Samuel
11.06.1897	GARTH MERTHYR	9	Shaft	Garth Merthyr Colliery Co.
18.08.1899	LLEST *	19	Explosion	Llest Coal Co. Ltd.
24.10.1900	GLENAVON	5	Inundation	Glenavon Rhondda Collieries Co. Ltd.
24.05.1901	UNIVERSAL *	81	Explosion	Universal Steam Coal Co. Ltd.
10.09.1901	LLANBRADACH No. 2 *	8	Explosion	Cardiff Steam Coal Collieries Co. Ltd.
04.03.1902	MILFRAEN	5	Shaft	Blaenavon Iron & Steel Co. Ltd.
03.06.1902	WINDSOR	6	Shaft	Windsor Steam Coal Co. (1901) Ltd.
04.06.1902	FOCHRIW No. 2	8	Explosion	Guest, Keen, & Nettlefold's Ltd.
03.09.1902	McLAREN *	16	Explosion	Tredegar Iron & Coal Co. Ltd.
01.10.1902	TIRPENTWYS	8	Shaft	Tirpentwys Black Vein Steam Coal & Coke Co. Ltd.
11.11.1902	DEEP NAVIGATION	6	Shaft	Ocean Coal Co. Ltd.
13.08.1904	NINE MILE POINT	7	Shaft	Burnyeat, Brown & Co. Ltd.
21.01.1905	ELBA	11	Explosion	Baldwins Ltd.
10.03.1905	CAMBRIAN No. 1*	33	Explosion	Cambrian Collieries Ltd.
11.07.1905	NATIONAL No. 2 *	119	Explosion	United National Collieries Ltd.
28.04.1906	DOWLAIS CARDIFF	5	Haulage	Guest, Keen, & Nettlefold's Ltd.
01.06.1906	COURT HERBERT	5	Explosion	Main Colliery Co. Ltd.
10.11.1906	ALBION	6	Explosion	Albion Steam Coal Co. Ltd.
16.02.1907	WAUNHIR	6	Haulage	Trimsaran Co. Ltd.
05.03.1907	GENWEN *	6	Explosion	David Harry & Bros.
10.11.1907	SEVEN SISTERS	5	Explosion	Evans & Bevan
14.12.1907	DINAS MAIN *	7	Explosion	Dinas Main Coal Co.
27.08.1909	ELY (NAVAL)	7	Shaft	Naval Colliery Co. (1897) Ltd.
01.10.1909	GRAIG MERTHYR	5	Explosion	Graigola Merthyr Co. Ltd.
29.10.1909	DARREN *	27	Explosion	Rhymney Iron Co. Ltd.
01.11.1909	TARENI	5	Inundation	South Wales Primrose Coal Co. Ltd.
18.05.1912	MARKHAM	5	Explosion	Markham Steam Coal Co. Ltd.
14.10.1913	SENGHENYDD (UNIVERSAL)*	439	Explosion	Lewis Merthyr Consolidated Collieries Ltd.
18.10.1913	GLYNEA	8	Explosion	Glynea & Castle Coal & Brick Co. Ltd.
26.04.1923	CAEDEAN	10	Haulage	Trimsaran Co. Ltd.

Date	Mine	No. killed	Cause	Owner
27.11.1924	KILLAN	5	Inundation	Killan Collieries Ltd.
01.03.1927	MARINE *	52	Explosion	Ebbw Vale Steel, Iron & Coal Co. Ltd.
10.07.1929	MILFRAEN *	9	Explosion	Blaenavon Co. Ltd.
28.11.1929	WERNBWLL *	7	Explosion	New Berthllwyd Gas Coal Co.
25.01.1932	LLWYNYPIA *	11	Explosion	Welsh Associated Collieries Ltd.
26.05.1936	LOVESTON	7	Inundation	Loveston Colliery Co.
10.07.1941	RHIGOS No. 4	16	Explosion	Clay, C. L., & Co. Ltd.
06.09.1955	BLAENHIRWAUN *	6	Explosion	National Coal Board
22.11.1957	LEWIS MERTHYR *	9	Explosion	National Coal Board
28.06.1960	SIX BELLS *	45	Explosion	National Coal Board
12.04.1962	TOWER *	9	Explosion	National Coal Board
17.05.1965	CAMBRIAN *	31	Explosion	National Coal Board
06.04.1971	CYNHEIDRE/PENTREMAWR *	6	Explosion	National Coal Board

The following disasters, outside the scope of the above table, all resulted in Special Inquiry Reports being issued and complete the list of all such reports issued since 1846.

Date	Mine	No. killed	Cause	Owner
14.01.1846	RISCA *	35	Explosion	Risca Colliery Co.
14.05.1900	CWM (MERTHYR) *	0	Explosion	Crawshay Bros Ltd.
28.02.1901	BLAENDARE SLOPE *	2	Explosion	Blaendare Co. Ltd.
26.06.1906	CARADOG VALE *	4	Inundation	South Wales United Collieries Ltd.
02.06.1941	LLANTRISANT *	4	Explosion	Powell Duffryn Associated Collieries
10.10.1952	BEDWAS *	1	Explosion	National Coal Board
21.10.1956	ABERFAN (Merthyr Vale Colliery)	144	Tip Slide	National Coal Board (Parliamentary Tribunal Rpt)
13.01.1954	GLYNCORRWG *	0	Explosion	National Coal Board

APPENDIX F – COMPARISON OF RCH DATA ON COLLIERIES

The following is a small sample of delayed recording of data by the Railway Clearing House, from the Port Talbot/Cymmer area. The extent of apparent late reporting, up to ten years in some cases, is both surprising and worrying. This illustrates the misleading nature of such records and the danger of using such information which may be several removes from the primary source. It was original suspicions on this, and railway company data, that caused me to look at colliery records in the first place.

MINING RECORD		RCH RECORDS	
COLLIERY	ABANDONED/NEW	STATED	LEAFLET DATE
Brynavon	Listed from 1912	New entry	24.01.1914
Brynavon	Not listed from 1914	Closed not recent	25.01.1917
Cedfyw Rhondda	Abandoned 21.12.1926	Closed	07.1928
Corrwg Vale	Abandoned 01.12.1925	Closed	07.1928
Craigavon	Abandoned 16.12.1906	Closed	25.01.1912
Craiglyn	Listed 1909	New entry1.9.1911	25.01.1912
Craiglyn	Closed 1927	Closed	01.1929
Cwmgwinea	Abandoned 29.02.1912	Closed	24.01.1918
Eskyn	Listed from 1910	New entry not recent	25.01.1917
Eskyn	Abandoned 01.09.1917	Closed	04.1927
Glyncorrwg	Not listed 1924	Closed	07.1928
Parc-y-Bryn	Abandoned 25.10.1924	Closed	07.1928
Ton yr Rhondda	Abandoned 26.06.1928	Closed	04.1930
Torymynydd	Listed from 1906	New entry 1907	26.10.1911
Treshenkin	Abandoned 27.10.1910	Closed	23.01.1913
Varteg (at Bryn)	Abandoned 25.01.1902	Closed	25.01.1912
Yniscorrwg	Abandoned 31.07.1925	Closed	10.1928

See section 14 of the 'Guidance Notes' for reasons for possible late reporting.

APPENDIX G – FAILED COMPANIES

All the following companies, whilst being Registered, apparently failed in that they never achieved an existence by the allocation of shares, or because they were unable to achieve their objectives in the acquisition of the desired property. The text in quotes is from letters in the appropriate National Archives BT31 files. It is not claimed that this list is exhaustive.

COMPANY (* Mentioned in main text)	REGISTERED	COMMENT	DISSOLVED
Abernant Anthracite Collieries Ltd.	08.05.1906	No details and does not appear in colliery listings.	23.02.1912
Alltygrug Anthracite Colliery Ltd.*	05.05.1911	To acquire Gilfach Goch Colliery at Ystalyfera. VL 9.6.1914	18.01.1921
Ammanford Anthracite Mines Ltd.	29.11.1988	No details and does not appear in colliery listings.	25.02.1992
Anthracite Coal Co. Ltd.	22.03.1881	To acquire Pantyffynon Collieries Co. & Gwaun cae Gurwen Co. Ltd.	02.07.1884
Anthracite Syndicate Ltd.	29.11.1921	No details.	10.02.1925
Atlantic Resolven Smokeless Steam Coal Co. Ltd.	16.07.1881	No shares list on file.	14.09.1888
Black Mountain Coal Ltd.	01.03.1983	Reg. as Garwyn Thomas Ltd. RN 8.6.1992, Last accounts to 31.8.1993. Petition 21.9.1995, RA 1.3.1996, COWU 29.2.1996. Does not appear in colliery listings.	08.01.2004
Black Mountain Anthracite Co. Ltd. *	07.10.1901	'As the minimum subscription was not forthcoming, this company did not proceed to allotment'.	13.01.1905
Black Rock Colliery Co. Ltd. *	11.10.1875	For Darranddu Colliery.	08.09.1885
Blackwood Colliery Co. Ltd.	21.12.1904	No details and does not appear in colliery listings.	24.02.1931
Blaenafon & Cefn y Van Freehold Colliery Co. Ltd.	04.03.1873	For Blaenafon & Cefn y Van Collieries.	13.01.1885
Blaenant Farm Colliery Co. Ltd.	09.08.1996	No details and does not appear in colliery listings. Last accounts to 30.6.2002 (dormant).	12.08.2003
Blaendare Colliery Co. Ltd. *	1982	No details and does not appear in colliery listings.	01.10.1991
Blaengraigola Colliery Co. Ltd. *	?	No details and does not appear in colliery listings.	14.10.1971
Blaengrennig Coal Co. Ltd. *	11.04.1996	No accounts presented to Companies House.	20.01.1998
Blaenhirwain Anthracite Collieries Ltd.*	29.01.1913	No details and does not appear in colliery listings.	04.04.1930
Braich-y-Cymmer Collieries Ltd. *	02.08.1898	Voluntary liquidation 24.2.1927	?
British Anthracite Colliery Co. Ltd.	21.10.1905	Voluntary liquidation 5.3.1908	13.01.1909
Briton Ferry Collieries Co. Ltd. *	20.06.1871	Court Order to Wind Up 26.5.1873	07.10.1904
Broad Oak Colliery Co. Ltd. (? South Wales)	?	Meeting to VWU 22.3.1905. Winding up meeting 22.12.1905.	?
Brookes Anthracite Syndicate Ltd. *	22.11.1904	To acquire Glangwendraeth Colliery.	08.01.1915
Brynafan Colliery Co. Ltd.*	22.08.1913	For Brynafon Colliery. Voluntary liquidation 2.3.1914	14.05.1915
Brynamman Anthracite Collieries Ltd.*	16.03.1906	No details	26.07.1912
Brynbach Colliery Co. Ltd.*	28.11.1908	Voluntary liquidation 20.8.1914	20.11.1914
Brynhenllys Colliery Co. Ltd. *	09.02.1923	Voluntary liquidation 15.12.1925	?
Bryn Steam Navigation Co. Ltd.	12.05.1915	No details and does not appear in colliery listings.	08.03.1935
Brynygroes Colliery Ltd.*	22.10.1918	Voluntary liquidation 1.12.1920	20.03.1925
Burry Port (Carmarthenshire) Coal & Ironstone Co. Ltd.	07.09.1860	'Company has never carried on business or even allocated shares'	07.03.1882
Buttery Hatch (Rhymney Valley) Colliery Co. Ltd.*	?	No Details	?
Caerbryn Colliery Co. Ltd. *	11.03.1881	Voluntary liquidation 19.8.1882	17.07.1888
Caerbryn Colliery Ltd.*	25.09.1900	'Although company was Registered, it did not go to allotment'	26.12.1902
Cardiff Merthyr Steam Colliery Co. Ltd. *	29.03.1866	Voluntary liquidation 4.5.1875	31.08.1883
Cardiff Rhondda Colliery Ltd.	04.04.1884	Voluntary liquidation 4.2.1888. Wound Up 29.7.1889	?
Cardiff-Rochefort Colliery Co. Ltd. *	18.05.1906	No Details	24.10.1916
Carmarthen Anthracite Ltd.	30.01.1908	Renamed Saron Anthracite Collieries Ltd.	31.12.1940
Cefnstylle Colliery Co. Ltd. *	26.09.1911	Voluntary liquidation 17.10.1913. Wound Up 9.6.1914	?
Cefn-y-Coed Colliery Co. Ltd.	07.03.1901	No details and does not appear in colliery listings.	30.01.1934
Coedcae Coal & Coke Co. Ltd. *	18.05.1874	Renamed Rhondda Valley Coal & Coke Co. Ltd. 2.12.1874. No returns after 1874.	28.04.1885

COMPANY (* Mentioned in main text)	REGISTERED	COMMENT	DISSOLVED
Consolidated Collieries Co. Ltd. *	12.03.1874	For New Forest and Bush Collieries. No papers after 7.1874.	28.04.1875
Corrwg Rhondda Coal Co. Ltd. *	16.09.1884	For Glyncorrwg Colliery. 'The company has never carried on any business'	08.12.1891
Crynant Colliery Co. Ltd. *	01.08.1874	No papers after 12.1875.	17.07.1885
Cwm Bryn Colliery Ltd.*	1978	No details and does not appear in colliery listings.	02.02.1988
Cwmnant Collieries Ltd.*	04.10.1923	No allotment details. 'This company is dormant and not carrying on any business' (at 10.8.1925)	18.02.1927
Cymmer Navigation Collieries Ltd.*	27.11.1900	For Cymmer Glyncorrwg Colliery Voluntary liquidation 11.09.1902 Wound Up 30.11.1903	?
Cymru Colliery Co. Ltd.	09.02.1996	No Details	03.11.1998
Davis' Rhondda Merthyr Steam Coal Co. Ltd.	01.09.1890	'Company never went to allotment.'	11.06.1895
Duffryn Mountain Colliery Ltd.	27.11.1865	No documents on file.	01.05.1883
Dunraven Adare Collieries Ltd.*	03.11.1876	No documents after Registration.	22.01.1886
Dyffryn Mountain Colliery Co. Ltd.	27.11.1865	No details and does not appear in colliery listings.	01.05.1883
Dyllas (South) Mining Co. Ltd.	04.09.1985	No details and does not appear in colliery listings.	21.02.1995
Ely Valley Colliery Co. Ltd.	21.01.1861	Winding up meeting 2.1.1862	?
Ely Valley Colliery Co. Ltd.	21.11.1866	No documents after Registration.	31.08.1883
Empire Collieries Ltd.*	14.02.1899	'No allotment of shares having been made.'	27.10.1905
English & French Collieries Co. Ltd.	01.12.1880	No documents after Registration.	05.06.1888
Eskyn Colliery Co. (1919) Ltd.*	02.04.1919	'The only business carried out was the hire of wagons.'	25.10.1932
Fforchneol Merthyr Colliery Co. Ltd. *	26.06.1884	No documents after Registration.	08.12.1891
Garnswillt Anthracite Colliery Co. Ltd.*	03.03.1925	Voluntary liquidation 12.3.1929	06.07.1929
Garw Coal Co. Ltd.	02.11.1904	No documents after Registration.	29.11.1907
Garw Valley Collieries Co. Ltd. *	30.01.1875	Court Order to Wind Up 18.2.1876	07.10.1904
Gellihir Colliery Co. (1914) Ltd.*	19.08.1914	No details and does not appear in colliery listings.	05.11.1943
Gellygron Colliery Co. Ltd.*	26.10.1904	'The company has never done any business. Co. lost law case.'	05.03.1909
Gellynudd Colliery Co. Ltd. *	04.08.1908	No details and does not appear in colliery listings.	11.10.1927
Gellyluog Colliery Co. Ltd.	28.11.1952	No details and does not appear in colliery listings.	16.01.1959
Gilvach Coal Co. Ltd.	23.04.1862	No details and does not appear in colliery listings.	?
Glamorgan Merthyr Colliery Co. Ltd.*	02.07.1870	No documents after Registration.	15.01.1884
Glamorganshire Consolidated Collieries Co. Ltd. *	11.04.1874	For Clyne Wood Colliery. No documents after 08.1874.	28.04.1885
Glanyreithin Anthracite Colliery Co. Ltd.	22.09.1906	No details and does not appear in colliery listings.	24.02.1911
Glynhir (Steam, Gas & House Coal) Collieries Ltd.*	25.10.1906	'Company never went to allotment.'	18.10.1910
Glyn Level Colliery Ltd.*	-	See under 'Pontypool Colliery Ltd.'	-
Glyn Main Coal Co. Ltd.	20.02.1907	Voluntary liquidation 14.4.1908, WU 31.12.1909	30.05.1911
Godreaman Graig Coal Co. Ltd. *	04.01.1924	Did not go to allotment.	16.04.1929
Gorsgoch Collieries Ltd.*	07.06.1923	Voluntary Liquidation 02.09.1924. Wound up 25.08.1925	?
Graig Forest Colliery Co. Ltd.*	29.10.1900	'Co. is not carrying on any business (at 17.11.1903)'	09.09.1904
Great Bettws Llantwit Colliery Ltd.*	12.04.1869	No documents after Registration.	13.01.1884
Grovesend Colliery Co. Ltd.*	04.12.1868	No documents after 12.1869.	05.06.1888
Guinea Wallsend Colliery Co. Ltd.*	21.03.1867	Voluntary liquidation 24.3.1869	31.08.1883
Gwalia Colliery Co. Ltd.*	08.04.1904	'Company has not carried on any business since Registration.'	07.05.1907
Gwendraeth Valley Syndicate Ltd.	12.11.1908	'No business has been done since Registration.'	23.06.1911
Gwrhay & Greenland Collieries Co. Ltd. *	06.01.1896	'The company was Registered speculatively and it has never acquired the collieries in question.'	14.05.1897
Hendregarreg Colliery Co. Ltd. *	3.11.1868	No documents after 2.1870.	31.08.1883
Hendre Owen Fach Colliery Co. Ltd.	1989	No details and does not appear in colliery listings.	09.07.1991
International Anthracite & Mining Co. Ltd.	12.12.1906	L. d. 15.6.1910 'Company is defunct'.	29.08.1911
Killan & Three Crosses Collieries Co. Ltd. *	11.06.1873	Last document on file Shares List dated 31.12.1875	28.04.1885
Landshipping Colliery Co. Milford Haven Ltd.*	31.10.1866	No shares list on file.	31.08.1883
Lanelay Colliery Co. Ltd. *	03.12.1866	No documents after Registration.	31.08.1883
Little Mountain Colliery Ltd.	27.07.1924	File destroyed.	14.11.1950
Llan Colliery Co. Ltd.*	21.12.1900	'Company is defunct. It was a failure from the start and they decided to let it go to the wall. No Winding Up proceedings have been taken.'	09.09.1904

COMPANY (* Mentioned in main text)	REGISTERED	COMMENT	DISSOLVED
Llanelly Anthracite Coal Co. Ltd. *	22.05.1872	For Rhos Colliery. 'No shares allocated and time expired.'	30.09.1884
Llangeinor Colliery Co. Ltd. *	28.03.1905	Voluntary liquidation 16.06.1910. Wound Up 31.03.1911	?
Llannon Anthracite Colliery Co. Ltd. *	15.06.1933	Does not appear in colliery listings. Vol. liquidation1 17.5.1945	?
Llantwit United Collieries Ltd.*	25.03.1902	For Gelynog Colliery.'Company formed to take over colliery, but arrangements fell through' .	13.01.1905
Llantwit Coal Consumers Co. Ltd. *	18.04.1873	For Llantwit Wallsend Colliery. 'Capital was never subscribed.'	13.01.1885
Llantwit Wallsend Colliery Co. Ltd.*	09.12.1863	For Gelynog coal field. No documents after Registration.	06.10.1882
Lletherlan Colliery Ltd.*	1985	No details and does not appear in colliery listings.	22.05.1990
Llwyn Mawr Colliery Co. Ltd.*	09.02.1907	Voluntary liquidation 27.11.1908.	30.01.1923
Llynvi Collieries Ltd.*	19.06.1912	See Llynvi Valley in the A-Z	05.11.1943
Lochners Navigation Coal & Coke Co. Ltd. *	10.1903	Purchase not completed. See Cymmer Glyncorrwg entry in the A-Z.	?
Maesmawr Llantwit Colliery Co. Ltd.*	21.12.1900	'Company is not carrying on any business nor is it in operation (at 28.8.1903)'	?
Morgan Varteg Colliery Co. Ltd. *	20.10.1980	Does not appear in colliery listings. See Bryn Varteg in the A-Z.	18.02.1986
Myrtle Hill Craig-y-Dinas Colliery Co. Ltd. *	07.03.1900	Does not appear in colliery listings. See Sylen Mountain entry in the A-Z	1911
Neath Abbey & Duffryn Estates Colliery Co. Ltd.	23.06.1884	'The company never came to anything.'	08.12.1891
Neath Collieries Ltd.	08.06.1874	No documents after 8.1874.	28.04.1885
Neath Merthyr Colliery Co. Ltd.*	13.02.1901	'Since the formation of the company, no operations whatsoever have been carried out.'	09.09.1904
Nelson Colliery Co. Ltd. *	20.10.1884	No documents after 11.1885.	22.06.1894
New Drym Anthracite Collieries Ltd.*	31.12.1900	'his company did not go to Allotment.'	18.11.1902
New Ffosfach Colliery Co. Ltd.*	05.08.1914	'Company never went to Allotment'	18.01.1918
New Great Western Coal Co. Ltd.	22.07.1909	No details and does not appear in colliery listings.	27.03.1953
New Hendreforgan (1919) Colliery Co. Ltd. *	07.01.1919	'Company has not carried on any business since Registration.'	24.02.1922
New Hendreforgan Collieries Ltd.*	21.09.1920	Renamed Gwys Anthracite Collieries Ltd. before registration.	?
New Rhondda Collieries Ltd.*	03.01.1913	For Whitworth Collieries.	15.12.1916
Oaktree Colliery Co. Ltd. *	1983	No details and does not appear in colliery listings.	14.09.1993
Panteg Collieries & Blaendare Brickworks Co. Ltd.	28.02.1921	No details and does not appear in colliery listings.	22.07.1960
Pantymoch Colliery (Port Talbot) Ltd.*	11.11.1957	No details and does not appear in colliery listings.	28.09.1962
Parc-y-fan Colliery Ltd.*	12.06.1922	No allotments on file.	31.03.1925
Patent Anthracite Fuel, Coke & Coal Co. Ltd. *	26.07.1884	Voluntary liquidation 15.6.1885	20.03.1906
Pembrokeshire Anthracite Steam Coal Co.	24.06.1853	No Details	?
Penclawdd Colliery Co. Ltd.*	23.01.1857	Voluntary liquidation 5.1.1860.	07.03.1882
Penclawdd (Cefn-m-Chen) Colliery Co. Ltd.	26.03.1896	No documents after Registration.	04.10.1898
Pencraig Colliery Co. Ltd.*	12.04.1977	No details and does not appear in colliery listings.	11.02.1986
Pengam Colliery & Brickworks Co. Ltd. *	11.09.1890	'Company was never in operation. The shares were not allotted'	15.08.1893
Penlan Colliery Co. Ltd. *	07.03.1919	Voluntary liquidation 17.11.1921	?
Penmynydd & Tylantwyn Colliery Co. Ltd.*	1965	Does not appear in colliery listings.	01.04.1982
Penrhiw Coal Co. Ltd. *	19.07.1894	For Penrhiw and Woodfield Collieries. 'No business has been done by this company and it is practically defunct or still born'.	15.09.1896
Pentrebach Colliery Ltd.*	30.03.1903	To effect agreement with R. J. Lloyd.	29.05.1906
Pentre United Steam Coal Collieries Co. Ltd. *	12.02.1868	For Pentre & Church Collieries. 'Company never formed.'	31.08.1883
Pen-y-Rhiew Colliery Co. Ltd.	29.09.1856	Voluntary liquidation 3.11.1858	03.05.1881
Pontardawe, Bryncoch & Graigola Railway & Collieries Co. Ltd. *	03.02.1894	For Bryncoch Little Pit and Graigola Level. 'The company did not go to allotment.'	15.90.1896
Pontardulais Coal & Brick Co. Ltd. *	08.10.1909	For Bolgoed Colliery. 'Company never took over the business contemplated nor possessed any assets'	27.09.1912
Pontlash Colliery Co. Ltd.*	08.06.1892	'No allotment took place or business carried out.'	15.09.1896

COMPANY (* Mentioned in main text)	REGISTERED	COMMENT	DISSOLVED
Pontypool Colliery Ltd.*	04.04.1901	Company was to have been called 'Glyn Level Colliery Ltd.' 'Company did not go to allotment.'	22.12.1903
Pont-y-Pridd Merthyr Colliery Co. Ltd.*	22.03.1864	Voluntary liquidation 19.12.1865	06.10.1882
Port Talbot Colliery Co. Ltd.	03.07.1899	'Company did not go to allotment.'	26.12.1902
Powell Aberbeeg Colliery Co. Ltd.*	22.12.1885	'Company was never floated.'	10.05.1892
Primrose United Collieries (1928) Ltd.*	25.09.1928	Court order to Wind Up 17.7.1929	10.05.1935
Pwll-yr-engine Colliery Co. Ltd. *	17.03.1857	No papers after 3.1858.	07.03.1882
Reynolton Colliery Co. Ltd. *	15.03.1904	'Company has never carried on any business.'	26.07.1912
Rhondda & Swansea Colliery Co. Ltd.*	5.12.1884	No shares list on file.	08.12.1891
Rhondda Valley Coal & Coke Co. Ltd.*	18.05.1874	Renamed from Coedcae Coal & Coke Co. Ltd. 2.12.1874. No returns after 1874.	28.04.1885
Rigos Anthracite Coal Co. Ltd.	4.11.1921	To acquire assets of New British Rhondda Colliery Co. Ltd.	07.03.1939
Rock Llantwit Colliery Co. Ltd. *	07.07.1902	No details and does not appear in colliery listings	19.03.1907
Rumney Valley Collieries Co. Ltd. *	29.09.1880	For Rudry and other collieries. No papers after Registration.	13.01.1888
Saron Anthracite Collieries Ltd.	30.01.1908	Registered as Carmarthen Anthracite Ltd.	31.12.1940
Sirhowy Navigation Collieries Ltd.*	04.12.1925	'To acquire Tunnel levels at Sirhowy. Never functioned after registration.'	11.06.1929
Skewen Main Colliery Co. Ltd. *	1965	Does not appear in colliery listings.	11.06.1982
South Llantwit Colliery Co. Ltd.	24.04.1902	'Objects for which the company was floated, lapsed. The seams of coal leased, worked out forty years previously and instead of coal the company went for old workings full of water'.	29.05.1906
South Wales Anthracite Ltd.	1985	No details and does not appear in colliery listings.	07.02.1989
South Wales Anthracite Ltd.	?	Petition presented 25.10.2001, Court hearing 05.12.2001 First meeting of creditors 5.2.2002, VL 5.2.2002, WU 12.11.2002.	?
Swansea & Neath Collieries Co. Ltd. *	21.11.1873	For Brynwillach Colliery and others. 'Company was never actually formed.'	28.04.1885
Swansea Bituminous Colliery & Fire Clay Co. Ltd.	17.10.1871	No documents on file.	30.09.1884
Swansea Vale Anthracite Colliery Co. Ltd.	1933	No details but see under Ystrad No. 1	?
Sylen Mountain Colliery Co. Ltd. *	22.02.1904	No details and does not appear in colliery listings	24.02.1911
Talyfan Colliery Co. Ltd.*	27.03.1905	No shares list on file.	04.10.1907
Tawe Vale Coal Co. Ltd.	08.03.1907	No details and does not appear in colliery listings.	13.08.1912
Tower Colliery Ltd.	28.11.1994	No Details	?
Trinant Colliery Co. Ltd.*	30.05.1924	'Arrangements fell through over Cefn Coch Colliery.'	22.12.1931
United Caepontbren Collieries Ltd.*	21.02.1908	'Company has not been proceeded with.'	10.03.1911
United Collieries & Coal Trading Co. Ltd.*	30.06.1881	For Aberdare Town Graig and Duffryn Merthyr Collieries. No shares list on file.	14.09.1888
Vale of Neath Coal Mining Co. Ltd.	04.08.1989	No details and does not appear in colliery listings.	?
Van Colliery Co. Ltd.*	25.02.1867	No shares list on file.	31.08.1883
Welsh Anthracite Collieries Ltd.	21.11.1910	Company renamed 'Welsh Anthracite Collieries & Roumanian Asphalte Co. Ltd.' 5.7.1911. ? active company	27.03.1914
Welsh Coal Mines Ltd.	01.09.1891	'Nothing has been done beyond Registration.'	24.09.1893
Welsh United Collieries Ltd.*	22.05.1895	For Lantwit Merthyr, Penrhiw & Woodfield Collieries. 'Nothing done since Registration.'	22.10.1897
Wenallt Coal Colliery Co. Ltd.	13.07.1860	Last document on file, Shares List 1.12.1866	?
Ynisdawela Collieries Ltd.*	16.03.1907	'This company never did anything beyond Registration.'	13.08.1912
Ynysmudwy Colliery Co. Ltd.*	08.12.1976	No details and does not appear in colliery listings.	14.04.1983

APPENDIX H – SOUTH WALES OPENCAST SITES

No apology is offered for the incomplete state of this appendix. It was not part of the objective to research opencast sites and this listing is a compilation of bits and pieces gleaned in going through other records. Perhaps one day someone will attempt to plot the details of the surprisingly large number of sites. Inevitably some will be duplications with a single site referred to by two names. Others essentially belong to a single large complex, which has seen various phases and extensions.

OPENCAST SITE, near		KNOWN OPERATION	OPERATOR (PP=Planning Permission)	LICENCE GRANTED	COMMENCED	ABANDONED
ABERCRAVE/GWAUNTON, Abercrave	B 43NE/SE	1964-72	Derek Crouch (Contractors) Ltd.			
ABERNANT, Aberdare	G 11NE/SE					31.01.1954
ABERNANT, Aberdare			See under Tir Ergyd			
ABERPERGWM, Glyn Neath						
ABERPERGWM EXTENSION 2, Glyn Neath	G 10NW					1950s
BANWEN RECLAMATION, Onllwyn	G 4SW	1993	Hawkins Plant Services			15.12.1994
BARAN MOUNTAIN, Pontardawe	G 2SW					
BENWARDS FIELD, Llanelly (Breck.)	B 47NE					27.02.1993
BETTING UCHAF, Cwmllynfell	G 2SE				06.1951	05.1952
BETTWS & EXTENSION						04.1947
BETTWS EAST	G 34NE		Ministry of Fuel & Power			08.1947
BLAENANT, Brynmawr	B 47NE	1972-74	Murphy Bros. Ltd.			23.04.1975
BLAENAU MAWR, Llandebie	C 48NW/SW					
BLAENAVON, Blaenavon						
BLAEN CYFFIN, (Llanhilleth)						03.12.1977
BLAEN CYFFIN EXTENSION, (Llanhilleth)						19.08.1978
BLAENDARE, Upper Race					14.01.1978	30.10.1982
BLAENHIRWAUN Nos. 1 & 2, Tumble	C 47NE & 48NW					
BLAENPERGWM, Glyn Neath	G 10NW		Ryan International P.LC.	23.1.1987	09.04.1987	22.10.1988
BLAENPERGWM SOUTH, Glyn Neath		1994-95	Glotec Mining Ltd.		06.01.1993	18.08.1993
BLAEN PIG, Waunavon						
BLAINA DEEP, Ammanford	C 48NE	1963-68	Sir Lindsay Parkinson & Co. Ltd.		1962	3.1968
BLAINA ZONE, Ammanford	C 48NE	1954	G. Wimpey & Co. Ltd.			
BRAWDS LEVEL, Seven Sisters			Ward Bros Mining Division Ltd.	01.02.1994	15.04.1994	27.07.2000
BRITISH RHONDDA, Rhigos	G 10SE/NE	1954-57	Sir Robert McAlpine & Sons Ltd.			1958
BROWN HILL, Brynamman ?	G 2NE					1960
BROWN HILL EXTENSION 1, Brynamman ?	G 2NE					1960
BRYNAMMAN, Brynamman	G 2NE					08.1950
BRYN DEFAID, Aberdare	G 11NE	1969-70	G. Wimpey & Co. Ltd.			01.1972
BRYNDU, Pyle	G 33SE	1958-61	Sir Lindsay Parkinson & Co. Ltd.		10.02.1961	31.03.1962
BRYNDU ADDITIONAL, Pyle	G 33SE					08.1955
BRYNDU EAST, Pyle	G 33SE					08.1955
BRYNDU ZONE, Pyle	G 33SE	1954-56	Wilson, Lovatt & Sons Ltd.			
BRYNGOLEU, Onllwyn	G 4SW	1972-73	G. Wimpey & Co. Ltd.			1974
BRYNGWYDDEL EXTENSION, Aberdare	G 11NE					05.06.1976
BRYN-GWYN, Aberdare	G 11SW	1955-64	R. M. Douglas (Contractors) Ltd.			
BRYN-GWYN & EXTENSION, Aberdare	G 11SW					
BRYNHENLLYS REVISED, Ystradgynlais		1995 1996 1997-04	Celtic Energy Ltd. Taylor Woodrow Civil Engineering Ltd. Celtic Energy Ltd.			2004
BRYN MORGAN, Cwmtwrch	G 3SW & G 2SE					18.08.1961
BRYN PICA, Aberdare	G 11NE/SE	1966-71	G. Wimpey & Co. Ltd.			
BRYN PICA COMPLETION, Aberdare	G 11NE/SE					11.1972
BRYN PICA EXTENSION SOUTH, Aberdare	G 11NE/SE	1976-80	G. Wimpey & Co. Ltd.			28.05.1982
BRYN SERTH, Tredegar	M 11NW/SW					08.1990
BRYNTEG, (Dylais Higher)	G 3SE					1951
CAE HARRIS, Dowlais	G 6SE/SW					1975
CAE HARRIS RECLAM. SCHEME, Dowlais	G 6SW 12NW					21.10.1987
CAE HELYG, Penygroes	C 48NW					02.1966

OPENCAST SITE, near		KNOWN OPERATION	OPERATOR (PP=Planning Permission)	LICENCE GRANTED	COMMENCED	ABANDONED
CAE MARI DWN, Merthyr	G 12NW					
CAPEL HEDRE, Ammanford	C 48NW					04.1954
CARREG PENTWYN, Cwmtwrch	G 3SW		Morris International Ass. Ltd.	07.12.1987	11.03.1988	18.01.1992
CARWAY		1954-56	Sir John Jackson Ltd.			
CARWAY GROUP & ADDITIONAL	C 53NE/SE 54NW/SW				09.10.1953	28.09.1957
CATTYBROOK			Discovery Aggregates (U.K.) Ltd.	08.09.1993	11.02.1994	
CEFN, Kenfig Hill	G 34SW					03.1952
CEFN ADDITIONAL, Kenfig Hill	G 34SW					03.1952
CEFN BYRLE, Seven Sisters	B. 43NE				05.1952	11.1953
CEFN EITHEN & HOLFEN FACH, Cross Hands	C 47NE	1954-55	Sir Lindsay Parkinson & Co. Ltd.			04.1956
CEFN RHIGOS, Rhigos	G 10NE					07.05.1987
CEFN SOUTH, Kenfig Hill	G 34SW	1966-68	Lehane, Mackenzie & Shand Ltd.			
CEFN UCHAF, Onllwyn - G. N.	G 4SW /B 44SW		Wimpey Construction (U.K.) Ltd.		08.09.1986	25.03.1988
CELLWEN, (Dylais Higher)						1948
COEDCAE MAWR, Brynmawr	B 47NE					27.06.1981
COLY UCHAF, Bedlinog	G 12SE					13.08.1963
CRYNANT, Crynant	G 9NE					04.1953
CWMAMMAN, Ammanford	C 49NW	1965-68	R. M. Douglas (Contractors) Ltd.			1968
CWMBLACKS, Aberdare			N.C.B. requisitioned 4.1951		30.06.1952	23.03.1953
CWMGARW, Brynamman	C 49NE					08.1953
CWM GORSE, Gwaun cae Gurwen	C 49SE					08.1952
CWM GORSE, Gwaun cae Gurwen	C 49SW	1971-73	R. M. Douglas (Contractors) Ltd.			1974
CWM GORSE, Gwaun cae Gurwen	C 49SW					1977
CYNHEIDRE, Pontyates	C	1995-96	Clay Colliery Co. Ltd.			31.03.1999
DAN-Y-BANC, Pontyates	C 54NW		Clay Colliery Co. Ltd.	22.04.1993	26.05.1993	
DDOLGAM, Black Mountain, Cwmllynfell	C 50NW					07.1964
DERLWYN, Glyn Neath	G 4SW & 10NW	1991-92 1993 1994-95 1996	A. G. K. Civil Engineering Ltd. No contractor at present Celtic Energy Ltd. Walters Mining Ltd.		22.10.1990	02.1997
DOWLAIS TOP, Merthyr	G 6SE					1969
DRAGON, Blaenavon				No rail traffic forwarded since 04.1944		
DREFACH, Raglan	G 35SW					1965
DRYM, Seven Sisters	G 3SE	1973-78	G. Wimpey & Co. Ltd.			1977
DRYM EXTENSION SOUTH, Seven Sisters	G 3SE		G. Wimpey & Co. Ltd.			1979
DUNRAVEN & HENDRE GOL, Glyn Neath	G 10NE	1954-56	Sir Lindsay Parkinson & Co. Ltd.			05.1957
DUNRAVEN DEEP EXT., Rhigos	G 10NW/NE/SE					1972
DUNRAVEN DEEP ZONE, Rhigos	G 10NW/NE/SE	1957-77	Sir Lindsay Parkinson & Co. Ltd.			
DYLLAS FARM, Merthyr	G 11NE		Walters Civil Engineering Ltd.			16.01.1993
DYNANT FACH, Tumble	C 47SE					30.01.1960
DYNANT FAWR, Tumble	C 47SE		Glendever Ltd. & Dynant Fach Mining Co. (Planning permission 15.3.1999) Stop notice issued 25.2.2003		1999	03.2003
EAST LODGE BRYNDU, Pyle	G 33SE					08.1955
EAST MERTHYR RECLAMATION, Merthyr		1995	Celtic Energy Ltd.			
EBBW VALE CEMETERY, Ebbw Vale	M 11NW/SW	1987	Blaenau Gwent Borough Council		28.11.1989	31.07.2002
ELWYN		3.2003	Ward Bros. Mining			
EMPIRE & EXTENSION, Glyn Neath	G 10NW					05.06.1963
FARTEG HILL ADDITIONAL, Ystalyfera	G 9NW		See under Treforgan			
FARTEG HILL, Ystalyfera	G 9NW					06.1954
FARTEG UCHAF, Ystalyfera	G 3SW & 9NW	1987	Crynant Mineral Supplies			12.09.1987
FFERWS HILL, Llandybie ?	C 48SE					26.02.1989
FFOREST GOCH, Neath	G 8SE/ 15NE				05.1961	03.1962

OPENCAST SITE, near		KNOWN OPERATION	OPERATOR (PP=Planning Permission)	LICENCE GRANTED	COMMENCED	ABANDONED
FFOS LAS, Kidwelly		1983-92 1993 1994-96 1995-01	Wimpey Construction UK Ltd. Wimpey Construction Ltd. Celtic Energy Ltd. Miller Mining Ltd.			24.10.1983
FFYNDAFF, Rhigos	G 10NE					early 1950s
FFYNDAFF, Rhigos	G 10NE/SE	1987-90	Currall, Lewis & Martin Ltd.		16.8.1988	23.11.1990
FFYNDAFF, Rhigos	G 10NE/SE	1981-88	Lehane, Mackenzie & Shand Ltd.			09.1988
FFYNDAFF ADDITIONAL, Rhigos	G 10NE/SE	1989-92 1993	Murphy Bros. Ltd. C. P. Holdings Ltd.			15.12.1994
FOUNTAIN, Bridgend	G 34SW	1965-68	Lehane, Mackenzie & Shand Ltd.			
FOUR WINDS, Dowlais	G 12NW					13.01.1962
GARNANT, Garnant	G 2NW	1988-92	Taylor Woodrow Construction Ltd.		13.05.1988	1993
GELLI FELIN FARM, Brynmawr	B 47NE					23.07.1983
GELLIARGWELLT UCHAF, (Gelligaer)	G 19SE					06.03.1976
GELLIWAROG FARM, Pontardawe	G 2SE					14.07.1987
GILFACH GOCH FARM, Ystalyfera	G 3SW					03.01.1987
GILFACH GOCH, Ystalyfera	G 3SW					04.1952
GILFACH IAGO, Saron	C 48NW/NE				11.1949	10.1950
GILFACH IAGO, Saron	C 48NW/NE	1988-92 1993 1994 1995-96	Wimpey Construction (U.K.) Ltd. Wimpey Construction Ltd. Celtic Energy Ltd. Miller Mining Ltd.		13.06.1988	18.09.1997
GILFACH-YR-ENCIL, (Merthyr)						11.08.1973
GILFACH-YR-HAIDD, Ystalyfera	G 3SW					03.1984
GINNEY COTTAGES, Cwm Mon.						15.08.1988
GLAN-LASH, Llandebie	C 48NW					07.1953
GLOBE INN, Gwaun cae Gurwen	C 49NW	1964	G. Wimpey & Co. Ltd.			27.07.1965
GLYN COED, Dafen	C 58NE/ 54SE		R. M. Douglas (Contractors) Ltd.			10.1946
GLYN GLAS, Llandebie	C 48NW/NE	1967-70	Lehane, Mackenzie & Shand Ltd.			1972
GLYN GLAS, Llandebie	C 48NW/NE	1971-73	Lehane, Mackenzie & Shand Ltd.			
GLYN GLAS EXTENSION N'TH, Llandebie	C 41SE & 48NE	1971-73	Lehane, Mackenzie & Shand Ltd.		1972	07.1974
GLYN GLAS REMAINDER, Llandebie	C 48NE					12.1982
GLYN GLAS SOUTH, Llandebie	C 48NE	1977-78 1979 1980-82	Shepherd Hill & Co. Ltd. G. Wimpey & Co. Ltd. Shepherd Hill & Co. Ltd.			12.1982
GLYN TAI, Saron	C 48NE					10.1951
GLYN TAI, Saron	C 48NE	1982-86	Wimpey Construction UK Ltd.			23.04.1986
GLYNEITHINOG, Glyn Neath	G 10NE					09.02.1973
GORS COLLIERY	G 3SW					1976
GORS COLLIERY EXTENSION	G 3SW					1976
GORS FARM & EXTENSION	C 47SE					03.06.1961
GRAIG ROAD, Glanamman	G 2NW					1963
GREAT MOUNTAIN, Tumble	C 47NE	1975-79	Murphy Bros. Ltd.			1978
GREAT WHITE TIP, Merthyr		1993 1994 1995	Wimpey Construction Ltd. Celtic Energy Ltd. Miller Mining Ltd.			
GRENIG, Glanamman	C 49NW					07.04.1959
GROVESEND, Pontardulais						01.06.1960
GURNOS, Ystradgynlais	G 3SW					15.10.1962
GWAUN CAE GURWEN EAST PIT		1954	R. M. Douglas (Contractors) Ltd.			
EXTENSION, Gwaun cae Gurwen	G 2NE	1989-90 1992 1993 1994-95 1995-00 1997-01 2001	A. F. Budge (Contractors) Ltd. R. J. Budge (Mining) Ltd. R. J. B. (Mining) Ltd. Celtic Energy Ltd. R. J. B. Mining (U.K.) Ltd. Celtic Energy Ltd. U. K. Coal Opencast Operations		09.05.1988	

OPENCAST SITE, near		KNOWN OPERATION	OPERATOR (PP=Planning Permission)	LICENCE GRANTED	COMMENCED	ABANDONED
GWAUN CAE GURWEN EAST PIT, Gwaun cae Gurwen	G 2NE	1981-86	Shand Mining			26.11.1987
		1987	Currall, Lewis & Martin Ltd.			
GWAUN CAE GURWEN REJECTS TIP, GcG	G 2NE	1986-87	Shepherd Hill & Co. Ltd.			
GWENDRAETH, Pontyates	C 47SW & 54NW					1963
GWRHYD UCHAF, Dowlais	G 2SE					04.07.1989
GWYNFRYN, Cwmllynfell	G 2NE					1966
HALF WAY HOUSE (Tir Edmund) (Aberdare)	G 11SE					06.1961
HELID, Rhymney		1992	Not named			
		1993	Coal Contractors Ltd.			
		1994-95	Celtic Energy Ltd.			
HELLAN UCHAF, Nant-y-Cafn		1994-96	James & McHugh Mining Ltd.	03.10.1994	26.10.1994	
HEN-DAI FARM & TOP HILL, Llancaiach	G 19NE/SE					30.07.1966
HENDRE FAWR, Glyn Neath	G 10NE	1965-71	Sir Lindsay Parkinson & Co. Ltd.			1972
HENDRE GOL			See under Dunraven			
HIRWAIN, Hirwain						07.1950
HIRWAIN COMMON EAST, Hirwain	G 35SW	1965	G. R. Wilkins & Co. Ltd.			31.03.1973
		1966-72	Lehane, Mackenzie & Shand Ltd.			
HIRWAIN COMMON NORTH 2, Hirwain	G 35SW					1978
HIRWAIN COMMON NORTH, Hirwain	G 35SW		Murphy Bros. Ltd.			1959
HIRWAIN COMMON WEST, Hirwain	G 35SW					11.1958
HOLFEN FACH, Cross Hands			See under Cefn Eithen			
HOSKIN	M 12SW					1954
HOSKIN VARTEG	M 12SW					31.03.1956
HOSKIN VARTEG, TAL-Y-WAUN	M 12SW					07.1960
INCLINE TOP, Merthyr	G 12NW	1992	Wimpey Construction Ltd.		01.1993	10.09.1993
JOHNSON'S LEVEL, Blaenavon	M 12SE					09.1992
KAY'S & KEARS, Blaenavon	M 12SE	1993	Taylor Woodrow Civil Engineering Ld.			
		1994	Celtic Energy Ltd.			
KENFIG, Kenfig Hill	G 34SW/34SW					09.1951
KENFIG ADDITIONAL, Kenfig Hill	G 33SE/34SW					10.01.1959
LAMBERT'S, Pontyates	C 53NE					13.03.1963
LAMBERT'S No. 2, Pontyates	C 53NE	1980-81	Lehane, Mackenzie & Shand Ltd.			08.1982
LION, Blaenavon			Sir Robert McAlpine & Sons Ltd.	First rail traffic forwarded 7.1.1944		
LLAETHDY, Pontyberem	C 47SE	1970-72	G. Wimpey & Co. Ltd.			1974
LLANGEINOR, Llangeinor	G 34NE				04.12.1957	17.05.1958
LLANGYNWYD, Maesteg	G 26SW/34NW				Spring 1945	27.02.1946
LLANILID, Llantrisant	G 35SE & 41NE	1970-86	Derek Crouch (Contractors) Ltd.			26.07.1986
LLANILID, Llantrisant	G 35SE & 41NE	1997-01	Hall Construction Services Ltd.			
LLANILID WEST REVISED, Llantrisant	G 35SE & 41NE	1992	Not named			
		1993	R. J. B. (Mining) Ltd.			
		1994-95	Celtic Energy Ltd.			
		1995-00	R. J. B. Mining (U.K.) Ltd.			
		2001	U. K. Coal Opencast Operations			
LLECHART FACH, Pontardawe	G 8NW	1987	J. D. Fuels Ltd.			17.05.1989
LLECHART FAWR, Pontardawe	G 8NE					11.02.1989
LLETTY'R CRUDD, Pontardawe ?		1994-95	C. Rees & Sons Plant Hire Ltd.	07.06.1993	03.09.1993	By 03.2003
LOWER RHAS BRYN OER, Rhymney	M 10SE		Coal Trading Opencast Ltd.		10.4.1979	14.12.1984
MAERDY EXTENSION, Groesfaen	G 19NE					06.08.1970
MAES-CADLAWR, Llangynwydd	G 34NW				09.1947	03.1949
MAESGWYN 18 FOOT, Glyn Neath	G 4SW & 10NW	1954	G. Wimpey & Co. Ltd.		04.1949	10.1955
MAESGWYN CAP, Glyn Neath	G 4SW & 10NW	1955-61	G. Wimpey & Co. Ltd.			
MAESGWYN CAP EXTENSION, Glyn Neath	G 4SW & 10NW	1962-79	G. Wimpey & Co. Ltd.		07.10.1955	1975
		1980-88	Wimpey Construction UK Ltd.			
MAESGWYN CAP EXTENSION 2, Glyn Neath	G 4SW & 10NW					1973
MAESGWYN CAP FURTHER EXT, Glyn Nth	G 4SW & 10NW	1983-87	Wimpey Construction UK Ltd.			13.05.1988
MAESGWYN DEEP, Glyn Neath	G 4SW & 10NW	1954-57	Sir Lindsay Parkinson & Co. Ltd.			

OPENCAST SITE, near		KNOWN OPERATION	OPERATOR (PP=Planning Permission)	LICENCE GRANTED	COMMENCED	ABANDONED
MAESGWYN SITES COMPLEX, Glyn Neath	G 4SW & 10NW					24.09.1966
MAESGWYN ZONE, Glyn Neath	G 4SW & 10NW			07.06.1946		1950
MAES-Y-MARCHOG, Banwen	G 4SW	1979	G. Wimpey & Co. Ltd.			30.10.1986
		1980-87	Wimpey Construction UK Ltd.			
MARGAM, Port Talbot [Same as Parc Slip W.]	G	2001	Celtic Energy Ltd. (pp 14.6.1996)			
MOUNTAIN PIT, Tredegar	M 10SE					09.1968
MOUNTAIN PIT FARM, Tredegar	M 10SE & 11SW					1974
MOUNTAIN ROAD, (Neath Higher)	G 10NW					04.1966
MYNYDD LLANHILLETH, Blaenserchan	M					
NANT HELEN, Colbren		1987-92	Fairclough Parkinson Mining Ltd.		06.1987	
		1993	Amec Mining Ltd.			
		1994-95	Celtic Energy Ltd.			
		1996	Amec Mining Ltd.			
		1997-01	Celtic Energy Ltd.			
NANT HIR COLLIERY			Ward Bros. Mining Division Ltd.	26.02.1993	24.03.1993	
NANT HIR EXTENSION		1996	Ward Bros. Mining Ltd.			
NANT MELYN			Energybuild (pp 14.10.2004)			
NANT-Y-CAFN RECLAMATION			Henlan Coal Ltd.			
NANTYGLO, Nantyglo ?						08.2002
NANT Y MYNYDD, Aberpergwm			Energybuild (pp 23.6.2005)			
NEUARDD ROAD, Merthyr	G 11NE		A. C. Yates & Co.			03.06.1961
NEUARDD ROAD EXTENSION, Merthyr	G 11NE		A. C. Yates & Co.			NR
NEW BRYNCETHIN, Bryncethin	G 34SE	1962-64	Wilson, Lovatt & Sons Ltd.			04.1965
NEW RHIGOS, Glyn Neath	G 10NE					1945
OAK VILLA, Pontyberem		1969-70	Derek Crouch (Contractors) Ltd.			11.1970
ONLLWYN, Onllwyn	B 43NE/SE					11.1949
ONLLWYN, Onllwyn	B 43NE/SE	1972-79	G. Wimpey & Co. Ltd.			05.1982
		1980-81	Wimpey Construction UK Ltd.			
PANDY, Glyn Neath	G 10NE					Early 1950s
PANTMAWR, Ystradgynlais	B 43SW	1962-63	Sir John Jackson Ltd.			21.09.1964
PANT-Y-FELIN, Tumble	C 47NE	1969	G. Wimpey & Co. Ltd.			09.1970
PANT-Y-GLO, (Rhymney)	M 10SE					1977
PANT-Y-WAUN, Dowlais Top	G 6SE					03.1961
PARK FARM, Tondu	G 34SW					03.1954
PARC LEVEL, Pen Rhiwfawr			S. & H. Plant Hire			2004
PARK SLIP, Tondu	G 34SW	1971-76	Lehane Mackenzie & Shand Ltd.			
PARK SLIP, Tondu	G 34SW	1997-01	Miller Mining Ltd.			
PARK SLIP EXTENSION, Tondu	G 34SW	1979	Shand Mining			05.07.1989
		1983-88	Lehane Mackenzie & Shand Ltd.			
PARK SLIP OCCS, Tondu	G 34SW					01.1979
PARK SLIP WEST, Pyle [Same as Margam]		1995-01	Celtic Energy Ltd.			
PEN BRYN OER, Rhymney	G 6SE	1987	Coal Trading Co. Ltd.			25.09.1988
PEN BRYN OER, Rhymney	G 6SE	1989-92	Coal Trading (Opencast) Ltd.		26.09.1989	12.09.1992
PENCOEDCAE, Nantyglo	M 10NE/SE					13.06.1987
PEN COED CAE FARM 2, Tredegar	M 10SE	1987	Thomkins			by 1991
PENGOSTO, Brynamman	G 2NE	1969-78	Sir Lindsay Parkinson & Co. Ltd.			1979
PEN-HEOL-ADAM & EXTENSION, Gelligaer						27.08.1966
PENLLERFEDWEN, Cwmllynfell	G 2SE					1963
PENLLERGAER GROUP, Pontardawe	G 14NE	1958-61	Sir John Jackson Ltd.			06.1961
PEN PERLYN, Gurnos		1955-60	Sir John Jackson Ltd.			02.05.1959
PEN PERLYN SOUTH WEST, Gurnos						02.05.1959
PEN RHIW FAWR, Cwmllynfell	G 2SE					06.1952
PENSTACK, Brynamman	G 2NE					03.1950
PENTWYN EXTENSION						11.1966
PENTWYN FOCHRIW, (Gelligaer						26.05.1973
PEN WAUN, Aberdare	G 11SW	1958-65	G. Wimpey & Co. Ltd.			1966
PEN WAUN YNYS, Brynamman	C 49NW/NE				07.1952	04.1953

OPENCAST SITE, near		KNOWN OPERATION	OPERATOR (PP=Planning Permission)	LICENCE GRANTED	COMMENCED	ABANDONED
PEN-Y-BRYN OER, Rhymney	M 10SE					09.1992
PEN-Y-FAN						11.1968
PEN-Y-FAN EXTENSION						11.1968
PONT HENRY, Pont Henry	C 47SW					17.03.1961
PONT YATES, Pont Yates	C 54NW	1965-66	R. A. Davies (Contracts) Ltd.			10.1968
		1967-68	Sir Lindsay Parkinson & Co. Ltd.			
PONTLOTTYN, Merthyr	G 18NE	1965-66	Sir Lindsay Parkinson & Co. Ltd.			
PWLLDU GROUP, Blaenavon	B 47NE/SE &					
	M 11NE/SE &					
	M 12NW/SW					
RAGLAN GROUP, Bridgend		1955-59	Sir Lindsay Parkinson & Co. Ltd.			1960
RHIGOS, Glyn Neath	G 10NE/SE					21.02.1976
RHIGOS ADDITIONAL, Glyn Neath	G 10NE/SE	1978-79	Lehane Mackenzie & Shand Ltd.			06.1980
RHIGOS ZONE, Glyn Neath	G 10NE/SE	1954-58	Sir Robert McAlpine & Sons Ltd.			
RHOS COLLIERY, Pantyffynon	C 48NW	1976-80	Murphy Bros Ltd.			07.1981
RHOS PANDY					02.1949	
RHOSAMMAN, Brynamman	C 49NE					07.1952
RHYD WEN, Blaen cae Gurwen	G 2NE					03.1953
RHYDW TUMP, Brynmawr	B 47NE					1964
RHYD-Y-BLEW, Tredegar	M 11NW	1970-73	Lehane Mackenzie & Shand Ltd.			
RHYD-Y-MAERDY, Ammanford	C 47NE	1976-78	G. Wimpey & Co. Ltd.			08.1979
RHYMNEY, Rhymney	M 10SE					11.1951
RHYMNEY, Rhymney	M 10SE	1970-76	Taylor Woodrow (Construction) Ltd.			1974
RHYMNEY & EXTENSION SOUTH, Rhymney	M 10SE	1977-78	Taylor Woodrow (Construction) Ltd.			
RHYMNEY EXTENSION EAST, Rhymney	M 10SE					
ROADSIDE POND Extension, Dowlais	G 6SE					1975
ROCK CASTLE EAST, Penygroes		1970-71	G. Wimpey & Co. Ltd.			
ROCK TIP, Glyn Neath	G 10NW	1981	Wimpey Construction UK Ltd.			12.1982
ROYAL ARMS EXTENSION SOUTH, Merthyr	G 6SE					1975
ROYAL ARMS GROUP, Merthyr	G 6SE	1958-75	Taylor Woodrow (Construction) Ltd.			1966
SARN HELEN, Seven Sisters		1996	Walters Mining Ltd.			
		1997	Glotec Mining Ltd.			
SARON, Pantyffynon	C 48NE					1962
SELAR, Blaengwrach		1997-98	Celtic Energy Ltd. (pp 3.11.1997)			
		2001	Celtic Energy Ltd.			
SILENT VALLEY, Ebbw Vale	M17SE		Walters Mining Ltd.	03.08.1994	10.10.1994	
SMITH'S COLLIERY, Llanelly		1990-91	Lehane Mackenzie & Shand Ltd.			
SYDDYN, Pembrey	C 53SE					07.10.1961
TALYWAIN, Abersychan		1956-59	Sir Robert McAlpine & Sons Ltd.			07.1960
THE LAURELS, Brynmawr	M 11NW/NE	1971	Murphy Bros Ltd.			1972
TIR GARW & PEN-Y-DARREN, Ystalyfera	G 3SW				05.1953	11.1953
TIR-ERGYD & ABERNANT						
RESIDUAL, Aberdare	G 11NE/SE	1954-56	G. Wimpey & Co. Ltd.			08.1959
TIR-ERGYD, Aberdare	G 11NE/SE	1958-65	G. Wimpey & Co. Ltd.			
TIRPENTWYS GROUP, Cwmffrwdoer	M 17SE 18SW	1954-61	Wilson, Lovatt & Sons Ltd.		17.11.1954	16.07.1962
	22NE 23NW					
TIR-Y-GOF, Cwmtwrch	B 43NW	1970-75	Sir Lindsay Parkinson & Co. Ltd.			1975
TRECASTLE, Llanharry	G 41NE	1972	Derek Crouch (Contractors) Ltd.			23.03.1972
TRECATTY, Dowlais	G 6SW/SE &	1975-79	Taylor Woodrow (Construction) Ltd.			
	12NW/NE					
TRECATTY, Dowlais	above	1996	Ward Bros Mining Ltd.			
TRECATTY EXTENSION, Dowlais	above	1980-83	Taylor Woodrow (Construction) Ltd.			19.09.1984
TREDEG, Ystradgynlais	B 43NW/SW	1978-80	Murphy Bros Ltd.			12.1981
TREDEGAR, Tredegar	M 10SE					02.1949
TREDEGAR PATCHES, Tredegar						07.1969
TREFORGAN & FARTEG HILL						
ADDITIONAL, Ystalyfera	G 9NW	1954	Sir Robert McAlpine & Sons Ltd.			1955

OPENCAST SITE, near		KNOWN OPERATION	OPERATOR (PP=Planning Permission)	LICENCE GRANTED	COMMENCED	ABANDONED
TRIMSARAN WOOD ZONE, Trimsaran	C 54NW	1958-60	Sir John Jackson Ltd.			1959
TUMBLE, Tumble	C 47SE	1965-66	R. A. Davies (Contracts) Ltd.			14.07.1967
TWLL-Y-CARN,	C 47SE		Vale of Neath Coal Mining Co.	30.11.1993	31.03.1994	13.09.1994
TY CROES, Ammanford	C 48SW	1970-76	Murphy Bros Ltd.			1975
TY TALWYN, Tondu	G 34SW	1954-55	Wilson, Lovatt & Sons Ltd.			25.04.1956
TY UCHAF, Tirydail	C 49NW	1972-75	G. Wimpey & Co. Ltd.			04.1976
TY'NTON GROUP, Llangynwyd	G 34NW	1957-58	R. M. Douglas (Contractors) Ltd.			2.10.1958
TYN-Y-CRAIG		1994-95	Walters Mining Ltd.	01.03.1994	07.03.1994	
TYN-Y-CWM GROUP, Pontyberem	C 47SW & 54NW	1962-68	G. Wimpey & Co. Ltd.			26.09.1963
VARTEG, ?		1954-55	Sir Robert McAlpine & Sons Ltd.			
VARTEG, Blaenavon		1987	Tillings & Desmond			
WATERFALL, Blaengwrach	G 10NE/SE	1958-61	Taylor Woodrow (Construction) Ltd.			28.06.1962
WAUNAVON, Blaenavon	B 47NE					10.1948
WAUN HOSCYN, Varteg						
WAUN LWYD DEEP EXTENSION, Gwys	B 43SW	1957-62	G. Wimpey & Co. Ltd.			
WAUN LWYD GROUP, Gwys	B 43SW	1955-56	G. Wimpey & Co. Ltd.			02.08.1963
WAUN LWYD NORTH, Gwys	B 43NW	1975	Sir Lindsay Parkinson & Co. Ltd.			13.05.1976
WAUN-Y-GILFACH, Llangynwyd	G 34NW					
WAUN-Y-GWAIR, DYNEVOR & DYLLAS, Llwydcoed	G 11NE				5.1948	04.1950
WELLINGTON, Glanamman	G 2NW					1974
WERNDDU ISAF						1986
WERNOS COLLIERY, Pantyffynon	C 48SE	1980-81	Wimpey Construction UK Ltd.			01.03.1983
YNYS FFORCH FAWR, Seven Sisters	G 9NE	1993	James & McHugh Mining Ltd.			
YSGUBORWEN, Aberdare	G 11NE/SE					08.1952
YSGUBORWEN PATCH, Aberdare	G 11SE					02.1993
YNYS DAWLEY, Seven Sisters			Newscheme Ltd.			2004

SOURCES & BIBLIOGRAPHY

A. PRIMARY MATERIAL USED FOR THE LISTING

Hunt's *Mineral Statistics* 1854-81 (Provision of data was voluntary)

List of Mines 1873-1938, 1940-45, 1948 (data was for 1947), 1950 (employment data was for 1948; remaining data for 1950) (Provision of data was mandatory)

List of Mines, Monthly amendment lists 6.1938 -10.1947 (a few missing) (Ref. Coal 17/264 at the National Archives. Not published)

Colliery Year Book and Coal Trades Directory (1939, 1942 & 1946)

Guide to the Coalfields (1949-50, 1952-97)

National Coal Board/Coal Authority Small Mines Licence records (At The Coal Authority)

Catalogue of Plans of Abandoned Mines, 1930 (and Supplements 1931-38) (Mines Dept (Board of Trade) and predecessors' publications)

Catalogue of Plans of Abandoned Mines, 1978 (& 1979 Supp.) (Internal lists issued by the South Wales Area of the National Coal Board)

B. OTHER MATERIAL

Primary

Annual reports issued by public Limited Companies. (at the Guildhall Library, London)

Children's Employment Commission (Parliamentary paper 1842)

Coal Authority Records ('C. A. ref' items)

Coal Commission papers (NA Coal, primarily Coal 17 series)

Company Registration Files and records (Companies House and the National Archives)

Fatal Accident Lists (H. M. Inspector of Mines) from 1850 to 1895 and non-Fatal Lists when provided.

Gloucester Carriage & Wagon Co. (Orders 1867-1927 courtesy of Ian Pope)

Great Western Railway Wagon Registers (some, courtesy of Ian Pope)

H.M. Inspector of Mines Annual Reports 1850-1938 (particularly 1891)

Home Office papers (NA Ref. HO 45 files)

Monmouthshire Wagon Co. (Orders 1855-1891 courtesy of Ian Pope)
National Coal Board papers (NA Coal, primarily Coal 4, 17, 44, 84 and 89 series)
National Coal Board, South Western Division, Licensed Mines Register (at Coal Authority)
N. C. B. South Wales Pit Closure Register 1947-80 (at Glamorgan Archives)
N. C. B. South Western Division Register of Plans of Abandoned Mines (at The Coal Authority)
Parish Production Lists, the only ones for which detailed data has been obtained;
Aberdare 1861-81, Llanwonno 1866-81, Ystradyfodwg 1866-1881, Merthyr 1866-75 and Gelligaer 1860-61, 64-65, 67-81 & 83-87, together with 1887 data for all four, plus Llantrissant in *The South Wales Coal Trade* by Wilkins 1888.
Railway private siding agreements and related papers. (Collections of author and J. W. Mann and records held at the NA and various County Archives)
Railway Company Minute Books (at the National Archives)
Aberdare Valley Rly: Board Minutes 1856-61 (Rail 3/1)
Barry Rly: Committee 1904-22 (Rail 23/11-13), Engineer's Reports 1897-1902 (Rail 23/20), Officials' Reports to Directors 1903-05 (Rail 23/22)
Brecon & Merthyr Rly: Directors 1867-1922 (Rail 65/2-11), Traffic & Works 1881-1922 (Rail 65/19-21), Engineer's Reports 1882-1911 (Rail 1057/146)
Burry Port & Gwendraeth Valley Rly: Directors 1888-1898 (Rail 89/1) and GM's Reports 1914-1920 (Rail 1057/451)
GWR: Board and numerous committees. (Rail 250 various references 1854-1947)
GWR & PT Rly: Officers' Meetings 1908-1921 (Rail 242/3)
GWR & R&SB Rly: Officers' Meetings 1906-1921 (Rail 243/3)
Llynvi & Ogmore Rly: Committee 1867-72 (Rail 382/1)
Llynvi & Ogmore & GWR: Joint Committee 1873-83 (Rail 381/1-3)
Llantrissant & Taff Vale Junction Rly: Directors and General 1861-79 (Rail 380/1)
Llanelly Railway & Dock Co.: Committee 1843-60 (Rail 377/2-4), Meetings of proprietors 1836-57 (Rail 377/8), Executive Committee 1854-73 (Rail 377/11-16) and various other papers under Rail 377
LM&SR: Traffic Committee 1923-1947 (Rail 418/75-87)
L&NWR: (Rail 410. Various references 1854-1923)
Midland Rly: Way & Works Committee 1861-1903 (Rail 491/96-122), Traffic Committee 1867-1923 (Rail 491/147-167)
Monmouthshire Railway & Canal Co.: Committee 1849-80 (Rail 500/8-20)
Neath & Brecon Rly: Directors 1862-1922 (Rail 505/1-8), G.M.'s Reports 1901-22 (Rail 1057/1483)
Port Talbot Railway & Dock Co.: Directors 1898-1922 (Rail 574/2-5) G.M.'s Reports 1896-1922 (Rail 1057/1528)
Rhondda & Swansea Bay Rly: Directors 1892-1922 (Rail 581/4-7)
Rhymney Rly: Directors 1853-1922 (Rail 583/1-11)
Sirhowy Rly: Directors 1860-76 (Rail 624/1-2)
South Wales Mineral Rly: Directors 1853-1922 (Rail 639/1-3)
Taff Vale Rly: Directors 1844-99 (Rail 684/2-10), Engineer's Reports 1854-58 (Rail 684/45), Traffic Committee 1891-1922 (684/14-21), Finance 1891-1907 (684/32-34)
Vale of Neath Rly; Directors 1851-66 (Rail 704/4-7)
Report of the Commissioners on matters relating to coal. (HMSO 1871)
South Wales District (Coal Scheme) 1930. (Minute books and papers at National Archives)
Stephenson & Alexander (Auctioneers) (Records from 1878 at GRO)
Western Wagon Co. (Orders 1878-1904 courtesy of Ian Pope)

Secondary

A(N&SW)D&R Co. List of Collieries 1902
British Railways, *List of Collieries* 10.1954
Directory of Mines & Quarries (1984, 88, 91, 94 & 98)
Directory of Quarries (1988-2001)
Memoirs of British Geological Survey No. 1 Newport (1909 & 1969), 2. Abergavenny (1927 & 1989), 3. Cardiff (1912 & 1988), 4. Pontypridd & Maesteg (1964 & 1988), 5. Merthyr (1904, 1933 & 1988), 6. Bridgend (1904 & 1990), 7. Ammanford (1907), 8. Swansea (1907), 9. West Gower & Pembrokeshire (1907), 10. Carmarthen (1909), 11. Haverfordwest (1914), 12. Milford (1916), 13. Pembroke & Tenby (1921) & Special (unnumbered) Gwendraeth Valley (1968)
Great Western Railway, *List of Collieries* 1907, 1924 and 1932 editions
International Guide to the Coalfields (1997-2012)
LM&SR *List of Collieries* 1924 and 1937
Railway Clearing House Distance Books 1852-1910 (NA Rail 1089 various references)
Railway Clearing House *Handbooks of Stations*, Appendices and leaflets.

C. NEWSPAPERS

South Wales Daily News/South Wales News (started 1872, renamed 9.4.1918) (1872-1928, & odd issues only 1900-20 at Cardiff Library)
Cambrian (1845-76, taken from the Swansea Library index)
Cardiff Times (1858-1884, 1893-94 at Cardiff Library)
Llanelly Guardian/Llanelly & County Guardian 1863-1925 (renamed 2.1.1879) (from the Llanelli Public Library index)
Llanelly Mercury 1891-1930 (from the Llanelli Public Library index)
Monmouthshire Merlin (odd issues at Newport Library)
South Wales Echo (odd issues)
South Wales Press 1898, 1908-14, 1925-32 (from the Llanelli Public Library index)
Star of Gwent (6.1853-62, 1864-65 at Newport Library)
The Times (www.infotrac.galegroup.com)
Western Mail (1879-1900) (www.infotrac.galegroup.com)
Plus, Many and varied on National Library of Wales Newspaper Website

D. JOURNALS

Coal & Colliery News (selected issues)
Coal & Colliery News Digest (selected issues)
Coal and Iron (1891-1913) (started 1891, after 1912 reporting of colliery events was very much reduced)
Colliery Guardian 1858, 1861-1990 (Not published 1859-60)
Engineer, The 1870-1900
Engineering 1867-1918 (started 1866. After 1915 reporting of colliery events was very much reduced)
Iron & Coal Trades Review (6.1899-1941) (Started 1866, but very little coal of interest prior to 1899)
Labour Gazette 1893-95
London Gazette 1840-2006 (www.gazettes-online.co.uk)
O'Connell's Coal & Iron News (selected issues)
Mining Journal 1849-51, 1853-1889 (after 1889 concentrated almost entirely on metal mining)

E. DIRECTORIES (The data is deemed to be for the year in brackets)

Despite the wide spread availability of the frequently issued *Kelly's Iron Trade Directories* and *Ryland's Directories*, little or no use has been made of them, as comparison with official Lists of Mines and other publications suggests that they are the least reliable of those that are available.

Year of publication (year of compilation)	Publisher	Coverage
1849 (1848)	Hunt	Bristol (and various Welsh locations) March & June editions
1850 (1849)	Hunt	Bristol (and various Welsh locations)
1850	Slater	South Wales & Monmouthshire
1850	Pigot	Monmouthshire
1850 (1849)	Hunt	Swansea & West Wales
1852 (1851)	Scammell	Bristol & South Wales
1852	Lascelles	Monmouthshire
1852-53 (1852)	Slater	South Wales & various English counties
1854	Pearse	Swansea
1856	Pearse	Swansea, Neath & Llanelly
1858	Bird	Cardiff & suburbs
1858-59 (1858)	Slater	North & South Wales, Monmouthshire & Bristol etc.
1859 (1858)	Slater	North & South Wales, Monmouthshire & Bristol etc.
1862	Morris	Hereford & Monmouth
1863	Wakeford	Cardiff
1865	Webster	Glamorgan, Monmouthshire & Bristol
1866	Harrod	Glamorgan, Monmouthshire & Bristol
1868 (1867)	Slater	North & South Wales, Monmouthshire & Bristol etc.
1869	Pearse & Brown	Swansea
1871	Kelly	South Wales & Monmouthshire
1872	Chalinder	Llanelly
1873	Butcher	Cardiff & Newport
1873-74 (1873)	Butcher	Swansea, Neath & Briton Ferry

1875	Worrall	South Wales & Newport, Mon.
1875	Mercer & Crocker	Monmouthshire, Herefordshire & Gloucestershire
1875-76 (1874)	Butcher	Cardiff, Newport, Pontypool & Pontypridd
1875-76 (1874)	Butcher	Swansea, Neath, Bridgend & Llanelly
1876	Mercer & Crocker	Glamorgan, Monmouthshire & others
1877	Owen	Glamorgan & Monmouthshire
1877 (1876)	Johns	Newport
1878	Owen	Glamorgan & Monmouthshire
1878 (1877)	Johns	Newport
1880 (1879)	Slater	North & South Wales, Monmouthshire & Bristol etc.
1880 (1879)	Johns	Newport
1880 (1879)	Butcher	Cardiff including Pontypridd
1881	Rylands	South Wales & Monmouthshire
1881-82 (1881)	Butcher	Swansea, Neath, Briton Ferry & Llanelly
1882 (1881)	Johns	Newport
1882-83 (1881)	Butcher	Cardiff including Pontypridd
1884 (1883)	Kelly	South Wales & Monmouthshire
1885	Wilson	Wales
1887	Owen	Cardiff
1891	Kelly	South Wales
1895	Owen	Cardiff
1895	Kelly	South Wales & Monmouthshire
1895	Potts	Great Britain & Ireland
1899	Wright	Swansea
1901	Kelly	South Wales & Monmouthshire
1906	Kelly	South Wales & Monmouthshire
1910	Kelly	South Wales & Monmouthshire
1914	Kelly	South Wales & Monmouthshire
1920	Kelly	South Wales & Monmouthshire
1923	Kelly	South Wales & Monmouthshire
1926	Kelly	South Wales & Monmouthshire
1934	Kelly	Monmouthshire
1937	Kelly	Monmouthshire

F. MAPS & PLANS

Primary

Ordnance Survey 6 inch and 25 inch maps, all editions of County series.
Ordnance Survey 6 inch maps endorsed with Abandoned Mines. (At the Coal Authority)
British Geological Survey 6 inch and 1:10,000 maps.
'Abandonment' and 'Mineral Takings' plans (At the Coal Authority)
South Wales Institute of Engineers, Transactions & Proceedings, various maps accompanying articles. Vols. 1-55 1857 to 1940.

Secondary

Gordon's Map of South Wales Coal Field. (Various editions c1895, c1901, c1913, c1921, c1922)
Campion's Map of South Wales Coal Field (Various editions during 1890s)
Johnston's Map of South Wales Coal Field (c1900-05)
Forster Brown's Map of South Wales Coal Field (1874) published as a plate appended to T. F. Brown 'The South Wales Coal-Field', South Wales Institute of Engineers Transactions, vol.9, pt.2, 1874, pp.59-129.

G. PUBLISHED MATERIAL

I have been aware of the very extensive work of Ray Lawrence for a number of years and his series of volumes on the mines of South Wales. However, I took an early decision not to make use of his researches in order to avoid any suggestion of extensive plagiarism. This work may well be the poorer in the light of that decision.

Big Pit Blaenafon - National Museum of Wales 1988
Burdett's Official Intelligence - 1883-1899 (Continues as the Stock Exchange Official Intelligence)
Cardiff & the Marquesses of Bute - J. Davies (1981)
Coal in South Wales - British Coal pamphlet 1989
Colliers' Strike in South Wales, its cause, progress and settlement - Alexander Dalziel, 1872

Cymmer Steam Coal - Insole 1880
Glamorganshire & Aberdare Canals - S. Rowson & I. L. Wright 2004
Glynogwr & Gilfach Goch - Meirion Davies 1981.
A Great Welsh Combine - Reprinted from *Syren & Shipping* 1910
History of Burry Port - R. G. Thomas (unpublished manuscript c1938, Llanelli Public Library, courtesy of R.P.J.)
The History of the Development of the Coal Industry of the Rhondda Valleys for the last 50 years - paper submitted to the Treorchy Eisteddfod in 1895. (Treorchy library)
History of Ebbw Vale - A. Gray-Jones 1970
History of Fochriw - Ifor Coggan
History of Bynea & Llwynhendy - B. & L. Local History Group 2000 (Coal section by M. V. Symons)
History of Mountain Ash, 1896 - W. Bevan, 1990 edition
History of the Pioneers of the Welsh Coalfield - E. Phillips 1925
History of Tredegar - D. & P. Powell, 1902
History of the Vale of Neath - D. Rhys Phillips, 1925
Horses to Barges - W. S. Morgan
The Industrial & Maritime History of Llanelli & Burry Port 1750-2000 - Craig, Protheroe Jones & Symons, 2002
Industrial Railway Soc. Bulletins - Published by the Industrial Railway Society
Neath Abbey & the Industrial Revolution - Lawrence Ince 2005
Old Aberdare, Vol. IV - Cynon Valley History Society 1985
Pembrokeshire. The Forgotten Coalfield - M. R. Connop Price 2004
Penallta Colliery - G. Salway
The Powell Duffryn Steam Coal Co. Ltd. 1864-1914 - Published by Powell Duffryn 1927
Proceedings of South Wales Institute of Engineers - 1857 to 1940
Records of the several Coal Owners' Associations of Monmouthshire & South Wales 1865-95 - Cardiff Library
Register of Defunct & other Companies - 1977 Ed. Published by the Stock Exchange
Returns of Joint Stock Companies - Parliamentary Papers 1866-1900
Short History of Dowlais Ironworks 1759-1936 - John A. Owen 1972.
Small Mines of South Wales - A. J. Booth (Vol. 1 1985, Vol. 2 1997)
South Wales Coal Annual - From 1903 to 1937, in particular, the Annual Diary 1904-23
South Wales Coal Field - Business Statistics Co. Ltd c1922
South Wales Coal Trade - Wilkins. 1888
Stock Exchange Official Intelligence - 1900-34 (continues as Stock Exchange Official Year Book)
Stock Exchange Official Year Book - 1935-40
Stock Exchange Year Book - 1875 to 1894 and various other years
Thomas-Merthyr Colliery Co. Ltd. - Ronald Llewellyn Thomas. (Merthyr Historian Vol. 25. Jan. 1947)
The Welsh Coal Fields - Reprinted from Syren & Shipping 1906
Welsh Mines Society Journal - Published by the Welsh Mines Society.

H. WEB SITES

www.bgs.ac.uk	Extensive records, including 'Lists of Mines' recently made available.
www.carmarthenshire.gov.uk	Planning applications
www.europa.eu.int	European Commission Grants
www.fochriwhistory.co.uk	History of Fochriw area, including coal in depth.
www.freepages.history.rootsweb.ancestry.com	Various colliery sites
www.gazettes-online.co.uk	London Gazette covering legal changes to companies.
www.glamarchives.gov.uk/collection/	Extensive on-line catalogue of Glamorgan Archives.
www.hse-databases.co.uk	Safety issues
www.infotrac.galegroup.com	Times Online, Western Mail & Bristol Mercury
www.llgc.org.uk/	Extensive on-line catalogue of the National Library of Wales
www.maps.nls.uk/index.html	Extensive on-line O.S. maps
www.nationalarchives.gov.uk	National Archives (formerly the Public Records Office)
www.parliament.uk	Hansard reporting
www.welshcoalmines.co.uk	Comprehensive cover of South Wales collieries
www.welshjournals.llgc.org.uk	Various articles
www.welshnewspapers.llgc.org.uk/en/home	Welsh newspapers (extremely extensive)
www2.swansea.gov.uk/_info/cambrian	Index to the Cambrian newspaper
www1.swansea.gov.uk/calmview/Record	Extensive on-line catalogue of West Glamorgan Archives.

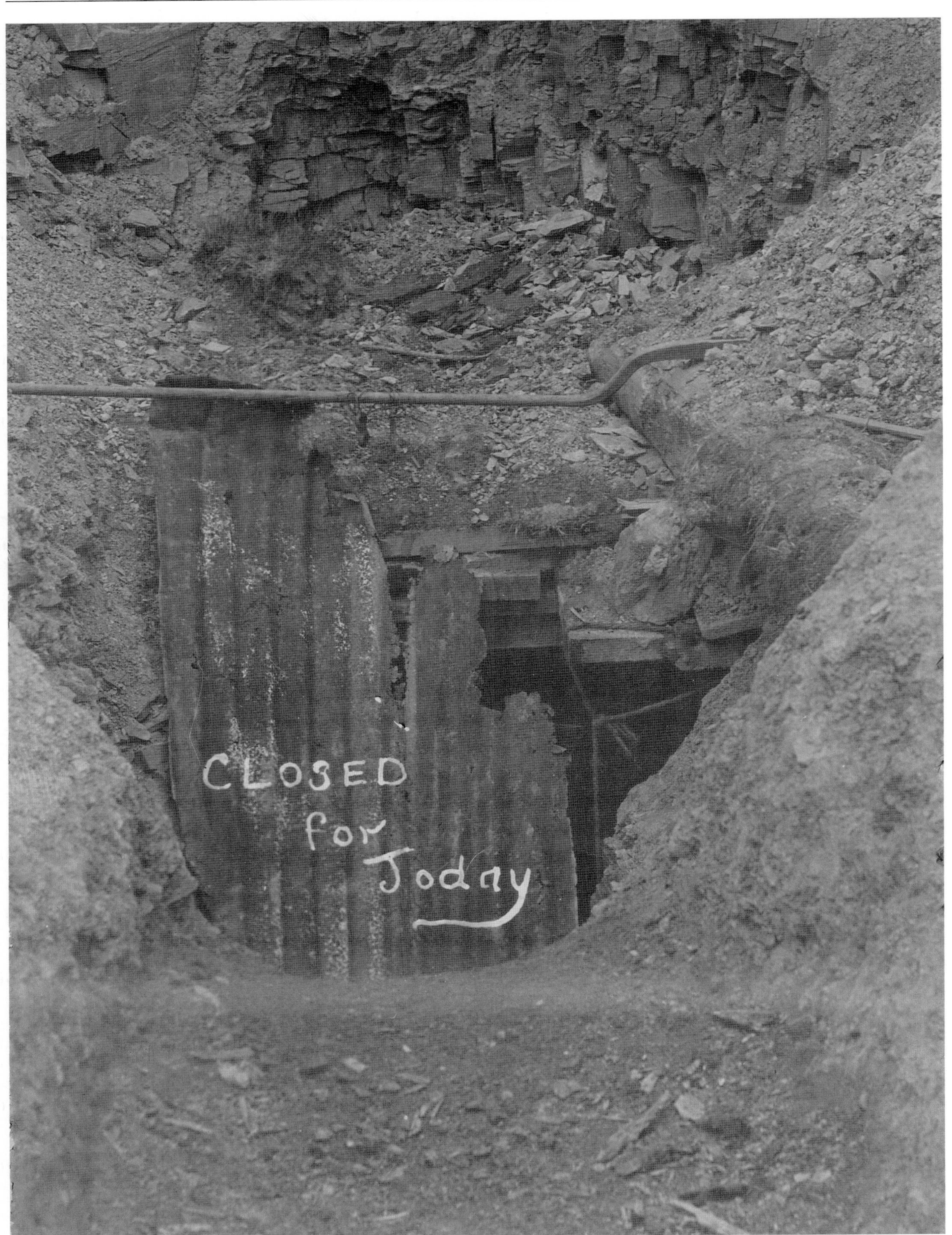
CLOSED
for
Today